Mná na hÉireann

MNÁ NA HÉIREANN

WOMEN WHO SHAPED IRELAND

NICOLA DEPUIS

MERCIER PRESS

IRISH PUBLISHER – IRISH STORY

MERCIER PRESS

Cork

www.mercierpress.ie

Trade enquiries to CMD BookSource,
55a Spruce Avenue, Stillorgan Industrial Park,
Blackrock, County Dublin

ISBN: 978 1 85635 645 9

10 9 8 7 6 5 4 3 2 1

A CIP record for this title is available from the British Library

Typesetting by Kieran O'Connor.
Printed and bound by J F Print Ltd, Sparkford, Somerset.

TABLE OF
CONTENTS

LEGENDS

Tryers of firesides,
twilights. There are no tears in these.

Instead, they begin the world again,
making the mountain ridges blue
and the rivers clear and the hero fearless –

and the outcome always undecided
so the next teller can say begin and
again and astonish children.

Our children are our legends.
You are mine. You have my name.
My hair was once like yours.

And the world
is less bitter to me
because you will re-tell the story.

Eavan Boland

**This book is dedicated to two inspirational Irish women –
my grandmother Ita O'Mahony and my mother Dolores Depuis.**

The big mistake to make in life is to go around asking for permission.

June Levine

I think being a woman is like being Irish. Everyone says you're important and nice, but you take second place all the time.

Iris Murdoch

Never doubt that a small group of thoughtful committed citizens can change the world. Indeed, it is the only thing that ever has.

Margaret Mead

INTRODUCTION

When I was a child, in the mid-1980s, my father returned from work at the CMP dairy plant in Cork city one evening with important news. He announced that he had been successful in his campaign as shop steward to win equal pay for his female co-workers. I remember being excited. Not because he had fought for the basic rights of women and won them, but because he had arrived home with a big box of chocolates under his arm, given to him by his appreciative female co-workers. Being five years of age at the time, I was too young to understand this momentous event that was to infinitely change the lives of women workers at the CMP. I barely gave it a second thought. It was only as I grew up and my father proudly reminded me of his victory time and time again that questions began to form in my mind, the most pressing one being: Why weren't women paid the same wage for doing the same job before then? And so began my discovery of the history, or should I say 'herstory', of female oppression, a journey of discovery that I am still undertaking today.

When I began learning about the history of Ireland at school, I noticed the same names repeating themselves over and over in my copy-books: Daniel O'Connell, Wolfe Tone, Charles Stewart Parnell, Big Jim Larkin, Michael Collins, Éamon de Valera and Patrick Pearse. When we studied poetry, it was always the works of Seamus Heaney, W.B. Yeats, Patrick Kavanagh and Michael Longley. When we studied literature, it was always

James Joyce, Samuel Beckett and Frank O'Connor. In music class we learned about Mozart, Handel and Bach. In maths class it was Pythagoras and Venn diagrams. In French we talked about Napoleon and David Hallyday. In religion, we learned about St Patrick but not St Brigid. Aside from a brief mention that Jesus' mother was a virgin and Mary Magdalen was a prostitute (the only two roles available to women in the Bible it seems), religion class was filled with the wonder and awe of Jesus Christ, his heavenly father and a host of male biblical characters who fought against lions and demons to make the Christian world what it is today. I was slowly but surely becoming indoctrinated into the long-held belief that men are the leaders, the revolutionaries, the healers, the teachers and the heroes. My inculcation in the patriarchal establishment was such that it took me a long time to ask: What in God's name have Irish women been doing since the beginning of time? Having finally asked the question, it has taken me much longer to find an explanation. This book is a small measure of my answer.

While *Mná na hÉireann* focuses on a selection of both well-known and lesser-known suffragists, feminists, pacifists, pragmatists and nuns, I am aware that some of the most inspirational Irish women are those who quietly go about their day-to-day business of raising families and contributing to the community. These everyday heroines pave the way for the change-makers and revolutionaries of our country.

This book is for mothers and daughters, grandmothers and granddaughters. It is a celebration of the strong unique bond that is passed down through the female line. It is in celebration of all the giantesses who have paved the way and on whose shoulders the women of Ireland now proudly stand. It is a tribute to the history of the Irish woman and it is a prayer to the future generations of *mná na hÉireann* that they will continue to be as inspirational as the women who came before them.

MARY AIKENHEAD

FOUNDRESS OF THE RELIGIOUS SISTERS OF CHARITY

—— 1787–1858 ——

Cork-born Mary Aikenhead was a woman ahead of her time. She was born during an era when women were expected to be subservient and quiet, yet Mary, with her unrelenting belief in Divine Providence and her devotion to 'God's nobility – the suffering poor', cast off the expected limitations of her sex as she set about establishing the Roman Catholic order of the Religious Sisters of Charity. She opened the first hospital in Ireland ever to be run by religious sisters or, more importantly, by women. Her belief that 'just because it has never been done before, there is no reason why it should not be done now' was put into practice time and time again, as she became the first religious woman in Ireland to visit prisoners in Kilmainham Gaol and the foundress of the first religious sisterhood to

set foot in Australia. A true feminist, she was fearless in challenging clerics about the just treatment of her congregation. In her seventy-two years, Mary reached out and touched the lives of many, lifting the spirits of the suffering poor and inspiring generations of women to do the same.

Mary's life began on 19 January 1787. She was the first-born child of Dr David Aikenhead, a wealthy apothecary and property owner of Scottish Protestant descent, and Mary Stackpole, an aristocratic Catholic from a wealthy merchant family.

She was fostered out to Mary and John Rourke, who lived on Eason's Hill, for the first few years of her life, although why this was done is unclear. This was to prove a fateful decision as Mary, baptised a Protestant, began to mix with the poorer Catholics in the Shandon area – a portion of society that she would have been cut off from had she spent these formative years with her aristocratic birth parents. When she was six, her parents brought her home to live with them. She was sent to a nearby school for the daughters of Protestant gentlemen, where she was to be prepared for life in genteel society.

When Mary was twelve, her mother's sister Rebecca Gorman returned from a stay at a convent in Bruges, where she had been leading a religious life. Rebecca was to have a huge influence on Mary, lending her religious books and often bringing her along to mass and benediction. On one of these occasions, Mary heard a sermon by Dr Florence McCarthy, coadjutor bishop of Cork, at the South Parish church. It was about the parable of Dives and Lazarus, in which an uncaring rich man ends up in a place of torment while a poor man inherits paradise. Having lived amongst both the rich and the poor, Mary felt called to act. Poverty was widespread in Ireland in the nineteenth century. Many people were unable to afford shelter, food, health-care or education, and children were frequently abandoned and left to fend for themselves. At the age of fifteen, Mary was received into the Catholic Church and developed an interest in the religious life. She considered joining the Presentation Sisters but was disheartened by the idea of enclosure, as she felt strongly about retaining the freedom to visit the sick poor in their homes.

Through the connections of her good friend Anna Maria O'Brien, Mary was introduced to Dr Daniel Murray, future archbishop of Dublin and a man who was to play a huge role in her life. Dr Murray was hoping to establish a congregation of religious sisters who would visit the poor in their own homes, similar to the French Daughters of Charity of St Vincent de Paul. To Mary's surprise, he proposed that since she had 'a great heart and a willing mind' she should lead this new venture as the first mother superior of the new congregation. Her claims of inexperience and a lack of training in the religious life were dismissed, and in 1812, unable to enter France because of the political climate, Mary and her companion Alicia Walsh entered the Bar Convent in York belonging to the Institute of the Blessed Virgin Mary. Mary took the name Sister Mary Augustine but was to be known throughout her life as Mrs Aikenhead. Three years later, Mary and Alicia (now Sister Mary Catherine) returned to Ireland where Dr Murray had prepared their first convent on North William Street off Summerhill in Dublin. The two women immediately set to work making the 'walking nuns' a reality.

In 1816, Pope Pius VII gave his approval to the establishment of the congregation, and on 9 December Dr Murray received the perpetual vows of Sr Mary Augustine and Sr Mary Catherine into the Pious Congregation of the Religious Sisters of Charity. The congregation's motto became *Caritas Christi urget nos* (the charity of Christ urges us). The constitution of the congregation called for vows of chastity, poverty and obedience, as well as a fourth vow obliging the sisters to devote their lives to the service of the poor. Though very short of funds and constantly relying on the 'rich bank' of God's providence, in 1819 Mary opened a second convent on Stanhope Street, where she personally instructed the novices. As the number of novices grew, Mary and the sisters, with the help of the Society of Friends and the Christian Brothers, opened new schools for the education of the poor on Gardiner Street (1830) and in Sandymount (1831). However, whilst visiting the sick poor, several of the young sisters picked up illnesses from which they eventually died, and it was Mary who nursed them day and night. But to every challenge and struggle, Mary's constant response was, 'God's will. Amen!'

At the age of forty-four, Mary's health began to fail and she spent most of the last thirty years of her life either in a wheelchair or on a couch, crippled with spinal problems, dropsy and eventually paralysis. It was under these difficult circumstances that she ran the congregation, mainly through the use of her 'lame pen'.

Mary's activity was unceasing. She directed her sisters in their heroic work during the cholera epidemics of both 1832 and 1833 and the famine in the 1840s. She undertook the management of many institutions, including a refuge for prostitutes on Townsend Street. She sent sisters to Australia in 1838 and to England in 1840, and she continued to play a very active role in organising the convents and raising money for the various charitable works in which the sisters were engaged. Many have said that she did her best work from her sickbed – an inspiring feat in itself.

From her own experience helping the sick poor, the majority of whom were Catholic, Mary began to recognise an urgent need for a hospital where Catholic doctors and nurses could be trained. She envisaged a hospital for patients of all creeds where both the poor and her own sisters, who were very susceptible to disease, could be treated. Even though the Act of Catholic Emancipation had

> SHE WROTE 4,000 LETTERS FROM HER SICKBED, WHERE SHE ALSO HAND-MADE BOLSTER SLIPS AND PILLOWCASES FOR THE HOSPITAL

been passed in 1829, Catholics were still excluded from positions of trust, including posts in public hospitals and schools of medicine. With this in mind, Mary appealed for donations to start a hospital for the most needy. She wrote 4,000 letters from her sickbed, where she also hand-made bolster slips and pillowcases for the hospital. In January 1834, her dream was realised when she opened St Vincent's Hospital in St Stephen's Green, Dublin. It was the first Catholic hospital in Ireland since the Reformation and the first to be run by religious sisters. Nursing as a profession in the modern sense was unknown at the time, but Mary Aikenhead helped to raise the level of respect and recognition awarded to nurses. It was recorded that the first operation at the hospital was performed on a little boy who lay in Mary Aikenhead's lap throughout the procedure.

In 1845, Mary moved to a house in Harold's Cross, Dublin, where she spent the last thirteen years of her life. The evening before she died she was told that a messenger had come from the Magdalen Asylum in Donnybrook to enquire how she was. Aware that the next day would be the feast of Mary Magdalen, always a special day of celebration for the residents, she replied, 'If I die tomorrow, do not tell the poor penitents until the day after as it would spoil their pleasure.' These were her last recorded words. She died at 3 p.m. on 22 July 1858, forty-three years after taking her vows. Such was her impact on the poor and working people of Ireland that a deputation from a body of Dublin workmen requested, as a favour, that they might be allowed to carry her coffin to the grave, and a farmer wrote in a letter to his cousin, 'In her, Ireland's poor have lost their best friend. No other woman ever did so much for them.' Since Mary's death her congregation has spread to many parts of the world, including Scotland, America, Venezuela, Zambia and Nigeria, where they continue to work in schools, hospitals and prisons.

DOCTOR JAMES BARRY

PIONEERING SURGEON

— 1799–1865 —

Doctor James Barry, born Margaret Bulkley, was the first woman in Britain to graduate in medicine, seventy years before women were actually allowed to study the subject in college. Rather than spend her life fighting for the right of women to become doctors, Margaret Bulkley sacrificed her own gender in her quest to become one of the most progressive military doctors of the nineteenth century. In her lifetime, Dr Barry greatly improved sanitary conditions for soldiers and their families. She performed one of the earliest successful caesarean sections in Africa, in which both mother and child survived. She prioritised the disenfranchised and the dispossessed: women, slaves, prostitutes, prisoners, lepers and children. She worked with compassionate concern for a better understanding of the mentally ill. She risked her professional standing time and again in a bid to revolutionise the standards of hygiene in military hospitals. She was also one of the most passionate early advocates of preventative medicine. Lost beneath mountains of military records for nearly 100 years, the details of the life of Margaret Bulkley, aka Dr James Barry, are as startling today as they were at the time of her death.

Margaret Bulkley was born in 1799 to Cork city grocer Jeremiah Bulkley and his wife Mary-Ann, sister of James Barry, the Irish painter and professor of painting at the Royal Academy of Art in London. When Jeremiah was imprisoned for debt, Mary-Ann took her two daughters to London where the young Margaret was introduced to her uncle's legendary friends: physician Edward Fryer, David Erskine Stuart, the Earl of Buchan, and General Francisco Miranda, the Venezuelan revolutionary. All three men were advocates of female education and saw a promising future for the young Margaret who showed an early interest in medicine. When James Barry died, he left provisions in his will for Margaret's education. Edward Fryer began to tutor her occasionally and General Miranda gave the young girl the full use of his extensive and celebrated library. Miranda also promised Margaret a job as a surgeon in Venezuela, but as women were forbidden from studying medicine at the time, it became clear that another course of action was needed.

In 1809, a young James Barry was accepted into the University of Edinburgh as a literary and medical student. Back in Ireland, Margaret Bulkley left all visible traces of her gender behind as she boarded the ship to Scotland with her mother. Margaret's mother fully supported her daughter's decision to enter university disguised as a male, and may have believed it was the only way this family of women could survive financially. However, in order to keep up the façade, they were forced to cut off all contact with family and friends, and upon boarding the ship to Scotland both would leave life as they had known it behind.

At university, Margaret showed great interest in the less popular fields of obstetrics and gynaecology. She also took classes in midwifery which at the time was seen as belonging in the lesser domain of women's work; the

Royal College of Physicians went so far as to ban its male licensees from practising it. When Margaret qualified with a medical doctorate in 1812, she was disappointed to find that her loyal patron Francisco Miranda had been imprisoned following the failure of his revolution, and so she was now faced with the prospect of looking for work.

The British army was seeking surgeons at the time and Margaret enlisted. There is a belief that she formed a relationship with a fellow student in Edinburgh who was later to die in the army, prompting Margaret to want to provide better care for soldiers. After working at St Thomas' Hospital in London and later in Plymouth, Margaret was posted to Cape Town, South Africa, where she made such an impression as a physician, surgeon and obstetrician that she was appointed medical inspector for the entire colony within a number of years. While in Cape Town, Margaret went beyond the call of duty by attempting to oversee every aspect of the medical system, from the inspection of drugs for sale to the checking of hygiene levels in jails. She also criticised local doctors for their blatant discrimination against lepers and prisoners. It was this radical enthusiasm for change and equality that marked her lifelong battle against the authorities.

MARGARET WAS CALLED TO THE AID OF A WOMAN WHO WAS DYING IN CHILDBIRTH. SHE MANAGED TO SAVE BOTH MOTHER AND CHILD, PERFORMING A SUCCESSFUL CAESAREAN SECTION

When it came to her patients, Margaret treated them all without prejudice. She became a lifeline for women who had never before been treated by a doctor with such an innate understanding of women, and as she never accepted fees for her private practice she was able to offer her expertise to the poorer women in Cape Town. Out of gratitude, the woman's father offered to reward Dr Barry financially, but she declined the money, requesting instead that as she had no children of her own the child be named after her. The request was granted and the newly born James Barry went on to become the godfather of James Barry Munnik Hertzog, the future prime minister of South Africa.

A student of tropical diseases, Margaret introduced the smallpox vaccination to Cape Town in 1822, twenty years before its introduction in England. As a military doctor, she was also constantly reforming and upgrading the living conditions of the troops and their families. At the time, soldiers were living in squalor, with little thought given to their diets and sanitation.

While Margaret's professional life was much-lauded, her personal life came under scrutiny when her relationship with the governor of the Cape colony, Lord Charles Somerset, caught the attention of the public. The pair became involved in a libel suit after being accused of having an 'immoral relationship'. A placard was placed on the Hout Street bridge in Cape Town in 1824, which alleged that the writer of the sign had seen Barry and Somerset engaging in buggery, an offence punishable by death at that time. Large sums of money were collected in an appeal to apprehend and convict the author of this libel, but the writer was never traced. Today, it is believed that when Somerset discovered Margaret's true sex they embarked on a passionate affair, which resulted in Margaret becoming pregnant. However, there are no known records indicating if the child was born alive.

After a short stint in Jamaica in 1829, Margaret took unofficial leave of absence and returned to England where she is believed to have taken care of the ailing Lord Somerset. Upon being asked by Director General Sir James McGrigor why she had taken unofficial leave, Margaret is said to have replied, 'I was fed up with my hair and wanted a proper haircut.' To which McGrigor responded, 'It would seem Sir, that your audacity is equal to the prodigious growth of your hair.'

Over the next few years Margaret was posted in

Mauritius, Trinidad, Tobago, Saint Helena and Malta, where she proved such a success that she was promoted to the highest rank a doctor could reach in those days – Inspector General of British hospitals. During the Crimean War she worked tirelessly to save the lives of soldiers, treating 462 wounded men from the war in Corfu. She then spent her three months' leave at Sevastopol in the Ukraine where she crossed paths with Florence Nightingale, who later referred to her as 'the most hardened creature I ever met throughout the army'.

In 1857, Dr Barry was sent to Canada where she was horrified to find that no provisions had been made to provide married soldiers with suitable quarters. Wives were obliged to live with their husbands in a room accommodating over twenty other single soldiers, and divided only by a thin curtain. In the face of great opposition, Margaret ensured the provision of special married quarters. A strict teetotaller herself, Margaret

IT WOULD SEEM SIR, THAT YOUR AUDACITY IS EQUAL TO THE PRODIGIOUS GROWTH OF YOUR HAIR

also began a huge campaign to clamp down on alcoholism amongst the soldiers. She saw this addiction as the single greatest contributor to accidental deaths, with many soldiers dying from hypothermia having fallen asleep in a drunken stupor. That same year, Florence Nightingale promoted her Royal Commission on Army Health which contained a large number of reforms first initiated by Dr Barry, though Margaret was to receive scant recognition for this.

Outside of her pioneering work in army medicine, Margaret became well known in her lifetime for her various quirks. She was a strict vegetarian and only drank goats' milk. To this end she brought her own goat everywhere she went. She defied anyone to comment on her feminine voice and features and launched many a duel with those who dared. Later in life Margaret suffered from chronic bronchitis and in 1864 she was forced to retire against her wishes. She returned to live at 14 Margaret Street, Cavendish Square, London, where her constant companions became her manservant John from Jamaica, a succession of dogs all called Psyche, a cat and a parrot. On 25 July 1865, following a severe outbreak of dysentery in

London, Dr James Barry died from the disease she had spent a large part of her life fighting.

The woman who took care of Margaret's deceased body later revealed her discovery that 'he' was in fact a 'she' who showed obvious signs of having been through pregnancy. When word of this began to circulate, the British army sealed away records of the surgeon's life for a period of 100 years. When historian Isobel Rae gained access to these records in the 1950s she slowly began piecing together the details of this extraordinary woman's life; a woman who rose through the ranks to become one of the most senior medical officers in the British military and who, through her pioneering advances in medicine, was responsible for saving the lives of thousands.

LOUIE BENNETT

FIRST FEMALE PRESIDENT OF THE IRISH TRADES UNION CONGRESS

— 1870–1956 —

Louie Bennett is not a well-known Irish historical figure and yet her influence on the workers' movement was such that during her thirty-eight years as general secretary of the Irish Women's Workers Union she successfully campaigned for many ground-breaking reforms, including better working conditions, better pay and extended paid annual holidays. She was the first elected female president of the Irish Trades Union Congress in 1932, serving a second term in 1948. An outspoken pacifist, Louie strongly disapproved of militant suffragette activities, but it was the suffrage movement that initially motivated her to enter the public political scene.

Louie's early life was one of middle-class privilege. Born Louisa Elizabeth Bennett on 7 January 1870 into a wealthy Protestant unionist business family

of staunch Victorian values, Louie grew up with nine siblings on Temple Road in Rathmines and later in Killiney, County Dublin. Her father ran the family business of fine-art auctioneers and valuers on Ormond Quay. After attending boarding school in England, where her latent nationalism developed to the point that she reputedly formed an Irish League in her school, Louie continued her education in London, before going on to study music in Bonn.

However, it was literature that most interested her in her early years, and it was through the representations of women's lives in the works of Charlotte Brontë, George Eliot and Henrik Ibsen that Louie first developed her ideologies on women's rights, describing Olive Schreiner's *Story of an African Farm* as 'a cry of rebellion against many things in heaven and earth, but most of all, against the injustice of woman's position in the world'.

In the late 1890s Louie acted as housekeeper for her brother Lionel while he worked as an engineer on railway construction in Northern Ireland. Louie continued to read voraciously and decided to embark on a career as a novelist, despite the advice of her writing tutor Barry Pain who cautioned her about the problems facing women authors. Unfazed by the apparent limitations of her sex in the literary world, Louie wrote her first novel, *The Proving of Priscilla*, which was published by Harpers in 1902. She followed this in 1908 with *A Prisoner of his Word*, a romance set during the 1798 Rebellion, in which her lead character Ross Lambart states, 'Great reforms are not effected at a blow; only by long and patient striving can a nation grow and gain greatness.' This was to prove a prophetic statement about Louie's future work as a trade unionist and social reformer.

Although Louie's career as a writer never fully took off, it wasn't long before the non-militant suffragette movement captured her imagination and

> **IT WAS THROUGH THE REPRESENTATIONS OF WOMEN'S LIVES IN THE WORKS OF CHARLOTTE BRONTË, GEORGE ELIOT AND HENRIK IBSEN THAT LOUIE FIRST DEVELOPED HER IDEOLOGIES ON WOMEN'S RIGHTS**

she began attending regular meetings. She became aware of the existence of numerous suffrage groups around the country and, being a highly organised and strategic thinker, she decided that these groups would be more effective if they were combined into one large group working towards a common goal.

In 1911, at the age of forty-one, Louie and her friend Helen Chenevix, one of the first female graduates of Trinity College, worked to combine fifteen suffrage groups in Ireland into the non-militant Irish Women's Suffrage Federation (IWSF), with both women becoming joint honorary secretary. That same year, Louie formed the Irish Women's Reform League (IWRL), the only women's rights society at the time not to contain the words 'suffrage' or 'franchise' in its title. Through the IWRL, Louie was able to promote a much broader range

SHE ESTABLISHED A NEW VIGILANCE SOCIETY … WHICH SAW MEMBERS OF THE IWRL PATROLLING THE STREETS OF DUBLIN AT NIGHT IN AN EFFORT TO PROTECT YOUNG GIRLS

of women's issues than simply the right to vote on the same terms as men. She instigated an investigation into working conditions in Dublin factories and reported her findings in the *Irish Citizen*, a suffrage newspaper that she would later edit. During this time she also established a lending library at the IWRL offices in Dublin, providing books described as 'covering all aspects of the women's movement', and she helped to establish a new vigilance society called the Girls' Protection Crusade, which saw members of the IWRL patrolling the streets of Dublin at night in an effort to protect young girls from dangerous situations.

Louie cited the 1913 Strike and Lockout in Dublin as a major influence on her work with the trade unions. Later in life, she recalled creeping 'like a culprit into Liberty Hall to see Madame Markievicz in a big overall, with sleeves rolled up, presiding over a cauldron of stew, surrounded by a crowd of gaunt women and children carrying bowls and cans'. Dismayed by the sight of starving women and children, Louie joined other IWRL members in an aid scheme to provide daily meals for strikers' families, and she appealed in the *Irish Citizen* for funds to relieve the distress of families affected by the strike.

In 1915 Louie became a member of the Women's International League for Peace and Freedom, which was set up by feminists from around the world who refused to let the outbreak of war in 1914 postpone their campaign for the vote. Many of the league's members linked the war and militarism in general with the fact that more than half the adult population were excluded from the political process because of their gender. Louie was upset by the way in which the question of suffrage was cast aside in the fight for Home Rule, declaring that 'women should never have abandoned their struggle for justice, war or no war'. As an Irish delegate of the league, Louie regularly travelled around Europe to discuss issues of peace and human welfare.

In 1916, urged on by Helena Molony, general secretary of the Irish Women's Workers Union (IWWU), Louie took on the daunting task of organising female workers, for, as she said later of that time, 'the Irish woman worker was a neglected factor in industry, exploited and shamefully underpaid'. Starting with 'the aristocrats of industry' – the women printers – Louie later recalled, 'I had absolutely no idea how to go about it. But I was burning with enthusiasm. I had no money. No office. No furniture. Nothing. But I went out and I got one member to start me off. I put her name down in a twopenny jotter and hoped fervently for more.' And so began a 'timid campaign' of waiting outside printers' workshops and thrusting handbills at uninterested women workers.

The following year Louie became general secretary of the IWWU and held this post until she retired in 1955 at the age of eighty-five. Within two years the IWWU membership had exceeded 5,000 and was being described by the *Irish Citizen* as 'a new force in Irish affairs which no class of politicians can ignore'. Louie visited factories, fruit farms, laundries and hospitals all over the country to observe working conditions first-hand. She consulted shop stewards regarding precise manufacturing requirements within specific industries so that she would be better prepared when it came to negotiating with employers.

In 1945 Louie experienced one of her finest moments in office when she led the laundry workers in a successful fourteen-week strike, demanding an extra week of paid holidays in the year, which would amount to a fortnight of holidays in total. Although Louie, who was nicknamed 'The Fighting Pacifist', was normally adamantly opposed to strikes, she endorsed them on this occasion, believing that workers' conditions were equally as important as their pay.

During her time with the IWWU, Louie campaigned vigorously for the raising of the school-leaving age, free school books, the provision of adult education, the provision of school meals, limiting juvenile employment, improving social services and health facilities, and the introduction of female factory inspectors to ensure that health and safety measures were met. On reflection, Louie stated that, 'The considerable reforms in working conditions that have been achieved in my thirty years' experience are largely due to the influence of women.'

Louie helped to achieve all of these reforms while attending to her other responsibilities. As an unmarried daughter, she provided care for her elderly mother and aunt, as well as her brother Lionel who suffered from arthritis. Throughout Louie's career she was also repeatedly forced to fend off derisive comments from those who felt that she was too middle class to be a spokeswoman for working women.

Upon her retirement in 1955, the woman described as the 'foster mother of thousands of Irishwomen' revealed in a press interview that although she was no longer working with the union, 'I'll never be able to stop worrying about my thousands of children in it'.

Louie lived in the family home until her mother's death in 1929. She then moved to St Brigids, the house next door to Helen Chenevix's home in Killiney, where she spent the next twenty-seven years until her death on 25 November 1956. She is commemorated by a seat in St Stephen's Green, Dublin.

EAVAN BOLAND

INSPIRATIONAL IRISH POET

— 1944– —

When Seán O'Riordáin wrote the poem *Banfhile* (*Woman Poet*) in the 1940s, which opened with the line 'A woman can be a poem, she can never be a poet ...' he was not to know that one of Ireland's most celebrated female poets was about to be born. Eavan Boland has since left her mark on Irish poetry in a way that no other female poet has over the last century. Boldly breaking through barriers established by a male-dominated literary tradition, she has focused specifically on female themes and preoccupations; reflecting the experiences of what one critic has referred to as 'women's secret history'. The first poet to examine the day-to-day milieu of the Irish female student, poet, wife and mother, Eavan has firmly adhered to her belief that it is the poetic tradition's ignorance of these experiences valued most by women that has led to a devaluation of her sex

in the world of poetry; women being mostly relegated to the place of passive muse or mother. In reclaiming the notion of what it is to be an Irish poet, Eavan Boland has given a voice to generations of Irish women.

Eavan Boland was born in Dublin on 24 September 1944. Her father Frederick Boland was an Irish ambassador and her mother Frances Kelly was a highly regarded post-expressionist painter. Eavan would later describe her mother as having been a 'transformative figure in my life. My mother was intensely supportive. As a painter herself, she believed in the imaginative life in a singular and radiant way.' Eavan moved with her parents to London when she was five and remained there for six years, after which her family moved to New York. In moving from place to place, Eavan's sense of language was continually 'overlaid by different places, accents and sounds. I think that's one of the reasons I read poetry as a child. It seemed to have a language of its own, always independent of place and change.'

IN MOVING FROM PLACE TO PLACE, EAVAN'S SENSE OF LANGUAGE WAS CONTINUALLY 'OVERLAID BY DIFFERENT PLACES, ACCENTS AND SOUNDS'

Eavan later returned to Dublin to complete her secondary education. During her first year back in Ireland she wrote 'the first poem that seemed real to me'. Entitled *Liffeytown*, it reflected the young poet's feelings about returning to Dublin. A year later she published a pamphlet of poems entitled *23 Poems*. 'It cost 30 pounds to publish. I think there were a hundred copies. My mother invested in them pretty heavily, and kept copies of them. I'm not sure anyone else did. But though it was a slightly offbeat thing to do as a teenager, I got confidence from doing it.' Eavan graduated from Trinity College with a BA in English literature in 1966. The young poet subsequently lectured at Trinity for a time but, frustrated by the rigid patriarchal structure in which poetry was being taught, as well as the lack of time she had to concentrate on her own poetry, she left and devoted the whole of 1967 to the study and writing of poetry. However, the more poetry Eavan studied and the more poets she met, the more she realised just how inaudible the voice of the Irish woman was in the long-established tradition of the Irish poet. Influenced by Sylvia Plath, Elizabeth Bishop and Adrienne Rich, Eavan found the courage to believe that being a woman need not limit her potential as a poet and in 1967 her first book of poetry, *New Territory,* was published by Dublin publisher, Allen Figgis.

In 1969 Eavan married novelist Kevin Casey and moved to the Dublin suburb of Dundrum, where she reared two daughters and began to write poetry about her domestic life; a subject that further differentiated her from Irish male poets. Her next three collections, *The War Horse* (1975), *In Her Own Image* (1980) and *Night Feed* (1982), quickly established Eavan as an important Irish poet whose female perspective opened up a whole new discourse within the realm of Irish poetry. In her collection *The War Horse,* 'The Famine Road' likens the suffering of a famine victim to that of an infertile woman, while in 'Child of Our Time' she examines individual responsibility in ignoring violence against children.

The reaction to Eavan's poetry in a male-dominated literary world was at first disparaging. 'Some responses were generous and accurate,' she recalls. 'But when I became more identified as a woman poet, and certainly wanted to be, a less critical and more emotive set of responses came into play. I often read attacks on my work that seemed to address some bias in the commentator on whether a woman poet, writing about the daily life of a woman, should really be considered seriously.' Undeterred, Eavan continued to explore the lives of women. In *Outside History* (1990), she mourned the lack of attention paid to women over the centuries. She also dealt with physical and emotional abuse, anorexia and the relationship between mothers and daughters.

As co-founder of the feminist publishing company, Arlen House, Eavan readily describes herself as a feminist, but makes the distinction that she is not a feminist poet. 'My poetry begins for me where certainty ends. I think the imagination is an ambiguous and untidy place, and its frontiers are not accessible to the logic of feminism for that reason.' One of her most famous feminist stances was against the under-representation of women in *The Field Day Anthology* of 1992, when not one of the twenty-eight sections was edited by a woman, and Eavan was one of only three featured female poets amongst thirty-four male poets. For her immeasurable contribution to the world of poetry, she was awarded the Corrington Medal for Literary Excellence in 2002.

Eavan Boland's poetry verbalises female experiences that were once considered either too banal or too embarrassing to be considered appropriate material for a poet. Through her honest explorations of marriage, motherhood, menstruation and mastectomies, she has given a voice to realities often silenced or slighted by myth – realities that define the lives of women.

CILL DARA

SAINT BRIGID KILDARE

NAOMH BRIGHID

SAINT BRIGID

FOUNDRESS OF THE FIRST RELIGIOUS ORDER OF WOMEN IN IRELAND

— *C.* AD 453–525 —

One of the most remarkable women of the fifth century, St Brigid, also known as Mary of the Gael, is still remembered and celebrated 1,500 years later, not only in Ireland but in many parts of Europe, particularly in Lisbon where Brigid's mother is believed to have been captured as a slave. As the only female patron saint of Ireland, St Brigid held more power in the Irish ecclesiastical world of her day than any woman alive today; her sphere of influence being such that her patronage covers a diverse range of subjects including babies, boatmen, children whose parents are not married, fugitives and midwives. Many miracles of healing are also attributed to Brigid who is said to have given sight to the blind, speech to the mute and a cure to the lepers.

Brigid was born around the year AD 453 at Faughart near Dundalk,

County Louth, a place long associated with Queen Medb. Her father Dubhthach was a pagan chieftain and her mother Broicsech was a slave. Brigid was influenced by the Christian preachings of St Patrick from a young age. In the *Book of Armagh*, there is a reference to the friendship that is said to have developed between the pair later in life: 'Between Patrick and Brigid, the columns of the Irish, there was so great a friendship of charity that they had but one heart and one mind. Through him and through her Christ performed many miracles.'

When Brigid came of age her father was keen to marry her off to a husband of a high standing in society, but this was not to be as Brigid was determined to preserve her chastity for God. A firm believer in prayer, Brigid prayed for God to make her physically unattractive to men. Her prayers were perhaps answered when she developed a pox that disfigured one side of her face, leaving the other side unmarked.

DURING BRIGID'S BLESSING AS ABBESS, SAINT MEL INADVERTENTLY READ THE RITE OF CONSECRATION OF A BISHOP. THIS COULD NOT BE UNDONE UNDER ANY CIRCUMSTANCES

Stories that testify to Brigid's generosity abound. When her ailing mother was sold to a nearby druid, and was unable to keep charge of the druid's dairy as was her duty, Brigid came to her aid. To help her mother who was living a life of great hardship as a slave, Brigid took over the running of the dairy, unbeknownst to the druid. Even though she often gave the produce away to the poor in the area, the dairy prospered and her mother was set free as a reward. Brigid would later be remembered as a patron saint of milk maids, dairy workers and cattle.

Despite her father's protestations, Brigid regularly donated many of his possessions to the poor who came knocking at their door. When Brigid gave away his jewel-encrusted sword to a leper, Dubhthach finally decided he had had enough and he gave his daughter leave to pursue her plan of forming the first community of nuns in Ireland.

Brigid followed Saint Mel into the kingdom of Teathbha which is made up of sections of modern Meath, Westmeath and Longford. She received the veil with seven other girls and each one selected a beatitude in which she wished to excel. Brigid chose 'Blessed are the merciful'. She asked the king of Leinster for land on which to build her new oratory and he promised her as much land as her cloak could cover. Six months later, Brigid returned with her cloak and in front of the king she gave the four corners of the cloak to four nuns who spread it out over the entire area of the Curragh, an area known then and now for horse racing. It was here in AD 485 that Brigid founded Cill Dara Abbey (church of the oak), the first double monastery in the world for both nuns and monks.

It is believed that during Brigid's blessing as abbess, Saint Mel was inspired by God and inadvertently read the rite of consecration of a bishop. This could not be undone under any circumstances. Hence, Brigid can be seen holding a bishop's staff in early pictures. Brigid appointed Saint Conleth as spiritual pastor and for centuries Kildare was ruled by a double line of abbot-bishops and abbesses who worked side by side healing the sick and helping the poor. The abbess of Cill Dara was regarded as superior general of all convents in Ireland, outranking bishops and with jurisdiction over all the churches in her area. Brigid became one of the most important Christian leaders in Ireland.

As the number of applicants to the monastery continued to grow, Cill Dara attracted many visitors from around the country who came seeking Brigid's advice and blessing. Many of them settled down in the area, giving rise to the nearby town of Kildare. Brigid founded a school of art, including metal work and illumination. The Cill Dara scriptorium produced the *Book of Kildare*, which according to Welsh historian Giraldus Cambrensis was 'the work of angelic, and not human skill'.

At the invitation of bishops around Ireland, Brigid travelled the country by chariot, converting pagans to the Christian faith and inspiring many women to join her congregation. She established convents in Longford, Tipperary, Limerick, South Leinster and

Roscommon. As it was a dangerous time for women to travel, she gained a reputation for fearlessness, leading to her patronage of travellers and sailors.

Brigid died *c.* 525 and was interred to the right of the high alter in Kildare cathedral. For many years afterwards, a fire was kept alight there in her honour. Her remains were later exhumed and transported to Downpatrick to lie alongside two other patron saints of Ireland, St Patrick and St Columcille. Brigid's feast day is celebrated on 1 February, when it is now customary to plait rushes into the shape of a cross, in remembrance of the cross Brigid made to convert a pagan druid on his deathbed. In her lifetime, Brigid was responsible for converting thousands of Irish pagan women and men to Christianity, changing the face of Ireland forever.

She remains one of Ireland's best-loved saints.

SISTER SARAH CLARKE

CAMPAIGNER FOR PRISONERS' RIGHTS

— 1919–2002 —

Sister Sarah Clarke was dubbed the 'Joan of Arc of English jails' for the years of work she dedicated to helping Irish prisoners being held in English prisons. Following the introduction of the Prevention of Terrorism Act in 1974 and the arrests that resulted from it, Sister Sarah became a lifeline for the falsely imprisoned members of the Guildford Four, the Birmingham Six and the Maguire Seven. While tirelessly campaigning for the prisoners' rights, Sister Sarah also looked after the prisoners' families when they arrived in England, acting as a guiding light for those who had been trying to feel their way in the dark.

Sarah Clarke was born on 17 November 1919, in the village of Eyrecourt in County Galway, where her parents ran a farm, a shop and a pub. From a young age she had wanted to become a nun but was heartbroken when it came to leaving her family behind. This sense of loneliness helped her empathise later in life with the Irish prisoners in Britain who had also been separated from their families.

On the day before the outbreak of the Second World War, Sarah joined the congregation of the La Sainte Union in Killashee, County Kildare, adopting the name Sister Mary Auxilius, though she would revert to her birth name later in life. She trained as a teacher and in 1941 she began working at a strict Catholic boarding school in Athlone where she remained for the next sixteen years. She was then transferred to the La Sainte Union's schools in Southampton and Herne Bay, Kent, before settling in the order's convent in Highgate, North London.

In the mid-1960s, at a time when the Vatican advised that the religious community should be aware of 'contemporary human conditions', Sister Sarah became the first Irish nun to study art at the Chelsea Art School, where she revelled in the cultural awakenings of the era, developed a life-long love for Johnny Cash and befriended art-student-turned-actor Alan Rickman. She hoped to use her skills in book illustration and religious decorative art when she left art school.

However, Sister Sarah would soon be taken down a very different path when the civil rights movement in Northern Ireland began to gain momentum, with numerous newspaper articles appearing about Bernadette Devlin's People's Democracy, alongside reports of a rising number of violent clashes between Catholics and Protestants. Sister Sarah kept herself informed about these developments, but it was a chance meeting on a train with a nationalist who had been attacked by loyalists as he marched in the 1969 Burntollet march from Belfast to Derry that had a profound effect on her. Soon afterwards, she sought the advice of both her mother provincial and her confessor, revealing that she felt she 'needed to do more than just pray for peace'. Her confessor pointed her in the direction of the Northern Ireland Civil Rights Association (NICRA), which was agitating against discrimination by the unionist government in Northern Ireland.

Sister Sarah was fifty-three years of age when she attended her first political meeting. It was to change her life. She was soon writing letters by the dozens to MPs who she believed would be sympathetic to the civil rights movement, but she received little encouragement or response. When the Prevention of Terrorism Act was rushed through parliament as a 'temporary measure' in the wake of the 1974 Birmingham pub bombings, it resulted in the arrests of hundreds of innocent Irish civilians. Sister Sarah decided to devote her time to tending to the needs of the newly imprisoned, as well as those of their families who often arrived in England oblivious as to why their loved ones had been arrested.

Over the next twenty-five years, Sister Sarah devoted herself to prison work. She arranged legal representation for those who needed it. She helped families locate prisoners who had disappeared into police custody. She visited prisoners and tried to reassure them. She attended court cases and took notes for relatives who couldn't afford to travel. She drove the prisoners' traumatised relatives from the airport or dockside to the prisons and back, and arranged their accommodation and meals while they were in England. As many of the prisoners' families were subject to harassment from an unsympathetic British public, Sister Sarah was granted her own flat in Kentish Town in London where she was able to accommodate the families herself. 'At that time you couldn't go into a café or even ask directions at a bus stop for fear of what people would say to you about the IRA,' explained Gerry Conlon's mother Sarah. 'Your legs would have turned to jelly.' Sister Sarah gave of her services indiscriminately and when asked in a television documentary how she could justify visiting murderers, she maintained that it was possible to 'hate the sin, but love the sinner'.

While working tirelessly on behalf of Irish prisoners, Sister Sarah frequently fell ill and at different times suffered from kidney stones, cancer, tuberculosis, polymyalgia and pleurisy. However, she never uttered a word about her own sufferings. When her eyesight failed and she was hit by a car, resulting in several broken bones and a shattered knee, Sister Sarah refused to waste any time in hospital and was immediately on the phone organising accommodation for families and campaigning for the release of prisoners.

At the age of sixty-five, she was barred from visiting prisons by the Home Office on the vague grounds that she was 'a security risk'. This meant that she couldn't attend the wedding of Guildford Four prisoner Paul Hill in Long Lartin prison, which upset her greatly. However, inspired by the biblical story of Daniel in the lion's den, Sister Sarah rose to great challenges in her long and inspired campaign for prisoners, and she would neither let herself be defeated nor lionised. Instead, she maintained a constant and focused fight for justice. She stood at the prison gates with the prisoners' family members, all the time keeping the momentum going.

One of the cases that most incensed Sister Sarah was that of the imprisonment of Belfast working-class family man Giuseppe Conlon, who later died in prison. He had been arrested after coming to London to visit his son Gerry, who was then under interrogation for the Guildford bombings. Giuseppe was sentenced to twelve years for possessing nitroglycerine allegedly passed to the IRA to make the bombs used at Guildford. As he lay dying he beseeched Sister Sarah to clear his name. Broken-hearted by the sufferings dealt to the Conlon family, Sister Sarah fought long and hard to honour Giuseppe's last request. The case was finally overturned in 1990. 'Without Sarah, I'd have been lost,' said Giuseppe's widow Sarah afterwards, 'and so would all of us. Without her, Irish prisoners would have been forgotten.'

AT THE AGE OF SIXTY-FIVE, SHE WAS BARRED FROM VISITING PRISONS BY THE HOME OFFICE ON THE VAGUE GROUNDS THAT SHE WAS 'A SECURITY RISK'

At the age of seventy-six, the now nearly blind Sister Sarah wrote her autobiography *No Faith in the System*. Using records that she kept in dozens of boxes at her flat in Kentish Town, Sister Sarah described in detail the horrific circumstances in which the Irish in England had found themselves over the past twenty-five years. During this time thousands of innocent people had been subject to false imprisonments, degrading strip-searches and violent interrogations while being denied proper legal representation. That same year, Sister Sarah, who was by now a veteran of police intimidation, was fingerprinted by the Special Branch at her home, before being forced to sign a statement she couldn't read. This was in connection to the escape of six men from Whitemoor prison five months earlier, after a gun and some Semtex had been smuggled into the prison. However, although Sister Sarah knew the families of the men involved, she had never been a visitor at Whitemoor.

In her final days, Sister Sarah is said to have spoken more freely about the family she left behind when she chose to enter the convent. It is clear that of all the sacrifices she made in her life, this was the one that caused her the most pain. Just before she died on 5 February 2002, at eighty-two years of age, she announced, 'I must go up the hill now and meet my mother.'

Before her death, the pope awarded Sister Sarah the prestigious *Pro Ecclesia et Pontificate* Cross in recognition of her work with prisoners and their families, and her pivotal role in the campaign to free those wrongly convicted of the Birmingham and Guildford bombings.

Sister Sarah Clarke played an important role in the campaign to free all those who were arrested and falsely imprisoned as a result of the Prevention of Terrorism Act. As well as being a religious woman of unwavering faith, she was also a practical woman who favoured direct action over prayer in the fight against wrongful persecution. When Irish people were denied their human rights and forced into degrading and heartbreaking circumstances, Sister Sarah Clarke stood beside them and lifted their spirits. She held their hands and assuaged their fears. She is remembered in the words of Giuseppe Conlon as a 'wee saint'.

MARGARET COUSINS

FIRST FEMALE MAGISTRATE IN INDIA

— 1878–1954 —

Margaret Cousins, better known as Gretta, was a lifelong campaigner for women's rights. In 1908 she established the Irish Women's Franchise League along with her husband James and fellow suffragette Hanna Sheehy Skeffington; its main aim being to persuade the government to grant women the right to vote. Margaret was also the treasurer of this group.

After moving to India in 1913, Margaret set up the Indian Women's Association to campaign for equal rights for women. She later became the first non-Indian member of the Indian Women's University at Poona, as well as the first female magistrate in India. A life-long theosophist, she was awarded the Founder's Silver Medal by the Theosophical Society in 1928.

Margaret Cousins, née Gillespie, was born in Boyle, County Roscommon, on 7 November 1878. Her father Joseph worked as a clerk at the Boyle courthouse and they were considered a wealthy family. As a young girl, Margaret attended the Boyle co-educational school and it was here that she first learned to play the piano, a talent she became renowned for later in life. Having won a scholarship, Margaret attended the Victoria High School in Derry. Later, she studied at the Royal Irish Academy of Music and graduated with a degree in music from the Royal University of Ireland. She began teaching music part-time and, at the age of twenty-five, married James Cousins, a Belfast-born, self-educated clerk and playwright.

From a young age, Margaret had felt an acute sense of injustice over women's exclusion from the process of choosing members of parliament to represent their interests. In 1908, dissatisfied with the level of attention awarded to women's suffrage within the Home Rule movement, she worked alongside Hanna Sheehy Skeffington to found the radical and militant Irish Women's Franchise League. The duo went on tour around the country, organising lectures and delivering heartfelt speeches. In 1910 Margaret travelled to England to join the suffragette movement and was arrested for taking part in a riot outside the home of the British prime minister on Downing Street. Margaret later described her month-long imprisonment in Holloway Jail as 'a living death'. In 1913 she was imprisoned twice for suffragette activities.

The Irish Women's Franchise League attracted publicity, both positive and negative, and during those censorious times they were often condemned for being 'unladylike' by nationalists who accused them of trying to deflect attention from what they saw as the more important matter of Home Rule:

> But the era of dumb, self-effacing women was over. Everywhere we explained that the Irish Women's Franchise League was not identical in its militant methods with the English suffragettes. We were not attacking shop windows; we had no Liberal by-elections, no Cabinet ministers in Ireland. We were as keen as men on the freedom of Ireland, but we saw the men clamouring for amendments which suited their own interests and made no recognition of the existence of women as fellow-citizens. We women were convinced that anything which improved the status of women would improve, not hinder, the coming of real national self-government. (Quoted from *We Two Together* by Margaret and James Cousins)

Margaret supported Irish independence but distrusted John Redmond's Home Rule Party as they had failed to support women's suffrage in the British parliament.

In 1913 Margaret went to London to lobby Irish MPs at Westminster to include the vote for all women in the Home Rule Bill. However, she would have to wait nine years for this dream to be realised. By this time, Margaret had grown weary of her fellow republicans' lack of interest in the campaign for women's votes and had left the country. She emigrated to India with her husband James, who had been offered the position of sub-editor for *New India*, a journal published by theosophists. Both Margaret and James had been students of theosophy, an ideology based on religious philosophy and metaphysics, for many years.

In India, Margaret became the mother of the modern Indian women's movement. In 1917 she was one of the founder members of the Indian Women's Association and from 1919 to 1920 she was headmistress of the National Girls' School in Bangalore. She was appointed the first woman magistrate in India in 1924 and held the position with distinction for many years, working to improve the welfare of children in her district. In 1926 she founded the All India Women's Conference, an organisation which today represents over one million women.

In 1932 Margaret was sentenced to a year in Vellore Women's Prison for openly protesting against new laws that prohibited people from speaking out against their government. While in prison, Margaret went on hunger strike in support of Gandhi's civil disobedience campaign. In October 1933, Margaret was released from Vellore and resumed her activities as an educationalist and campaigner for women's rights. Around this time, she also set up the Children's Aid Society.

In 1943 Margaret was left paralysed after a stroke. She died in Adyar, Tamil Nadu, in India, on 11 March 1954. She is commemorated in her native Boyle by a plaque unveiled by former Irish President Mary Robinson in 1994. One of the few Irish women to have inspired change both inside and outside of Ireland, Margaret Cousins helped set the wheels in motion in the fight for women's right to vote, a right that many Irish women take for granted today. Imprisoned time after time for daring to stand up for what she believed in, Margaret's actions have ensured the fairer treatment of women in both Ireland and India.

EILEEN DESMOND

IRISH POLITICIAN AND SOCIAL WELFARE REFORMER

—— 1932–2005 ——

Eileen Desmond was a woman of great resolve. Over the course of more than twenty years in the political arena, she boldly championed the right of women to equal pay, divorce and contraception. Following Constance Markievicz, she became the second woman to hold a senior cabinet post in Ireland. One of her greatest achievements was an unprecedented increase of 25 per cent in social welfare payments during an economic depression.

Eileen Harrington was born on 29 December 1932, in Kilcolman, a rural townland about eight miles from the small fishing town of Kinsale, County Cork. Her mother Ellen Harrington, née Walsh, was a seamstress and her father Michael was a postman and part-time fisherman. Eileen grew up in a

council cottage with her sister Patricia, who was thirteen months her junior. The family compensated for what they were unable to afford by growing their own vegetables and keeping hens. Eileen inherited a respect for education and an interest in world events from her father, while her mother taught her the importance of questioning rules. Although Ellen was a religious woman, she was never one to adhere to strict religious regulations. When Eileen was eleven her father went blind from glaucoma and she later recalled that from this point on she felt a deep sense of familial responsibility.

Eileen was educated at the Convent of Mercy in Kinsale before enrolling at St Vincent's School on St Mary's Road in Cork city, where she was one of only two female students to sit the Leaving Certificate. At the age of seventeen she moved to Dublin by herself, where she took up the position of civil servant with the Department of Posts and Telegraphs. In Dublin, surrounded by the tenements and slums of the late 1940s, Eileen experienced real poverty for the first time in her life and was deeply affected by it. She became a volunteer with the Legion of Mary and took a night-time course in social studies.

At the age of nineteen, Eileen met Dan Desmond, a TD from Crosshaven, who offered to drive her home for Christmas. At the time very few people owned cars and so a lift from a TD was considered a big deal. A relationship soon blossomed between the pair and they were married in 1955. As a result of the marriage bar that prohibited married women from working as civil servants, Eileen was forced to resign from her job. She now devoted herself to raising their two daughters, and in her free time she attended to the administration side of her husband's political work, as well as nursing him during his frequent bouts of ill health. They had been married only eight years when Dan, by then deputy leader of the Labour Party, died from a clot in his heart while being treated in hospital for tuberculosis. Eileen was left a widow with two young children at the age of thirty-two.

Dan's death caused a by-election in the mid-Cork region and Eileen, who was recovering from tuberculosis at the time, was asked to run. Having acquired a working knowledge of the political world, Eileen put her name forward and soon became one of the youngest members of the Dáil. However, her first foray into the political world caused a stir, with Taoiseach Seán

Lemass threatening to call a general election if the Fianna Fáil candidate Flor Crowley was beaten. When Eileen won on transfers, Lemass followed through on his threat and called for the dissolution of the Dáil before Eileen could take her seat. However, following another vigorous campaign, Eileen topped the poll again and was re-elected for the second time in a year.

From the outset, Eileen was devoted to improving the lot of women. She was angry at the marriage bar and the huge differences in pay between women and men working in the same jobs. She wanted to put an end to discrimination and financial injustice.

SHE WAS HIGHLY VOCAL ON THE ISSUE OF LEGALISING CONTRACEPTION IN IRELAND, A PUBLIC STANCE THAT RESULTED IN HER BEING DENOUNCED FROM THE PULPIT FOR PROMOTING IMMORALITY

One of her major roles during the early years was in helping illiterate people to fill out social welfare and medical card forms. Her sense of kindness and sensitivity attracted the disenfranchised who had been cast aside by various politicians in the past.

In the 1970s Eileen worked with Labour senator Mary Robinson in the landmark case of Cork woman Josie Airey who took the Irish government to the European Court of Human Rights and successfully challenged the lack of free legal aid in civil cases. Before this case, Josie had been unable to obtain a legal separation from her violent husband because she couldn't afford to pay the necessary legal fees. This ground-breaking case led to the establishment of the family law courts.

Eileen was instrumental in introducing divorce bills to Catholic Ireland, providing the framework for the eventual lifting of the ban on divorce in 1995. She was highly vocal on the issue of legalising contraception in Ireland, a public stance that resulted in her being denounced from the pulpit for promoting immorality. She was also involved in pressuring the then minister for health, Charlie Haughey, to improve the working conditions of nurses and to elevate nursing to the standard of a profession in Ireland. As Eileen's sister Patricia was a nurse, Eileen heard first-hand about the mistreatment nurses were all too often subjected to from the hierarchy of the medical world.

Eileen was elected to the European parliament in the 1979 European elections for the Munster constituency. She relished the opportunity to mix with the left-wing liberals of Europe who believed that anything was possible. She returned to domestic politics in 1981 when a Fine Gael/Labour Party coalition came to power and appointed her minister for health and social welfare, making her the second woman to hold a senior cabinet position since Countess Markievicz was elected minister for labour in the first Dáil of 1919. Eileen was now in a position to impact upon national legislation. However, a few weeks after her appointment her health failed and she suffered a life-threatening nose haemorrhage. Despite this, when a major political dispute meant that without her crucial vote the government would fall, Eileen was taken by ambulance from Cork to Dublin and carried into Leinster House on a stretcher. This incident became a source of great conflict within Eileen's family who feared she was sacrificing her health in her dogged pursuit of better rights for her constituents.

While still recovering from her illness, Eileen set about tackling the double portfolio of health and social welfare. She announced a new national poverty organisation, the Combat Poverty Agency and, during a severe economic recession, she fought for and gained a historically high 25 per cent rise in social welfare payments. During the abortion debate, Eileen made it perfectly clear from the outset that she was pro-choice, despite the fact that TDs suspected of not supporting the pro-life movement received mountains of hate mail and harassing phone calls. As a female representative of a rural constituency, she risked losing the support of some of the more conservative voters, but she was never one to be swayed when it came to her convictions. At a debate in the Dáil, she declared, 'We already have a ban on divorce in our constitution and it has done untold damage over the years. Under no circumstances will I support another constitutional ban on an issue that affects the lives and health of women.' While 140 members of the Dáil voted for the referendum, including eleven women, only eleven members voted against it, and Eileen was the only woman amongst those eleven.

Guided by her principles of equality and justice, Eileen was known for her common sense and steely determination, but she was also known to those closest to her as a shy and private person. During her time in politics, fellow member of the Labour Party, Fergus Finlay, described her as the 'quietest and most unassuming member of the parliamentary party', but that 'when it was an issue that involved conviction, rather than some question of tactics, Eileen's contribution frequently settled the discussion'.

Eileen retired from full-time politics at the 1987 general elections for health reasons. During her retirement she devoted herself to her grandchildren and often travelled to Bermuda to visit her daughter Honor. She was also proud to watch her daughter Paula become the first mayor of County Cork in 2002.

Eileen died suddenly on 6 January 2005. She was seventy-two years of age. At her funeral Senator Michael McCarthy, the Labour Party senator for Cork South West, gave a moving oration about her life and work in which he praised 'her formidable but understated abilities' and declared that 'her legacy is to *mná na hÉireann*, who have a shining example of what can be achieved, whatever the barriers or prejudice, to advance the interests of all of us'.

Eileen believed that people who grew up beside the sea, as she had, would always harbour a desire to push boundaries and to discover what lay beyond the horizon. In her long and varied career, during which she furthered the rights of women and the disenfranchised, while raising two girls and battling severe illness, Eileen Desmond proved this to be true.

BERNADETTE DEVLIN McALISKEY

CAMPAIGNER FOR CIVIL RIGHTS

— 1947– —

Bernadette Devlin was one of Ireland's most revolutionary political idols in the 1960s. During the civil rights movement in Northern Ireland, she was unflagging in her efforts to fight for the rights of Catholics. When she took her seat in the House of Commons on the eve of her twenty-second birthday, she became the youngest MP ever to enter parliament and her maiden speech was described as 'electrifying' by Tory minister Norman St John-Stevas. She came to embody the new Northern Ireland of the swinging

sixties, replete with revolutionary swagger, bold brilliance and an invigorating belief in the power of ideas to change the world.

Born on 23 April 1947 in Cookstown, County Tyrone, Bernadette Devlin was the third of six children. Her mother Elizabeth Bernadette Devlin, better known as Lizzie Devlin, came from a farming family who were firmly against their daughter marrying labourer John James Devlin, the road-sweeper's son, as they felt he was not good enough for their daughter. The sense of discrimination that marked the beginning of her parents' marriage stayed with Bernadette throughout her life. Although her father died when she was nine and her mother died when she was nineteen, both parents instilled in her a belief in equality and a sense of republicanism unfettered by bourgeois respectability or unmitigated violence. Bernadette attended St Patrick's Academy in Dungannon before continuing on to Queen's University, Belfast, in 1965, where she studied psychology.

In 1968 the civil rights movement changed the face of Northern Ireland, as thousands took to the streets in protest about the discrimination against Catholics in Northern Ireland. 'One man, One vote' became the calling-card that whipped thousands of beleaguered Catholics into action, including the young Bernadette Devlin who took part in the first civil rights march from Coalisland to Dungannon in August 1968. Two months later she took part in a second civil rights march in Derry, which resulted in a mass outbreak of violence that saw members of the police force attack peaceful civil rights demonstrators.

On her return to Queen's, Bernadette co-founded a student-led civil rights political party called the People's Democracy (PD). The party actively supported the campaign for civil rights for Northern Ireland's Catholic minority, believing that such rights could only be achieved through the establishment of a socialist republic.

On New Year's Day 1969, the People's Democracy organised a march from Belfast to Derry, modelled on Martin Luther King's civil rights march in the United States. From start to finish, Bernadette and the other marchers were viciously attacked by police and unionist mobs.

In February, Bernadette stood in the Northern Ireland elections and secured the highest vote amongst the eight People's Democracy candidates. After one failed attempt, she became the youngest woman ever elected to the

British parliament in April 1969 and the youngest MP elected in over 200 years, following an unprecedented turnout of 91.5 per cent in her mid-Ulster constituency. Upon entering parliament she declared, 'My constituency, as far as I can see it, is of ideas'. Over the subsequent months Bernadette addressed many open-air meetings in England, rallying support for the civil rights movement. She campaigned for the release of the imprisoned Pentonville dockers. On May Day 1969, she told the *Socialist Worker*, 'I'm against all repressive laws which attack my people – the poor, the workers and small farmers, British or Irish, Catholic or Protestant, black or white'.

In August 1969 Bernadette became involved in the Battle of the Bogside, a confrontation widely viewed as marking the beginning of the Troubles in Northern Ireland. When a group of nationalists began protesting against the marching of the unionist Apprentice Boys' parade in Derry through the predominantly nationalist Bogside area, a riot broke out which lasted three days, prompting the police to flood the area with tear gas. During the riots, Bernadette became a pivotal figure, urging the construction of barricades to block the entrance of police to the Bogside area. A month later, she travelled to New York and was carried through the city on the shoulders of proud Irish-Americans. When she was later awarded the keys to the city of New York by the mayor, Bernadette famously handed them over to the Black Panther Party. On her return to Ireland, Bernadette was imprisoned for six months for her role in the Bogside riots.

Bernadette's popularity quickly soared and she came to be seen as the politician of the people. In an interview with the *Socialist Worker* she explained why she believed she had inspired so many people: 'I was working class. I was a student, a woman. I wasn't seen as respectable. I was also a single mother while I was in parliament, which at the time was heretical. I think that touched a chord with a lot of young people, not to be afraid, not to be deferential and not to know your place.' Around the country, young women were shocked to see one of their own being elected to parliament. But while Bernadette looked like her peers, dressing according to the styles of the 1960s, in parliament she discovered that 'long haired, short-skirted women whistling in the corridors' were not encouraged.

Bernadette was addressing the crowd at a civil rights rally in Derry on 31 January 1972 when the British army opened fire on protesters. On this day, which would later become known as Bloody Sunday, Bernadette witnessed the shootings of twenty-seven protesters. She later told the Widgery Inquiry, 'The only clear memory I have – which I have now as I speak of it – is terror. That is all I remember, sheer terror.'

Days later, Bernadette punched Tory home secretary, Reginald Maudling, in the House of Commons. She claimed he had lied about the British army's role in Bloody Sunday during a statement to parliament in which he declared that the British had fired only in self-defence. When later asked if she regretted this attack, Bernadette replied, 'I'm just sorry I didn't grab him by the throat.'

In the early 1980s Bernadette became a prominent figure in the Smash H-Block Campaign, which supported the hunger strikers. As a result, on 16 January 1981, loyalist paramilitaries broke into her home in County Tyrone and shot Bernadette and her husband Michael. The couple had to be flown by helicopter to Belfast where they were treated in intensive-care facilities. It took them both a long time to recover from this ordeal and Bernadette took a step back from politics after this incident. However, in 1996 she returned to her original civil rights agenda when she co-founded the South Tyrone Empowerment Programme (STEP) to provide community development and training services for individuals and groups across the south Tyrone area. That same year, Bernadette's daughter Róisín McAliskey was arrested on an extradition warrant issued in Germany, having been accused of taking part in a 1996 mortar attack on a British military base at Osnabrück despite the lack of any actual evidence of her involvement. During her imprisonment, the then-pregnant Róisín was strip-searched seventy-five times in the space of four months, while her mother fought a vigorous campaign for her release. The British Home Secretary eventually vetoed the extradition on health grounds, but Róisín was arrested in 2007 on a European arrest warrant for the same offence. In November 2007, the extradition bid was again refused.

Bernadette Devlin McAliskey has been one of Ireland's most vocal agitators for civil rights. Honoured in murals across Northern Ireland, she has been pivotal in providing a legacy of change and female empowerment. In her quest for civil rights and an end to state violence, racism and prejudice, she has become one of Ireland's most inspirational women.

MÁIRE DRUMM

REVOLUTIONARY REPUBLICAN

— 1919–1976 —

Máire Drumm was a passionate republican leader, best known for her rousing rebellious speeches and her street politics. During the 1960s and 1970s she could be found standing on the street corners of Belfast or Armagh urging listeners to stand up to the British authorities. Speaking the language of the working class, she reawakened passionate patriotism in a people demoralised by bigotry, discrimination and inequality. One of the greatest orators of her time, Máire is remembered by many for her eloquent recital of Brian na Banban's poem 'Ireland's Enemy'.

Like Constance Markievicz, Máire put herself at the forefront of the republican cause when women were not expected to, and championed the rights of women throughout her life while maintaining her campaign for justice. 'Women are at last breaking the chains of being slave to slaves,' she said. 'We must make sure we never go back to being slave to slaves; but be the leaders and policy-makers of a new Ireland.' Her dual pillars of feminism and nationalism were later united in an interview by the BBC when, having been asked for her opinion on birth control, she replied, 'My family planning was always taken care of by the British government in that they interred my husband Jimmy on such a regular basis that contraception in my marriage ceased to be a problem.'

As vice-president and one-time acting president of Sinn Féin, Máire inspired a generation of women to aim for the highest echelons of the political world and to stand up for their rights as Irish women. During the internments of 1971, when 451 suspected members of the IRA were detained without trial at the Long Kesh Detention Centre, Máire arranged for the transportation of prisoners' wives and mothers to England, where they staged a protest on Downing Street. Many of these women had never before left Northern Ireland but were inspired to follow Máire's lead.

Máire was known to advocate the rights of loyalist communities who were suffering because of the bitter sectarian violence, and during her time as vice-president of Sinn Féin she met with loyalist paramilitaries in a bid to end the violence. She remained a constant campaigner for prisoners' rights and was known in her lifetime as 'Mother of the Prisoners'.

Born Máire McAteer in Killean, Newry, County Armagh, on 22 November 1919, Máire was the eldest of four children, brought up in an area steeped in the republican tradition. Her mother had been actively involved in the War of Independence and the Civil War. After attending a convent grammar school in Newry, Máire moved to Dublin and joined Sinn Féin. She then moved to Liverpool where she became active with the Gaelic League. After two years, Máire returned to Belfast and took a job at a grocer's shop on the Crumlin Road. Around this time she also developed a strong interest in camogie, and later worked in an administrative capacity with her club Gael Uladh and the Camogie Association of Ireland.

While visiting republican internees at Belfast Prison, Máire met her husband Jimmy Drumm, whom she married in 1946. The couple set up home in Andersonstown, West Belfast, and reared five children together: Seamus, Margaret, Catherine, Seán and Máire Óg.

In the 1960s Máire was involved in the civil rights movement to end discrimination within Northern Ireland. As sectarian violence between nationalists and unionists escalated, Máire worked tirelessly to re-house the thousands of nationalists who had been forced to flee their homes; her own home soon becoming affectionately known as Drumm's Hotel due to the seemingly endless stream of refugees arriving on her doorstep.

But it was during the Lower Falls curfew in July 1970 that Máire really made her mark. In defiance of British troops, she led over 1,000 women pushing prams laden with food and medicine into the Lower Falls, where sixty civilians had been badly injured and children as young as two were suffering from the effects of tear gas. This bold and daring move brought an end to the curfew and became one of the most historic female-led marches against violence in Northern Ireland.

In 1971 Máire experienced her first of two arrests for publicly protesting against internment. In 1972, in response to Operation Motorman, which saw the British army take control of areas believed to be under the influence of the IRA, Máire spoke out against the new military occupation of schools and public halls, as well as the field outside her home in which the British had constructed an observation post. She also led the protests in 1973 when Belfast republican Liz McKee became the first woman internee.

During their marriage, Máire's husband Jimmy was detained without trial for thirteen years in total, leaving Máire to rear a family of five on her own. At one point Máire's husband had the dubious distinction of being the most frequently jailed republican in Northern Ireland. She later watched as her beloved sons Seán and Seamus and her daughter Máire Óg were also detained without trial. She endured almost weekly raids on her house, as well as the persistent threat of death at the hands of loyalist paramilitaries.

In October 1976 Máire's health began to fail and she was admitted to the Mater Hospital, Belfast, to undergo surgery on her eyes. On 28 October three loyalist paramilitaries entered her ward dressed as doctors. They shot Máire dead while she lay recuperating in bed, injuring a nearby female patient in the attack.

The fact that Máire was murdered by paramilitaries is a testament to her influence on the community. In killing Máire, they laid to rest one of the nation's most inspirational speakers, who consistently fanned the flames of republican sentiment. As a wife, mother and member of the community, Máire was dedicated to change. She refused to silently endure the bigotry, discrimination and violence meted out to the people she loved most, and as a woman of her word she acted upon her convictions. Today, Máire's words live on in the many murals dedicated to her across Northern Ireland.

BIDDY EARLY

LEGENDARY HEALER

—✦— 1798–1874 —✦—

Biddy Early was a healer and herbalist whose success was such that she is the best remembered Irish folk healer of the nineteenth century. Tales of her healings were originally passed down in the oral tradition but nearly twenty years after Biddy's death, folklorist Lady Augusta Gregory compiled a collection of these stories for publication.

During her lifetime Biddy gained a wide-ranging reputation as a powerful healer, capable of healing animals as well as people. This was very important at the time as the rural community relied heavily on animals for their livelihood. Biddy was also said to be capable of fixing other problems associated with farm life including the restoration of spring wells. She was known for giving out herbal cures in small sachets and liquid potions in small bottles, accompanied by strict verbal instructions as to how they should be administered since Biddy could neither read nor write. She spoke mostly in Irish but had a working knowledge of English and it is thought that she could speak Shelta, the language of the ancient mystics and the Irish travellers. Commonly known as 'The Wise Woman of Clare', Biddy was also said to be extremely intuitive, which helped both her in diagnosing ailments and in uncovering the ulterior motives of some of her visitors. Many people believed that she could tell if someone had visited a doctor or priest before consulting her. With the aid of a dark blue-green glass bottle, it is said she could see visions of the past, present and future, and could tell when a stranger was travelling a long journey to seek her help, often walking halfway herself to meet them. Biddy's kindness further enhanced her legendary status. She never accepted money for her cures, preferring token gifts of food or alcohol, and she always gave any leftovers away. The door to her house was always open and she gave shelter to many a weary traveller.

Another great power which Biddy was accredited with was the ability to communicate with fairies and assuage their infamous wrath. Biddy claimed to have been able to speak to the fairies in their own language since she was a little girl. She was often asked for help by those who believed themselves to have been bewitched by the 'little people'. In one story, Biddy was visited by a man whose entire herd of cattle had been cursed by the fairies and fell ill as a result. Upon gazing into her bottle, Biddy saw that the farmer had planted a whitethorn bush along a fairy path in his field. She instructed him to go home and remove the bush. As soon as he had done this, his entire herd immediately returned to full health.

> **SHE NEVER ACCEPTED MONEY FOR HER CURES, PREFERRING TOKEN GIFTS OF FOOD OR ALCOHOL**

Biddy was born in Faha Ridge in 1798. Her father John Thomas Connors was a poor farmer while his wife Ellen Connors was a skilled herbalist. Ellen often reverted to her maiden name Early after she was married, prompting her loyal daughter to do the same in later life. It is believed that Biddy's powers may have been passed on to her through the female line, with her mother teaching her all about the use of native herbal cures, a skill for which she was renowned. Both of Biddy's parents died when she was sixteen, her mother of malnutrition and her father of typhus, and Biddy, unable to keep up the rent on the family home, went to work at a poorhouse in Gurteenreagh. It was here that she met her first husband, Pat Malley, a man twice her age. Pat already had a son from a previous marriage and the three of them went to live in a three-room cottage in Feakle. Soon afterwards Biddy gave birth to her first and only child, a son she named Paddy.

It was in Feakle that Biddy first earned a reputation for her cures. Allowing her clients to choose their own method of payment, Biddy's home soon filled up with the common trade items of the day – whiskey and poitín. The men of the house were understandably happy with this business arrangement but sadly, five years into the marriage Pat Malley died from alcoholism. Shortly after Pat's death, at the age of twenty-five, Biddy married her stepson John Malley, who was much closer to her own age than his father had been.

IN 1869, AT THE AGE OF SEVENTY-ONE, SHE WAS MARRIED FOR THE FOURTH AND FINAL TIME

It is believed that Biddy's son Paddy died at the age of eight from typhus and some believe that he gave Biddy her powers upon his deathbed so that she could earn a living. Another story describes Paddy winning Biddy's treasured glass bottle in a game of hurley against a mysterious team of strangers who subsequently disappeared. But there are other accounts of Paddy leaving home as a young man, frustrated with the constant stream of visitors to his home. The one thing that is clear is that Paddy did not feature in Biddy's life for very long after her second marriage.

When John Malley also died from alcoholism, leaving her widowed for a second time, Biddy wed a young man called Tom Flannery. The couple moved to a house in Kilbarron overlooking a lake that was to become known as Biddy Early's lake. It was around this time that Biddy's reputation expanded and many well-known people began seeking her advice, among them Daniel O'Connell, otherwise known as the Irish Liberator.

The Catholic Church soon began openly condemning Biddy's work and discouraging people from visiting her. Most priests came from a middle-class background and placed great emphasis on education. They were eager to put an end to the era of folk cures and superstitions. However, most of the locals believed Biddy to be a good and powerful person and they took no heed of the Church's warnings. When Biddy was accused of witchcraft in 1865 and brought before a court in Ennis, nobody would testify against her and the charges were eventually dismissed due to lack of evidence.

In 1868 Tom Flannery died, leaving Biddy widowed for the third time. In 1869, at the age of seventy-one, she was married for the fourth and final time to Thomas Meaney, a man in his thirties who, it is said, married her in exchange for a cure. However, Biddy is remembered as being a beautiful woman who retained her good looks throughout her life, always looking much younger than her years. Biddy and Tom lived together in her cottage in Kilbarron until, one year into their marriage, Tom died from over-consumption of alcohol. Biddy died in April 1874 and was buried in Feakle graveyard in County Clare. During her funeral a local priest remarked, 'We thought we had a demon amongst us in poor Biddy Early, but we had a saint, and we did not know it.'

While many of the details of her life are clouded by conflicting accounts, the one certainty is that Biddy Early was indeed a healer whose gifts, whether given to her by her son, the fairies or through instruction from her mother, were powerful enough to make her a legend.

ANN LOUISE GILLIGAN AND KATHERINE ZAPPONE

THE FIRST SAME-SEX COUPLE TO SEEK LEGAL RECOGNITION OF THEIR MARRIAGE IN IRELAND

—·— 1945– AND 1953– —·—

The names Ann Louise Gilligan and Katherine Zappone were first brought to the attention of the media and the majority of the public when they decided to seek legal recognition of their Canadian marriage in 2004. Prior to this both women had already gained respected reputations in the fields of theology and education, and were known as the co-founders of The Shanty Education Project – a voluntary organisation they established in 1986 to provide education and support to the residents of West Tallaght.

ANN LOUISE AND KATHERINE MET IN 1981 WHEN THEY WERE THE ONLY TWO CANDIDATES CHOSEN TO STUDY FOR A DOCTORATE IN THEOLOGY AT BOSTON COLLEGE

At the time, a policy of emptying inner-city Dublin of the under-educated and the unemployed had resulted in the relocation of 28,000 people to new housing ghettos in the four West Tallaght areas of Jobstown, Fettercairn, Brookfield and Killinarden. These areas had no amenities, infrequent bus routes and 70 per cent unemployment. Living in Brittas in County Dublin, not far from these housing estates, Katherine and Ann Louise witnessed the devastating effects that low employment, poverty and a lack of education opportunities were having on the residents of these severely disadvantaged areas. They became especially aware of the problems faced by the women in these areas, whose confidence and communication skills had often been eroded by their struggle with poverty and isolation.

Being firm believers in the power of education to transform lives, and as feminists who wanted to empower other women, Ann Louise and Katherine opened their new home to the women of West Tallaght, and organised free classes in confidence-building, organisational skills, feminist theology and spirituality. They arranged free childcare so that more mothers could take advantage of this second chance at education. The Shanty also offered the women of Tallaght a calm alternative to their sometimes traumatic home lives.

It wasn't long before Ann Louise and Katherine realised that their home wasn't large enough to satisfy the ever-increasing demand for courses, so after much fundraising and with the support of the burgeoning Shanty community, they converted the four-door garage adjoining their house into a designated educational space which they called The Muse. Eight different courses were soon being offered, ranging from literacy training through to diploma courses accredited by Maynooth University.

Over the next ten years The Muse flourished, but it also became evident that for real change to occur within the area, a centre of change and development would need to be constructed in the geographical heart of the community. Ann Louise, Katherine and The Shanty Education Project management team began to lobby for state funding. They were just preparing to march on the Dáil in September 1999 when they were awarded €1 million to build An Cosán, a multi-purpose facility in Jobstown with an in-house childcare unit called Rainbow House. An Cosán now offers education and training to over 400 adults every week, as well as early-childhood education and out-of-school education for 100 children. The Shanty Education and Training Centre, which encompasses The Muse, An Cosán and Rainbow House, has gone on to win numerous awards and is recognised as a model of best practice in the community and voluntary sector.

Throughout the entire venture, Ann Louise and Katherine have maintained that it was the strength of their loving and supportive relationship that inspired them to press on and realise their goals in community and education work.

Ann Louise and Katherine met in 1981 when they were the only two candidates chosen to study for a doctorate in theology at Boston College. There was an instant connection between the pair, which was enhanced by a shared love of theology, social justice and feminism. A relationship blossomed and six weeks after they met, Ann Louise and Katherine decided they wanted to spend the rest of their lives together. On 16 October 1982, they gathered twelve of their closest friends together to witness their life-partnership vows, and the exchange of rings on which they had inscribed 'God is love – KAL'.

Before meeting Katherine, Dublin-born Ann Louise had spent many years in a convent before realising that she didn't have the strength of faith required to fully commit to a religious life. However, she remained interested in the possibility of communal living and spent some months working in a kibbutz in Israel. She taught in secondary education for a few years before being offered a position in St Patrick's College, Drumcondra, where she continues to teach to this day. Influenced by her powerful mother and grandmother, Ann Louise was taught from an early age to be independent of thought as well as financially independent. Growing up, she was involved with The Samaritans and St Vincent de Paul, but it was during her final year at school in Loreto College, Foxrock, in 1963, that a fundamental shift in her way of viewing the world occurred. A priest was invited to teach students at the school about the social encyclicals, which Ann Louise describes as 'the best-kept secret of the Catholic Church'. From this point on, Ann Louise was imbued with a heightened social consciousness. She would go on to work in the area of teacher education at both undergraduate and postgraduate level for over thirty years.

Like Ann Louise, Katherine was also inspired by religion from a young age. Born in Washington in 1953 she attended mass every day before school and during playtime she would pretend to be a priest. She later studied medicine at Gonzaga University where her one non-science class was the Letters of St Paul. Her lecturer Fr Vincent Beuzer SJ saw a born theologian in Katherine and encouraged her to major in theology. Having completed a master's degree in religious studies in 1978, Katherine moved to New York where she chaired a department of religion for the Marymount School of New York. Here, she strove to make religion more relevant to the lives of rich young women from wealthy families, often bringing her students to Maryhouse, a Catholic Worker hospitality house for women and children, where they served lunch to the homeless. In September 1981, having ended a secret relationship of thirteen years with another woman, a heartbroken Katherine arrived in Boston. Over the next eleven years she lectured and developed courses in theology all over the world. She published widely in the areas of feminism, ethics, equality issues, spirituality and education.

Katherine taught part-time in Trinity College, Dublin, for nine years but, following a long and unsuccessful battle to see her years of dedicated work rewarded with a full-time post, she decided to enter a master's degree programme in business administration in UCD. This qualification subsequently led to her appointment as chief executive of the National Women's Council in Ireland, and later to her position as a public policy research consultant.

On 13 September 2003, Ann Louise and Katherine were legally married in Vancouver, Canada. They had been living together for twenty-three years. Upon returning home to Ireland, where they were both Irish citizens, they contacted the Revenue Commissioners to inform them of their marriage and to claim the various tax allowances to which married couples are entitled in Ireland. The Revenue Commissioners informed them that their claim for allowances had been rejected. This decision was made on the basis that although the tax legislation does not define husband or wife, the *Oxford English Dictionary* defines 'husband' as a married man, and 'wife' as a married woman. Ann Louise and Katherine, a couple who had devoted most of their adult lives to enhancing the conditions of the oppressed, now felt the full weight of oppression bearing down on this important area of their lives. They researched the decision and discovered that unless their Canadian marriage was recognised in Ireland they would not be entitled to the benefits enjoyed by heterosexual married couples in the areas of healthcare, taxation, maintenance, citizenship, property and inheritance rights.

TAKING THEIR CASE TO COURT WOULD MEAN REVEALING THEIR SEXUALITY TO THE NATION

Taking their case to court would mean revealing their sexuality to the nation. Also, as an employee of the Catholic-run St Patrick's, there was a fear that Ann Louise could lose her job. However, the pair felt strongly that they were being denied their constitutional right to equality and so they decided to take action. They consulted Phil O'Hehir of Brophy Solicitors, and barristers Ivana Bacik, BL, and Gerard Hogan, SC, who in November 2004 brought proceedings on their behalf to the High Court, challenging the decision of the Revenue Commissioners not to recognise their Canadian marriage. It was argued before the High Court that Katherine and Ann Louise had a constitutional right to equality – a right to marry, property rights, and family rights – under the constitutional protection of the family in Article 41. It was argued that these rights had been breached by the failure of the Revenue Commissioners to recognise their marriage. It was also argued that the failure to recognise their marriage breached their rights under the European Convention on Human Rights. After losing their case in the High Court, Ann Louise and Katherine appealed to the Supreme Court. As this book is going to press, the case is still pending. In 2008 the couple wrote a joint biography called *Our Lives Out Loud* in which they detailed the events leading up to the court case.

Brave and pioneering, Ann Louise Gilligan and Katherine Zappone have consistently stood by their convictions and, when necessary, acted upon them. As founders of The Shanty Education Project they are responsible for providing second-chance education and a new lease on life to thousands of women in West Tallaght. As the first same-sex couple to seek legal recognition of their marriage in Ireland they have been instrumental in rallying the Irish gay and lesbian community in the direction of legislative and social change. They serve as role models for a younger generation of gays and lesbians who will benefit greatly from the changes in society made as a result of the controversial KAL case.

MAUD GONNE

IRISH REVOLUTIONARY

—— 1865–1953 ——

Maud Gonne is remembered first and foremost as the muse of celebrated Irish poet W.B. Yeats, but this limited recollection does a great disservice to her memory. Maud was one of the original Irish freedom fighters, her life's work devoted to freeing Ireland from English rule. A lifelong campaigner for the alleviation of the plight of evictees, prisoners and children, Maud was instrumental in organising a scheme to feed the starving school children of Dublin, which later resulted in the extension of the 1906 Provision of School Meals Act to Ireland. A true feminist, she was also responsible for publishing *Bean na hÉireann*, the first Irish newspaper for women. As an artist she created many children's illustrations of Celtic legends, and through her work with Inghinidhe na hÉireann she was responsible for training a generation of actresses who later made the Abbey Theatre famous.

Born Edith Maud Gonne in Surrey on 20 December 1865, Maud was the eldest daughter of Captain Thomas Gonne, a wealthy British army colonel of Irish descent, and his wife Edith Frith Cook. When Edith died of tuberculosis in 1871, Maud and her younger sister Kathleen were sent to France to be educated by a governess, before moving with their father to his new post at the Curragh, Kildare, in 1882. In Kildare, Maud enjoyed her teenage years, frequently hosting parties and indulging her love of horse-riding. But her carefree attitude was to change upon the death of her father from typhoid in 1886. Maud later recalled that his dying wish was that he could have done more to fight the many injustices he had witnessed in Ireland. Opening her eyes for the first time to these injustices, Maud decided to honour her father's wish and to fight against them on his behalf.

Around this time Maud went to live with an uncle in London, where she became frustrated by English ignorance of the struggles of Irish tenant farmers. Having suffered a near-fatal lung haemorrhage, she returned to France to recuperate and it was here that she met and fell in love with Lucien Millevoye, the married French editor of the liberal newspaper *La Patrie*. Lucien and Maud shared similar views on nationalism and they decided to fight together for the French recovery of Alsace-Lorraine from Germany and the liberation of Ireland from England's clutches.

Maud returned on many occasions to Ireland where she campaigned for the release of Irish political prisoners who had been imprisoned for 'treason' in their fight against British oppression. In Donegal she organised protests against evictions and helped to rebuild some of the burnt-out houses of the evictees with her bare hands. To avoid arrest, Maud returned to France where she spread word of the mistreated poor farmers of Ireland through her newsletter *L'Irelande Libre*.

Maud first met writer William Butler Yeats in 1889; Yeats later described this meeting as the time when 'all the trouble of my life began'. He fell instantly in love with the six-foot tall beauty who he believed hailed from a 'divine race'. Maud later helped Yeats found the National Literary Society of London in 1891, the same year she refused his first marriage proposal. Under Maud's influence, Yeats became involved in Irish nationalism, later joining the Irish Republican Brotherhood.

During the 1890s Maud travelled extensively throughout England, Scotland, Wales and North America campaigning for the nationalist cause. In 1897, in protest against Queen Victoria's diamond jubilee, a monarch Maud dubbed 'The Famine Queen', Maud draped a black cloth over a coffin and paraded it through Dublin city in true theatrical fashion.

Between 1893 and 1895, Maud gave birth to two children with Millevoye: a son Georges, who died of meningitis when he was eighteen months old, and a girl called Iseult. Heartbroken by the loss of her son,

> MAUD [WAS] DESCRIBED BY KATHLEEN CLARKE AS 'A CAGED WILD ANIMAL' DURING THEIR INTERNMENT IN HOLLOWAY JAIL

Maud carried Georges' booties with her for the rest of her life and was buried cradling them in her arms. At the time, unmarried mothers in Ireland were ostracised from society and so Maud always referred to her son as her adopted child and to her daughter as her 'kinswoman'. In 1899 her relationship with Millevoye ended.

Maud co-founded the Transvaal Committee which supported the Afrikaners in the Boer War, and on Easter Sunday 1900, she founded Inghinidhe na hÉireann (Daughters of Erin). This was a revolutionary women's society that provided a place for female nationalists who felt unwelcome in male-dominated nationalist groups. Through the society, Maud offered Irish classes and drama classes to the likes of Sara Allwood who later became an Oscar-nominated actress. One of Inghinidhe na hÉireann's early activities was called The Patriotic Treat. As Queen Victoria treated 15,000 Dublin children to buns in Phoenix Park, Maud and her women upstaged the monarch by giving 30,000 people bread and butter in Clontarf Park. By now, Maud had become a national heroine. In April 1902, her legend was cemented when she played the personification of a mourning Mother Ireland in Yeats' play, *Cathleen Ní Houlihan*.

In 1903 Maud married Major John MacBride who, as a young man, had fought on the side of the Afrikaners in the Boer War. The couple were wed in Paris. The following year their son Seán was born; Seán would go on to win the Nobel Peace Prize in 1974 as one of the founders of Amnesty International. The marriage was short-lived and John soon returned to Dublin. However, Maud, afraid that she might lose her son in a custody battle if she returned to Ireland, remained in Paris where she worked with the Red Cross during the First World War. Following John MacBride's death in the wake of the 1916 Easter Rising, Maud returned to Ireland but was imprisoned shortly afterwards for six months in Holloway Jail alongside Hanna Sheehy Skeffington, Kathleen Clarke and Constance Markievicz, for her part in the anti-conscription movement. In 1922, along with her old friend Charlotte Despard, Maud founded the Women's Prisoner Defence League, which arranged for food, clothing and other necessities to be brought into the jails for prisoners. The league was banned a year later and Maud was imprisoned for smuggling goods into prisons. Along with ninety-one other women, Maud went on hunger strike and was released after twenty days. She was greeted at the prison gates by seventy-nine-year-old Charlotte Despard who had waited there for the entire twenty days in protest.

Until her death on 27 April 1953, Maud continued to support the republican cause and to work for the fair treatment and release of prisoners.

Maud Gonne, described by Kathleen Clarke as 'a caged wild animal' during their internment in Holloway Jail, was ferocious in her undertakings, prowling through life with a hunger to fight injustice and ignorance. She lives on through the poetry of Yeats and through the many changes in society she helped bring about.

LADY AUGUSTA GREGORY

MOTHER OF THE IRISH LITERARY REVIVAL

—⊷ 1852–1932 ⊷—

L ady Augusta Gregory was responsible for both stimulating and preserving Ireland's rich cultural heritage. Her contributions to Ireland's
literary legacy are endless: she collected the ancient stories of the
seanachaí, nurtured the creative talents of W.B. Yeats and Seán O'Casey, co-
founded the Abbey Theatre, and kept a twenty-year diary of the happenings
during the Irish literary revival – the only record of these events to be written by
one of the chief protagonists of the era. Through all of this, Lady Gregory promoted
a new source of national pride that stemmed from a culture of storytelling.

Lady Gregory was a prolific storyteller who travelled the length and breadth of the country seeking out the *seanachaí* and their stories, which she published in several of her bestselling books. Such was her dedication to the Abbey Theatre that in 1919, at the age of sixty-seven, Lady Gregory made her stage debut in the *Countess Kathleen*, standing in for an actress who failed to show up.

As the mother of the Irish literary revival, Lady Gregory opened her home at Coole Park to the leading literary figures of the day, including the writer George Bernard Shaw who later described her as 'the greatest living Irishwoman'.

Born Isabella Augusta Persse on 15 March 1852 in Roxborough, County Galway, Lady Gregory was the youngest daughter of an Anglo-Irish landlord family. Her father Dudley Persse had been twice married and had sixteen children, thirteen of whom belonged to Isabella's mother Frances Barry, who was originally from Cork. Isabella later learned from her nurse that shortly after she was born her mother, disappointed at not having had a boy, threw a quilt over her head and would have suffocated her had a member of the household staff not come to her rescue. It was into this unwelcome atmosphere that Isabella was born. Isabella found a more motherly figure in her nurse Mary Sheridan, a staunch, Irish-speaking Catholic who introduced her to the world of Irish mythology. Isabella's mother forbade her from reading novels until she was eighteen and so she turned instead to the *seanachaí*, the oral tradition of Irish story-telling, for entertainment. Mary Sheridan also introduced Isabella to the less fortunate world of the poor locals, instilling in her a deep sense of social awareness. As Isabella grew up she spent her time teaching Sunday school, helping the sick and the poor on her father's estate and fulfilling her familial obligation of nursing her brothers, many of whom were alcoholics.

In 1880, when Isabella was nearly twenty-eight years old, she married Sir William Henry Gregory, a widower with an estate at Coole Park, County Galway. As the wife of a knight, she gained the title Lady Gregory, as well as the approval of her mother for landing 'the big man'. Prior to this, her mother had let it be known that she didn't think her daughter attractive enough to ever marry.

Sir William, who was thirty-five years his wife's senior, was a well-educated man with many literary and artistic interests, and his home at Coole Park housed a large library and extensive art collection. He also had a house in London, in which the newlywed couple hosted a weekly salon frequented by many of the leading literary and artistic figures of the day, including Robert Browning, Henry James and Lord Tennyson.

The couple had been married for a year when Lady Gregory gave birth to their only child, a son called Robert who later died serving as a pilot during the First World War. The couple travelled frequently and Lady Gregory's first publication to appear under her own name was *Arabi and His Household*, a pamphlet published in 1882 in support of Egyptian nationalism.

In 1892 Sir William Gregory died, prompting Lady Gregory to wear black for the remainder of her life. She returned alone to Coole Park where she devoted herself to editing her late husband's autobiography. Her next publication was a 4,000-word essay called *A Phantom's Pilgrimage; or Home Ruin*, which was an anti-nationalist pamphlet against William Gladstone's proposed second Home Rule Bill; this was a clear indication of Lady Gregory's unionist leanings at the time.

LADY GREGORY'S INTEREST IN CELTIC MYTHOLOGY AND THE IRISH-SPEAKING WORLD OF HER NURSE MARY SHERIDAN WAS REIGNITED DURING A TRIP TO THE ARAN ISLANDS

In 1893 Lady Gregory's interest in Celtic mythology and the Irish-speaking world of her nurse Mary Sheridan was reignited during a trip to the Aran Islands. On her return, she took lessons in the Irish language at Coole and began collecting folk material, which would result in a number of publications, including *A Book of Saints and Wonders* (1906), *The Kiltartan History Book* (1909) and *Cuchulain of Muirthemne* (1902). The latter became the primary source of information on the heroes of the Red Branch line of Ulster kings, and was frequently used by Yeats and many other writers in their poetry and plays. In an introduction to one of Lady Gregory's most popular works, *Gods and Fighting Men* (1904), Yeats described the book as 'the best that has come out of Ireland in my time'. In 1894 Lady Gregory's literary research had a huge influence on her political beliefs when, while editing a selection of letters written by Sir William Gregory's grandfather, later published as *Mr. Gregory's Letter-Box 1813-30*, Lady Gregory became so convinced of the politics of these letters that she changed her allegiances from unionist to nationalist.

A few years later Lady Gregory met the aspiring writer W.B. Yeats for the first time at her neighbour Edward Martyn's house. Following a series of thought-provoking conversations about the need to reawaken Ireland's pride in its literary achievements, the Irish Literary Theatre was born. It opened in 1899 with Martyn's *The Heather Field* and Yeats' *The Countess Cathleen*, which Lady Gregory co-wrote. During this time Lady Gregory provided Yeats with money, a home, food and much of the dialogue he was to use in his plays. Yeats acknowledged Lady Gregory's patronage later in life when he said, 'I doubt if I should have done much with my life except for her firmness and care.' The Irish Literary Theatre was soon replaced by the Irish National Theatre Society, and in 1904 the doors of the Abbey Theatre were opened, with Yeats, J.M. Synge and Lady Gregory serving as its first directors.

In 1907, following the riots provoked by the opening of Synge's *The Playboy of the Western World*, riots that Lady Gregory described as 'the old battle between those who use a toothbrush and those who don't', Lady Gregory took the play on tour to America where she is said to have hidden amongst parts of the set during riots in New York and Philadelphia, while urging the actors to continue with their lines. She also began to produce material for her beloved theatre, writing over twenty plays including the one-act farce *Spreading the News* (1904), as well as *The Rising of the Moon* (1907) and *The Workhouse Ward* (1908). As she continued her fundraising efforts on behalf of the Abbey Theatre, she was ostracised by unionists who were aware of her nationalist sympathies, and frowned upon by nationalists who were aware of her unionist background.

Lady Gregory remained an active director of the theatre until ill health led to her retirement in 1928. Late in life she translated four of Molière's plays into the Galway dialect, completing the last translation when she was seventy-four years old. She also wrote a two-volume study on the folklore of her native area called *Visions and Beliefs in the West of Ireland*. Lady Gregory continued to read plays submitted to the Abbey until her death from breast cancer in 1932. Having transcribed hundreds of oral stories into the written form for the first time, thus preserving a collection of myths and legends that had been passed down orally from generation to generation since the earliest days of Irish civilisation, Lady Gregory was responsible for resurrecting in the public imagination the lives of such figures as Biddy Early and St Brigid amongst others. Inscribed on her tombstone is the fitting tribute: 'She will be remembered forever.'

VERONICA GUERIN

JOURNALIST WHO DIED EXPOSING DUBLIN'S DRUG DEALERS

— 1958–1996 —

'Shaped philosophy that she wanted to get the truth.'
This is how Veronica Guerin is remembered by an editor of *The Sunday Business Post*, the national weekly that launched her career as a journalist in 1990. With no formal training behind her, Veronica used the powers of persuasion that later made her famous to talk her way onto the staff of one of the country's most prestigious newspapers. Throughout her brief six-year career as a journalist, Veronica was fearless in her pursuit of the truth, unmasking the dangerous criminals of Dublin who proceeded to threaten her life and the safety of her family. Veronica was not easily intimidated though and the year before her death her bravery earned her the prestigious International Press Freedom Award from the Committee to Protect Journalists.

Veronica, also known as Ronnie, was born on 5 July 1958 in Artane, County Dublin. She was one of five children born to Christopher and Bernie Guerin. At the age of fifteen, Veronica revealed her powers of perseverance when she ignored the pain of a slipped disc in her back to play in the All-Ireland youth soccer finals. She studied accountancy and political research at Trinity College and after graduating went to work for her father's accountancy firm. When her father died unexpectedly in 1981, Veronica left accountancy. She worked for Fianna Fáil for a while before devoting her energies to the establishment of a public relations firm that would ultimately prove unsuccessful. However, it was through her work with Fianna Fáil and her PR firm that Veronica met many journalists and began toying with the idea of writing for newspapers herself.

At the age of thirty-one, with absolutely no experience in journalism, Veronica talked her way into the position of business writer for *The Sunday Business Post*, where her background in accountancy and her eye for a story set her on

> AT THE AGE OF THIRTY-ONE, WITH ABSOLUTELY NO EXPERIENCE IN JOURNALISM, VERONICA TALKED HER WAY INTO A POSITION AS BUSINESS WRITER FOR *THE SUNDAY BUSINESS POST*

the trail of those involved in the murky world of financial corruption. After three years she joined the *Sunday Tribune* as a reporter and built up her career writing about Catholic Church sex scandals and corporate fraud. It was here that she developed a reputation for 'door-stepping' – dropping in on her criminal subjects in their own homes.

In 1994 Veronica became an investigative journalist with the *Sunday Independent*. Specialising in crime stories, Veronica made a name for herself by launching a one-woman crusade against Dublin's violent inner-city drug gangs. She visited areas of Dublin that had been crippled by the drug trade and was horrified by the number of children dying from heroin overdoses in needle-strewn wastelands, while the men who profited from their deaths walked free. At the time there were over 8,000 drug addicts in Dublin alone, while over a dozen gangland killings remained unsolved. Outraged by the gardaí's inability to bring these dangerous men to justice, Veronica used the pages of the *Sunday Independent* to name and shame those involved. To circumvent libel laws she identified pivotal members using street-names and pseudonyms such as The Penguin, The Coach, The Boxer and The General.

Veronica boldly introduced herself to the more sinister members of the drugs world, offering them a chance to tell their side of the story in return for leaking inside information to her. Using known criminals as her sources, she was able to expose the finer details of the criminal hierarchy. However, these exposés made it increasingly hard for the criminals to operate and Veronica soon began receiving death threats. In October 1994 two bullets were fired through the window of her cottage in north Dublin as she played with her young son Cathal. On 30 January 1995, the day after she had published an article profiling The Monk, a man suspected of planning the biggest robbery in Irish history, Veronica opened her front door to find a man pointing a handgun at her head. After an excruciating minute he lowered the gun and shot her in the thigh. Leaving hospital that evening on crutches, Veronica asked her husband Graham to take her to visit every crime boss she knew. She wanted to let them know that she could not be intimidated. 'I vow,' she said, 'that the eyes of justice, the eyes of this journalist will not be shut again. No hand can deter me from my battle for the truth.'

Fearing for Veronica's life, the *Sunday Independent* installed a security system in her house and arranged for her to be kept under twenty-four-hour protection by the gardaí. Several days later Veronica requested that this protection be removed. She felt that it hindered her efforts to gather information from criminals as they were refusing to speak to her if she was seen in the company of the police.

In September 1995 Guerin paid a visit to ex-convict John Gilligan at his stud farm in the countryside. She proceeded to question Gilligan on how he was able to afford such a luxurious lifestyle with no apparent income. Gilligan responded by ripping open Veronica's shirt to check if she was wearing a hidden microphone, which she was not, before proceeding to beat her savagely. During a subsequent telephone conversation, Gilligan threatened to kill Veronica and harm her six-year-old son if she published anything about him in the newspapers. Veronica worried about her son's safety but, haunted by the drug-addled children she had seen, she was determined that her own child would not grow up in a crime-infested city where the authorities appeared to be unable to deal with the drug epidemic.

In the last articles she wrote before her murder, Veronica exposed herself to libel charges by putting real names and faces to the nicknames. She forced criminals, whose identities had previously been known to relatively few, into the public arena and thereby hampered their illegal activities. Her exasperation with the gardaí's apparent powerlessness had reached boiling point.

On the afternoon of 26 September 1996, two days before she was due to speak at a Freedom Forum conference in London on the subject of 'Dying to Tell a Story: Journalists at Risk', Guerin was driving alone in her car, when she stopped at a traffic light on the Naas dual carriageway and made a quick call to a friend on her cellular phone. While she laughed and chatted, two men on a motorcycle pulled up alongside her car and smashed her side window. One of the men opened fire, shooting

SHE FORCED CRIMINALS, WHOSE IDENTITIES HAD PREVIOUSLY BEEN KNOWN TO RELATIVELY FEW, INTO THE PUBLIC ARENA

Guerin numerous times in the neck and chest, killing her almost instantly. According to figures compiled by the Committee to Protect Journalists, Veronica was the twenty-fourth journalist that year to die in the line of duty and she was the first journalist murdered in the Republic of Ireland. As a mark of respect, her funeral was attended by the then Irish president, Mary Robinson, and a minute's silence was observed around the country.

Veronica changed the face of investigative journalism in Ireland. In death, she achieved what she had worked tirelessly to achieve in life; the dissolution of Dublin's most powerful drug gangs. It took her high-profile death, rather than the deaths of the countless children that had fuelled her initial outrage, to finally propel the authorities into action. Veronica's murder led to the largest criminal investigation the gardaí had ever mounted in the Republic of Ireland, resulting in over 150 arrests. Realising the potential of using tax-enforcement laws as a means of deterring and punishing criminals, the Irish government established the Criminal Assets Bureau (CAB) and implemented the Proceeds Against Crime Act 1996. Many Dublin criminals subsequently fled the country to avoid arrest. To help prosecute these men, the first ever Witness Protection Programme was set up in Ireland.

In a joint statement issued by leading editors in Ireland and Great Britain following her death, Veronica was described as 'a brave and brilliant reporter who was gunned down for being tenacious'. Her pursuit of justice in the face of intimidation made her one of the most remarkable women of the twentieth century.

ANNA HASLAM

PIONEERING SUFFRAGETTE

— 1829–1922 —

A nna Haslam was the founding member of numerous social, suffrage and union associations in Ireland and England. She promoted women's education, helped to establish centres of learning for women and successfully campaigned for the right of women to be eligible for election as county councillors. Described by her colleagues as 'one of the giants of the women's cause', Anna took part in virtually every campaign for women's rights in Ireland during the latter half of the nineteenth century.

Anna Maria Fisher was born in Youghal, County Cork, in April 1829. She was the second youngest of seventeen children born to Abraham Fisher of Youghal and Jane Moore of Neath in southern Wales. Anna's parents were wealthy Quakers who owned a corn-milling business and were engaged in a wide range of philanthropic activities, including the anti-slavery movement and the international peace movement. As a young girl, Anna also became interested in social and volunteer work and she helped in a soup kitchen in Youghal during the Great Famine of 1845–1849. She also started up an industry with her sister, teaching young girls how to knit and crochet and then arranging for the sale of their products. Anna regularly attended Quaker provincial meetings, and later described her religion as her training in gender equality, as the Quaker faith afforded more rights to their female members than any other faith at the time.

Anna was educated at Quaker boarding schools in Waterford and in Yorkshire, England. After graduating from school, she returned to Yorkshire in 1853 as a teacher at the Ackworth School. It was here that she met fellow Irish Quaker and teacher, Thomas Haslam. They married in a civil ceremony in Cork a year later and moved to Dublin shortly afterwards, where Thomas worked as a book-keeper. By this time Thomas had left behind the structured Quaker life and had been disowned by his monthly meeting group in London as a result. As Anna and Thomas had married in a civil ceremony, Anna was also expelled from the society. However, they had already benefited greatly from the educational and feminist teachings of the Quaker faith and continued to live according to these teachings for the rest of their lives.

Thomas, who was a dedicated feminist, assisted Anna in her efforts to gain the female vote. Anna later remarked that marriage brought her 'a most valuable helper' in her husband. It is believed that the Haslams determined early on in their relationship that they were not financially secure enough to raise children and so their marriage was largely celibate.

Having had the opportunity to avail of a high-quality education, Anna was adamant that this right should be open to all women. In 1861 she was part of a group that founded the Irish Society for the Training and Employment of Educated Women, later called the Queen's Institute, Dublin. This was a pioneering technical institute for women that led to Anne Jellicoe's founding of the Alexandra College for the Higher Education of Women in 1866 and the Alexandra High School for Girls in 1873. Anna also played a role in the successful campaign to have the Intermediate Education Act of 1878 and the Royal University Act of 1879 extended to girls. For the first time, girls were able to compete on equal terms with boys in public-school examinations and women were allowed to study for degrees in the Royal University. Anna later helped to set up the Association of Irish Schoolmistresses and Other Ladies Interested in Education which served to protect and promote the educational interests of women.

Throughout the 1860s and 1870s, Anna worked to gain access for women to medical degrees, and in 1874 she helped found the London School of Medicine for Women. She worked on the Married Women's Property campaign which called for an end to the law that declared all of a wife's earnings, inheritances and property to legally belong to her husband. Anna also became secretary of the Women's Vigilance Committee, which worked for the 'health and safety of women and girls, and the purification of the moral atmosphere of society'.

One of Anna's longest-running campaigns was that of the repeal of the Contagious Diseases Acts, which took her eighteen years to achieve. The Contagious Diseases Acts were passed in the 1860s in an attempt to curb the spread of venereal diseases in the British army. They provided for state regulation of prostitution in designated areas which included Cork, Cobh and the Curragh in County Kildare. Compulsory medical examinations were also implemented where any woman was suspected of being a prostitute and, if she was found to be suffering from a venereal disease, she was obliged to receive medical treatment. Anna and Thomas saw prostitution as a threat to family life and feared that these Acts gave recognition to the practice. They believed these Acts made women out to be commodities that could be cleaned up and passed on, and that by eradicating venereal diseases, the Acts were eliminating one of the 'natural penalties' that resulted from prostitution. While Anna spoke widely on the subject and wrote numerous letters to MPs, Thomas collected signatures from over a hundred doctors for a petition to repeal the acts.

In 1866 Thomas' health failed and Anna set up a stationery business on Rathmines Road to provide them with an income. As Thomas was never able to work again, Anna ran the stationery business for the next forty years while continuing to engage in the struggle for women's rights.

In 1866 the suffrage movement in England sent out a petition calling for the inclusion of women, on the same terms as men, in an impending act to extend the male franchise. In a fortnight they had collected 1,499 signatures. Amongst the fifteen Irish names collected was that of Anna Haslam and she later dated the beginning of her involvement in the suffrage campaign to this time. When the petition was rejected, the suffrage movement proposed an amendment of the word 'man' to 'person' the following year. When this too was rejected, organised suffrage action began in England and quickly spread to Ireland. As reforms in either country required laws to be passed by the all-male parliament in Westminster, women in Ireland and England decided to unite. In England the National Society for Women's Suffrage was founded in 1867.

In 1876 Anna founded the Dublin Women's Suffrage Association (DWSA), the city's first permanent suffrage organisation and the first such organisation to have a long-lasting impact in Ireland. Thomas, meanwhile, continued to write and publish pamphlets on the suffrage movement, including a number of editions of a newsletter called *The Women's Advocate*, which promoted suffrage events and organisations. While the right to vote was extended to men who had no property, women remained disenfranchised, leading Anna to declare that it 'is not easy to keep our temper when we see the most illiterate labourer, with no two ideas in his head, exercising the very important function of self-government while educated women capable in every way of giving a rational vote are still debarred'. The Dublin Women's Suffrage Association began to expand throughout the country, gradually becoming the Irishwomen's Suffrage and Local Government Association (IWSLGA) in 1901, which attracted both nationalists and unionists alike. Around this time Anna became immersed in unionist politics, taking part in the anti-Home Rule campaign with the Women's Liberal Unionist Association.

In 1908 the IWSLGA lost some of its momentum when the more militant Irish Women's Franchise League (IWFL) was founded by Hanna Sheehy Skeffington and Margaret Cousins. Three years later the most militant event of the suffrage campaign occurred when English suffragette Emily Davison ran onto the racetrack at the Epsom Derby and threw herself under the king's horse. She died from her injuries a few days later. With the eyes of the world now upon them, the suffrage movement began to pick up momentum. In 1911 they achieved a momentous victory when women were made eligible for election as county councillors. However, it was another seven years before substantial headway was made, and the right to vote was extended to women over the age of thirty.

In 1918, at the age of eighty-nine, Anna Haslam voted for the first time. She was given a place of honour in the voting hall and was surrounded and cheered on by a group of women who handed her a bouquet in the suffrage colours of purple, green and white. Unfortunately, her husband Thomas had died the year before and did not live to see the fruits of over forty years of their combined labour. Anna died on 22 November 1922, the same year the newly formed Irish Free State gave the franchise to all women and men over twenty-one years of age.

Through her life's work, Anna Haslam helped to change the position of women in Irish society forever. While running a demanding business and providing for her husband, she devoted her life to furthering the cause of women in education and politics, and was proactive in bringing about the changes she felt were necessary in society. When the vote was finally extended to all women over the age of twenty-one in 1922, it was in no small part due to the inspirational work of Anna Haslam.

LADY MARY HEATH

IRISH AVIATRIX AND RECORD-BREAKING ATHLETE

— 1896–1939 —

'Flying is so safe a woman can fly across Africa wearing a Parisian frock and keeping her nose powdered all the way,' said Limerick-born aviatrix Lady Mary Heath after her record-setting trip as the first pilot to fly a small open cockpit aeroplane solo from Cape Town to London in 1929. Mary is said to have crossed the Sahara armed with a shotgun, a couple of tennis rackets, six tea gowns, a Bible and a fur coat. She apparently passed the time by eating chocolate, reading a novel and trying to put on tights mid-flight in preparation for her arrival. It isn't hard to

imagine then why this six-foot-tall queen of the skies attracted so much public interest in the mid-1920s and for a period of five years was one of the best-known women in the world.

Mary's life was full of world firsts. She was Britain's first female javelin champion and set a disputed world record for the high jump (it was claimed that Hilda Hatt's jump a year earlier was higher), while her 100-metre hurdle time of sixteen seconds remained the Irish record for forty-one years. As a founding member of the British Women's Amateur Athletic Association in 1922, she was instrumental in successfully campaigning for women to be allowed to compete at the Olympic Games in 1928. However, when she found out that women would be allowed to compete in only six events, and not in an equal number of events to men, she quickly withdrew her support. Her book *Athletics for Women and Girls* (1925) was the first of its kind written for women athletes by a woman athlete and became the required text of the time. In 1926 Mary became the first woman to hold a commercial flying licence in Britain, followed shortly afterwards by fellow Irish aviatrixes Sicele O'Brien from Limerick and Lady Mary Bailey from County Monaghan. Mary was also the first woman to parachute from an aeroplane in Britain, touching ground right in the middle of a football field during a match. Following her pioneering flight from the Cape, she became the first woman to gain a mechanic's qualification in America where she became known as 'Britain's Lady Lindy', a reference to American aviator, Charles Lindbergh.

Mary never publicly discussed her tragic start in life when, in 1897, her father John Peirce-Evans, a notoriously violent man who suffered from mental illness, had beaten her mother Theresa Mary Peirce-Evans to death with a stick at their home in Knockaderry, County Limerick. At the time Lady Mary, born Sophie Catherine Theresa Mary Pierce-Evans, was only a few months old. Her father, claiming not to have 'wilfully murdered' his wife, was found guilty of murder and spent the remainder of his life in a psychiatric facility for the criminally insane.

Mary was sent to live with her grandfather and aunts in Newcastlewest. Educated at St Margaret's Hall on Mespil Road in Dublin, Mary proved to be a determined and headstrong individual from the start. She enrolled in the Royal College of Science in 1914 where she became the first Irish woman to graduate with a degree in agricultural science. During this time she also nurtured her love of sport by competing with the college hockey team and she often wrote articles for the student magazine.

During the First World War, Mary spent two years as an ambulance driver attached to the Royal Flying Corps, based first in England and later in France. But when the war ended and women who had been given a taste of the freedom of being able to drive and earn their own money were told to return to the kitchen, the recently married Sophie Mary Eliott-Lynn refused to follow orders. She was determined to make her own living. However, when she applied for a grant to complete her science degree after the war, a degree she was studying for so that she could follow her husband to Africa and make her own living on the land, she was turned down on the grounds that she was a married woman and therefore had no need for further skills.

In 1925 Mary became interested in flying and, as the first female member of the London Light Aeroplane Club, she made her maiden flight in August of that year. This was the age of the great air shows when aviation was something of an international obsession. While the wealthy took to the skies, those without wealth settled for the sport of spectatorship. Mary soon

AS THE FIRST FEMALE MEMBER OF THE LONDON LIGHT AEROPLANE CLUB, SHE MADE HER MAIDEN FLIGHT IN AUGUST 1925

became a favourite amongst fans, competing in air races around Europe and setting altitude records. She had qualified for a private flying licence in 1925 but shortly afterwards she applied to the International Commission for Air Navigation for a commercial licence only to be told that women were banned from commercial flying. True to form, Mary fought this ban, even proving that she was capable of controlling a commercial aircraft during 'that time of the month'. In 1926 she became the first British-based female pilot to be granted a commercial licence and this decision resulted in the ban being lifted on female pilots. That same year she set a world altitude record for light planes by reaching an altitude of over 16,000 feet.

In 1928, after her first husband William Eliott-Lynn drowned, Mary married Sir James Heath, a man forty years her senior, who indulged her love for flying by buying her her own plane. From this point on she was unstoppable. She travelled to South Africa with her new husband and while there she set her sights on a new goal. In January 1929, without either a radio or a comprehensive map, the thirty-one-year-old Lady Heath charted her own 10,000-mile route from Cape Town to London. Having initially estimated that the journey would take three weeks, she didn't touch down in London until three months later, sunburnt but wearing a fur coat.

Lady Heath was now a worldwide celebrity, and she regularly gave lectures on the art of flying, a sport she described as being 'so safe'. However, in 1929, at the peak of her success, she was badly injured in a plane crash while practising for the National Air Races in Cleveland, Ohio. She was unconscious for three weeks and hospital-bound for two months. She had a steel plate inserted into her skull and never fully recovered from this accident.

In 1931 Lady Mary filed for divorce from Heath in Reno, charging extreme cruelty. This divorce was not recognised, but when Mary married G.A.R. Williams in November 1931, Heath was granted a *decree nisi* on the grounds of adultery.

Lady Heath eventually returned to Ireland with her third husband Reggie Williams, an aviator from Trinidad. She went to work training pilots for the Iona National Air Taxis based in the Kildonan Aerodrome in Finglas; a company which was later replaced by Everson Flying and later again by Dublin Air Ferries. She founded the National Junior Aviation Club and trained the generation that would later join Aer Lingus. She is said to have landed her plane in every field in the country during this time, including Larkin's Field in Ballybunion, which was home to a woman she loved like a mother, her beloved Aunt Cis. Lady Heath was also known to occasionally whisk daring spectators up into the clouds and back, bestowing a legacy of skyward memories upon the people of County Kerry.

When Dublin Air Ferries went bankrupt in 1938, Lady Heath was left jobless and penniless. Following the breakdown of her third marriage and the onset of a debilitating drink problem, she returned to London where she died in May 1939 after falling down the stairs of a tram car. She was forty-two years of age. Since her death, her achievements have been remembered mostly by aviation and athletics fans, but there is no doubt that Lady Mary Heath is one of the most inspirational women ever to have spread her wings in Ireland.

NORA HERLIHY

PIONEER OF THE CREDIT UNION MOVEMENT IN IRELAND

—— 1910–1988 ——

Nora Herlihy's name has become synonymous with the foundation of the credit union, one of Ireland's most successful financial institutions. Nora promoted this institution throughout Ireland in 1958 to encourage people to assert more control over their finances and to curtail exploitation by money-lenders who maintained a persistent threat over the lives of the poor in 1950s' Ireland. Nora did this at a time when women were expected to assume a subservient role in society and leave financial matters to the men.

Nora, a dynamic and entrepreneurial woman, witnessed great poverty during her time working as a teacher in Dublin. She witnessed first-hand the devastating effects poverty had on her students, leading to sickness, malnutrition, inadequate clothing and housing, and the inevitable emigration of a parent or the entire family. Both urban and rural Ireland in the 1950s had been devastated by low wages. Less than 10 per cent of the population had continued on to second-level education and only 2 per cent had third-level qualifications. The welfare state had barely commenced. Most people did not have access to affordable credit or mortgages and were being preyed upon by illegal money-lenders. Deeply affected by this, Nora was spurred on to look for answers to the widespread problem of financial mismanagement and poverty.

Born on 27 February 1910 in the village of Ballydesmond in north Cork, Nora was the third child in a family of twelve. After attending boarding school at the Sisters of Mercy Secondary School in Newcastlewest, Nora followed in her father's footsteps by training to become a teacher at Carysfort College. She graduated on 4 July 1931, coming first overall in her final examinations. Nora began her teaching career in Ferrybank, County Waterford, but it wasn't until 1936 that she found a permanent position at the Irish Sisters of Charity School at Basin Lane in Dublin. It was here that Nora first encountered the negative effects money-lending and pawn shops were having on the community. At the time, there were pawn shops on over forty streets in Dublin.

A firm believer in lifelong learning, Nora enrolled in the first adult education course to be set up in Ireland at UCD. It was here that she met Tomás Ó Hogáin, a social economics student, with whom she first discussed the idea of 'financial co-operation' that had been operating successfully in America since 1908. Tomás invited Nora to a meeting about the co-operative system with Seamus P. MacEoin in December 1953. Here, Nora discovered the possibilities a credit union could offer; by taking part in common activities and goals, individuals could reclaim their financial independence. Three months later, on 6 March 1954, Nora and Tomás set up the Dublin Central Co-operative Society (DCCS) with the aims of creating employment through workers' co-operatives and neutralising the forces which caused emigration. Nora was then asked by the US-based Credit Union National Association to form a sub-committee to examine the structure of credit unions and their prospective function in Ireland. A week-long event was organised at the Daonscoil in Skerries in 1957, during which Muriel Graham of the Irish

Women's Association was present. The public's unbridled enthusiasm for the credit union idea led Nora, Seamus and Seán Forde to form the Credit Union Extension Service (CUES). After carrying out further extensive research on a voluntary basis, Nora concluded that credit unions had an important role to play in Ireland, and the credit union movement was born. In December 1957 Seán Lemass, the then minister for industry and commerce, appointed Nora as the only woman to serve alongside twelve men on a special committee to advise on legislative changes that would help to foster co-operative enterprise in non-farming sectors.

In 1958 the first two Irish credit unions were founded under Nora's guiding influence, one within a co-operative in Dublin and the other at Donore Avenue, a large urban community in the centre of Dublin city. In what was a recurring pattern around the country, the impetus for the founding of a credit union at Donore Avenue came from a group of women, in this case led by sisters Eileen and Angela Ní Bhrion. Nora, a member of the Irish Countrywomen's Association, established ties early on between the credit union movement and the Irish women's movement, and she was invited to talk to various women's groups throughout the country on the practicalities and benefits of credit unionism.

In 1960 Nora was instrumental in setting up the Civil Service Credit Union and the Irish League of Credit Unions. She became secretary of the latter union and operated out of the living-room of her house in Dublin for many years, where she is said to have worked morning, noon and night at this unpaid position. The Irish credit union movement started without any funds, relying solely on volunteers. While keeping on her position as a full-time teacher, Nora used her own money to fund the development of the movement. She played a large part in securing the 1966 Credit Union Act, and stood by President Éamon de Valera's side as he signed into law the act which set out how the movement would be governed and controlled.

Nora encouraged credit unions to develop their role in employment creation and emphasised the importance of education. As a result of her outstanding qualities of leadership in democratic adult associations, she became the first Irish person to be awarded a traineeship by the Credit Union National Association. She was sent on a three-month training programme to America, where she visited Madison, Alabama, Texas, Oklahoma, Toronto and New York. At its meeting in March 1963, the board of the Credit Union League of Ireland unanimously voted Nora Herlihy the person who had made the greatest individual contribution to the movement in Ireland.

Nora continued to promote and establish credit unions all over the country until her death on 7 February 1988, which happened to be the twenty-eighth anniversary of the founding of the Irish League of Credit Unions. Nora's pivotal role in ensuring the spread of the credit union movement throughout Ireland has enabled generations of Irish people to escape the poverty cycle and to become more self-sufficient in their financial management. Today, there are 521 credit unions in Ireland affiliated to the Irish League of Credit Unions, with nearly 3 million members nationwide.

GARRY HYNES

FIRST FEMALE RECIPIENT OF THE TONY AWARD FOR DIRECTING

— 1953– —

Garry Hynes is an award-winning Irish theatre director. She has built her career on a multitude of challenging and engaging theatrical works that have re-established Ireland as the home of a great literary and theatrical tradition. Like Lady Augusta Gregory before her, she is one of the few Irish women to have ever reached a position of power within the Irish theatre domain, most notably by taking over as artistic director of the Abbey Theatre in 1991. When she co-founded Druid Theatre in 1975, Garry quickly revolutionised a stagnant Irish theatre scene by seeking out and directing plays which represented Irish women in the truest sense.

Geraldine, or Gearóidín, Hynes was born on 10 June 1953 in Ballagha-derreen, County Roscommon. She moved to Galway with her family at the

Foundling by George Bernard Shaw, Sundance
Farrell, Master of Two Servants by George Mully,
Geography of a Horse Dreamer by Sam Sheppard,
Dick by Richard Maher and Roger Mitchell, Accidental
by J M Synge, Playboy of the Western World by J M Synge
Sheridan, Rising of the
Lady Gregory, A
Murphy, Same
Aron, Beggars
the Western
by
Waiting for
Theatre)
by Tom
Factory Girls
Western
Thee Dr Fell
Fo, Little
by Ken
Ken
Sisters
Anouilh
Look Back
Difficulty
Paul Vincent
by David
Gaslight by
Habits by
and Roger
Woods 1993
George Fitzmaurice
There are
Playboy of the
Pig's Dyke by
O'Flatharta
The Blue

age of thirteen, where her father earned a living organising vocational training courses. Garry was educated at the Dominican convent in Galway. She had seen only a handful of plays by the time she enrolled in University College Galway (UCG), but this was enough to give her a taste for theatre that has never left her. She quickly joined the UCG Drama Society where she realised that, although she desperately wanted to be a part of the world of theatre, she was terrified of acting. It was then that she began to contemplate the idea of working as a director. Having revealed her ambition to the Drama Society, she was asked to direct Terence Rattigan's *The Browning Version*. However, from the beginning she struggled with the casting. But, determined not to miss out on her first opportunity to direct a play, Garry installed herself in the college library and immersed herself in its theatre section until she found a play she felt she could confidently direct – the result being Brian Friel's *The Loves of Cass Maguire*. From that point on, Garry devoted all of her time and energy to the theatre. She spent the summers of 1971–75 working in a clerical office in New York as part of a student summer programme. While there, she went to see every play she could, revelling in the experimental nature of America's thriving theatre scene. She then spent her winters in UCG directing her own versions of the plays she had seen in New York, all the time trying to recreate the exciting atmosphere she had experienced during those summers.

In 1975 Garry graduated from college. She wanted to continue working in the theatre, but as Galway had no professional theatre company of its own, she decided to start one with her drama society peers Mick Lally and Máire Mullen. With a grant of £1,500 from the Irish Arts Council, Druid Theatre was born, with Garry Hynes as its first artistic director. The fledgling company started small but soon developed a reputation for innovative and unsentimental work. On their first trip abroad in 1980, Druid won a Fringe First at the Edinburgh Festival for *Island Protected by a Bridge of Glass* and *The Pursuit of Pleasure*, both of which were written by Garry with help from the company. *Island Protected by a Bridge of Glass* told the story of legendary pirate queen Granuaile, while *The Pursuit of Pleasure* explored the life of Oscar Wilde. Over the following years Garry tackled plays by a number of Irish writers, but her next great success was the Druid production of Synge's *The*

Playboy of the Western World, which *The Irish Times* described as the 'definitive' production.

In 1984 Garry began directing plays for Ireland's national theatre, the Abbey. Considered Ireland's most promising director at the time, Garry was offered the position of artistic director of the Abbey in 1986, but as she was dedicated to her work with Druid and she had begun directing work for the Royal Shakespeare Company, she turned down the position. However, when the Abbey came knocking again in 1990, she felt the timing was right. The position was viewed by many as a graveyard for Irish theatre directors, with the theatre having gone through six artistic directors in seven years, but Garry relished the challenge it posed and she took up the mantle in January 1991. By the time of her departure in 1994, the Abbey's *Dancing at Lughnasa* had won an Olivier Award in the West End and three Tony Awards on Broadway. Deborah Warner's production of *Hedda Gabler* won a second Olivier Award, and the Abbey regained its reputation as a writers' theatre, premiering new work by Tom Murphy, Marina Carr and Jimmy Murphy. Despite these accolades, from Garry's first day at the Abbey she was the subject of derogatory media attacks on her talent and ability. Like Lady Augusta Gregory before her, she refused to let this shake her. Theatre critic Colm Tóibín believes that Garry attracted so much criticism because: 'One, she's a woman, and two, she doesn't suffer fools gladly. That's difficult in any society.'

In 1995, having left the Abbey, Garry embarked upon what was to be the most successful collaboration of her career. While reading through unsolicited scripts that had been sent to Druid over the previous year, she stumbled upon *The Beauty Queen of Leenane*, *A Skull in Connemara* and *The Lonesome West*, three plays by an unknown writer in London called Martin McDonagh. From the very first page of each script Garry found herself excited by the richness and vivacity of the language. She travelled to London to meet the young Irish writer and immediately offered to option the production of all three plays – an unprecedented commitment to an unproduced playwright. Three years later Garry's faith in the writer paid off when she became the first woman ever to receive a Tony Award, for directing Martin McDonagh's *The Beauty Queen of Leenane*.

Since her early days of watching the best and the worst of experimental theatre in New York, Garry Hynes has never been afraid to set herself challenges. This was most clearly seen in 2005 with the premiere of *DruidSynge* at the Galway Arts Festival. *DruidSynge* was a cycle of all six plays written by John Millington Synge and directed by Garry Hynes, shown one after the other in a singular theatrical experience. This *tour de force* was later described by *The Irish Times* as 'one of the greatest achievements in the history of Irish theatre'. That same year, Garry received a special tribute award for her contribution to the Irish theatre industry, and the following year she was honoured with the Freedom of the City of Galway.

Garry Hynes continues to create theatre that is provocative, challenging and relevant. By opening her doors to a new generation of previously unheard of Irish playwrights, she has cultivated a renaissance in modern Irish theatre writing, and through her astute direction of these new plays, she has introduced stories of modern Ireland to the worldwide stage.

MOTHER JONES

PROMINENT AMERICAN
LABOUR ORGANISER

—— 1830–1930 ——

There is no better introduction to labour-organiser Mother Mary Jones than her own words: 'I'm not a humanitarian. I'm a hell-raiser.' In over fifty years spent campaigning to improve the working conditions of children, miners and textile workers, Mother Jones was frequently imprisoned, and she made such an impact on the labour movement in America that she was once denounced in the US Senate as 'the grandmother of all agitators', and described as 'the most dangerous woman in America'.

Mother Jones was born Mary Harris on 1 May 1830 on the north side of Cork city. Her paternal grandfather had been a freedom fighter and was hung for his political activities. Her father Richard Harris, a Catholic tenant farmer, was forced to emigrate to Toronto, Canada, with his wife Ellen Harris, née Cotter, and their young family in 1835 to escape their impoverished circumstances. Here, Mary's father began working as a labourer on railroad construction and made enough money to put his daughter through school. When she graduated at the age of seventeen, Mary went to work as a schoolteacher in Memphis, Tennessee. Here, she met her husband George E. Jones, an iron-moulder and organiser of the Iron Moulders' Union, who taught her a great deal about the workings of unions. However, tragedy soon befell Mary and her family when in 1867 a yellow fever epidemic washed through Memphis killing her husband and their four young children within the space of a week. Devastated, Mary laid her family to rest before going out to help in the homes of others who had been affected by the fever. She then moved to Chicago where she ran a successful dress-making business. However, tragedy struck again in 1871 when the Great Chicago Fire destroyed both her home and her business, forcing her to camp beside the lake with all of the other homeless citizens.

It was during this ordeal that Mary decided to join the newly formed Knights of Labor, a secret society that was organising textile workers in Chicago, and she also became active in the labour movement. Her rousing speeches soon attracted the attention of labour leaders and she was called to speak in different states across America. Over the next fifty years Mary travelled the length and breadth of the country, living alongside the workers in tents and shacks, and showing up 'wherever there is a fight'. Her work varied from delivering speeches to recruiting members to the union, and from educating children to organising soup kitchens. The song 'She'll Be Coming 'Round the Mountain' is said to have been written about Mary's travels through the Appalachian mountain camps.

In the 1890s Mary became an organiser for the United Mine Workers Union. By now in her sixties and sporting a head of bushy white hair, Mary became affectionately known as 'Mother Jones' by other union leaders. In 1898 she helped found the Social Democratic Party and in 1899 she mobilised the miners' wives to march with brooms and mops to block strike-breakers from entering mines during the United Mine Workers' strike in Pennsylvania. She used such tactics many times throughout her career as an agitator. This was a time when unionisation was regularly suppressed by the brute force of the police, federal troops and armed militia, but Mary held fast to her maxim: 'Pray for the dead and fight like hell for the living.' When Mary faced trial for ignoring an injunction banning meetings by striking miners, the West Virginia district attorney Reese Blizzard said of her, 'There sits the most dangerous woman in America ... She crooks her finger – 20,000 contented men lay down.'

Incensed by the recruitment of child labour, Mary went to work in a number of textile mills where she was able to witness for herself the extent of the damage being done to children as young as six, who were routinely losing limbs to factory machinery. One textile mill she worked in employed 75,000 workers, 10,000 of whom were children under the age of ten working illegally. In 1903 Mary led the 'March of the Mill Children' from the textile mills of Kensington, Pennsylvania, to President Theodore Roosevelt's home in Long Island, New York, brandishing banners that declared, 'We want to go to school and not the mines!' Although the president refused to meet with the marchers, the incident brought the issue of child labour to the forefront of the public agenda and a child labour law was passed that raised the minimum age of workers from twelve to fourteen.

Mary helped form the radical labour organisation, the Industrial Workers of the World (IWW), one of the most influential labour agitation forces in American history. Her fellow IWW-founder Elizabeth Gurley Flynn, a nationally known labour organiser, described Mary as 'the greatest woman agitator of our times'. However, the one right Mary had no interest in agitating for was the right of women to work. 'I am not a suffragist,' she once said, 'nor do I believe in "careers" for women, especially a "career" in factory and mill where most working women have their "careers". A great responsibility rests upon women – the training of the children. This is her most beautiful task.'

Mary played a major role in a miners' strike in Paint Creek, West Virginia, in 1912. During the strike, men employed by the mill-owners released machine-gun fire on strikers and their families. When a company guard was killed, Mary was arrested and, at the age of seventy-eight, she was found guilty of murder and sentenced to twenty years in prison. This decision was subsequently overturned when a senatorial investigation found proof of her innocence. Five years later she was again sentenced to twenty years in prison for leading a protest against the conditions at the West Virginia coalfields. Released soon afterwards, Mary succeeded in opening up an investigation into these hazardous conditions.

In 1914 a dispute about membership of the United Mine Workers Union erupted in Ludlow, Colorado, and soldiers opened fire on a tent colony, killing miners and their wives and children. Horrified, Mary persuaded President Woodrow Wilson to insist that the owners and workers negotiate a truce. Mary's meeting with Colorado mine-owner John D. Rockefeller Jr prompted Rockefeller to visit his mines and to introduce much-needed reforms. Mary went on to participate in the strikes of garment workers and streetcar workers in New York, and in the steel workers strike in Pittsburgh in 1919. She was still working amongst striking coal workers in West Virginia at the grand old age of ninety-three. A year later, in 1924, she was involved in her last labour dispute, which was fittingly a dressmakers' strike in Chicago where she had run her own dress-making business many years earlier. Shortly after celebrating her one-hundredth birthday, Mary Harris Jones died on 30 November 1930.

Mother Jones continues to be a source of inspiration and strength to workers across the world today. In her lifetime she was responsible for raising the minimum age of child labour in many American states, giving countless children the opportunity to escape the perils of factory work and continue their schooling. A fearless leader, Mother Jones often ventured where others feared to tread, risking imprisonment and death in her pursuit of better rights for workers and children. Five years before she died, Mary published her autobiography, in which her words of strength and hope for the workers of the future are as empowering today as they were in 1925:

> In spite of oppressors, in spite of false leaders, the cause of the workers continues onward. Slowly his hours are shortened, slowly his standards of living rise to include some of the good and beautiful things in life. Slowly, those who create the wealth of the world are permitted to share it. The future is in labour's strong, rough hands.

NAN JOYCE

CAMPAIGNER FOR TRAVELLERS' RIGHTS

— 1940– —

Nan Joyce was one of the first travellers to publicly campaign for travellers' rights in Ireland. Since the early 1980s, Nan has been responsible for creating a culture of traveller awareness in Ireland. She has given a voice to the disenfranchised travelling community who for many years have suffered degradation and abuse.

The travelling community is estimated to make up less than 0.5 per cent of the population of Ireland. As a result, their needs have often been neglected by the settled majority. They have been subjected to explicit prejudice, often being refused service in pubs, shops and hotels. The mortality rate of infant travellers is three times that of the settled population. The life expectancy of traveller women is fifteen years less than their settled counterparts, while

the life expectancy of traveller men is ten years less than settled men. This is due in part to the extraordinary stress members of the travelling community are forced to live under as a result of constant harassment from the public, as well as the shortage of suitable, safe and sanitised halting sites available to them. When Nan Joyce entered the public realm in the 1980s, she became one of the first people to draw the attention of the Irish public to the day-to-day horrors experienced by members of one of Ireland's oldest communities.

Nan was born in Clogheen, County Tipperary, in 1940, to a young travelling couple, John O'Donoghue and Nan McCann. She was the second of nine children. During Nan's early years, her family were 'hunted from place to place' and Nan remembers children running past their camp 'afeared [*sic*] of the travellers'. Nan's father, a horse trainer who was said to always have a whip in his hand, was an avid reader and he taught his children the history of all the castles and landmarks they passed on their travels. By reading medical books, he was able to deal with many of the illnesses that befell his children. As well as speaking Cant, the language of the travellers, Nan's father could read and write in both Irish and English. Nan's mother on the other hand was illiterate and relied on her husband to fill out forms for her.

During her younger years Nan remembers being welcomed by many who were glad to see the travellers coming, as traditionally being tinsmiths and carpenters, they were often asked to mend pots and kettles by people living in remote areas. When Nan was twelve her father died in a police cell and her mother was sent to prison when she was caught trying to steal metal waste to sell to support her family, leaving Nan with little choice but to assume the role of matriarch of the family. For the next few years she roamed the country, tending to the needs of her siblings. She later married another traveller, John Joyce, with whom she would have eleven children.

Nan Joyce first came to the attention of the world in the 1980s when her family were forced from their halting site in Clondalkin, County Dublin, by council bulldozers. They relocated to a community in Tallaght that was already home to eight other travelling families. Nan enrolled her children in the local school and was just beginning to adjust to her new surroundings when a group of angry residents from Tallaght began threatening her and the other traveller families, giving them forty-eight hours to leave the area.

When they refused to leave, the group of residents distributed leaflets through the doors of Tallaght's settled inhabitants, advising the men to gather up their hurley sticks and leave their women and children at home. They then proceeded to march outside Nan's trailer, chanting 'Out! Out! Out!' at the various travelling families, many of whom had terrified elderly parents living with them. 'Some of the children were very nervous,' remembers Nan. 'My little boy Richard wouldn't go to school, he was saying, "Mammy, what about all the people – they'll kill me …"'

However, some settled people from Tallaght came to the defence of the travellers and stood with them. Gay Byrne also supported the travellers, broadcasting his morning radio show from the halting site. During the show, Nan spoke publicly for the first time about the injustices that the travelling community were being subjected to. She was surprisingly forgiving when it came to the Tallaght residents who had threatened her family. 'A lot of them had been moved out there from the inner city,' she said, 'and they had no jobs and no shops and they were stuck in the house all day. We all need someone to kick. Travellers are very forgiving. We haven't done half the harm to settled people that they have done to us.' Nan regularly read the local newspapers and was horrified by the way they represented the travelling community. 'I wouldn't wonder for the settled people to be against us because they were hearing nothing but bad about us,' she said. The high rates of illiteracy amongst the travelling community had meant that for a long time travellers were denied access to the dominant means of self-representation. But Nan was to change this. She wrote a travellers' manifesto, in which she outlined the needs of travellers, and delivered it to the offices of all the local newspapers. Next, she helped form the Travellers' Rights Committee in conjunction with members of both the travelling and settled community. She held meetings outside her caravan where she tried to get other travellers involved. She visited schools, convents and colleges all over the country, helping to re-educate the public on the travellers' history and heritage. She was shocked when a student at UCC once asked her if travellers ever married. It was clear that even though Ireland was becoming more multi-cultural, it was neglecting its own homegrown traditions and cultures. Nan and the Travellers' Rights Committee led various pickets, marches and pony-drawn carts right up to the Dáil. Nan became so well known that holidaymakers and students from America, China and India began calling to her caravan to have their pictures taken with her.

Nan was the ideal spokesperson for the plight of the travelling community as she had endured and survived so many hardships herself. Alongside the psychological damage of facing constant prejudice and intolerance, Nan had lived by her share of roadsides that lacked adequate facilities, leaving her and her family open to the effects of extreme weather conditions, disease and despair. As a result, two of Nan's daughters suffered nervous breakdowns at different times and were committed to psychiatric hospitals. Another of Nan's daughters developed severe lead poisoning and was forced into long-term care in a home after batteries were dumped at their roadside camp. During the 1982 bin strike, strangers dumped their uncollected trash at Nan's camp, leading to an infestation of rats. This resulted in the death of her one-year-old grand-daughter, Anna Marie, who contracted meningitis from the rats.

During the general election in 1982, the Travellers' Rights Committee put Nan forward as their candidate. To bolster support, Nan made a documentary for the BBC in which she went out onto the streets of Dublin petitioning the public for their votes. Wearing a hidden microphone and followed by secret cameras, Nan met many people who wished her well and

NAN RAN AGAINST A CANDIDATE WHOSE ELECTION PROMISE WAS TO 'GET THE KNACKERS OUT OF TALLAGHT', AND MANAGED TO WIN TWICE AS MANY VOTES AS HIM

promised her their vote, but she also met those who called travellers 'dirt' and 'filth' and said that 'they should be burned'. Nan ran against a candidate whose election promise was to 'Get the knackers out of Tallaght', and managed to win twice as many votes as him. Her success was short-lived, however, when a few weeks after the election she was arrested and wrongly charged with the theft of jewellery. She was placed in a dirty police cell and the only towel she was given to wash herself with was covered in blood. This arrest was widely reported in the newspapers and Nan was dubbed the Tinker Queen. The charges were eventually dropped due to lack of evidence when the case came to court, and many believe that Nan was set up because of her public campaigning. This event did much to dampen her confidence.

However, in 1983 Nan attended a seminar Trócaire was holding in Galway, with Father Mernagh and Mervyn Ennis. The trio attended a human rights workshop with Seán MacBride, son of Maud Gonne. Nan made such an impact on her group that when it came time for each workshop to nominate a chairperson to represent them, Nan was selected to speak in front of thousands of bishops and humanitarians from all over the world. Her speech received a standing ovation. 'You people are very concerned about the Third World,' she said, 'I think you should also be concerned about us, we are the fourth world. We live among rats in camps or caravans ... our children suffer from as many diseases as the children of the Third World.' A subsequent article published by *The Irish Times* on 18 June 1983 declared that, 'Mrs Joyce had an extraordinary impact on the seminar, receiving more applause than anyone else who presented reports.'

The Travellers' Rights Committee evolved into the first travellers' rights organisation, called Minceir Misli, in 1983, through which Nan continued her work. She published an account of her life in the book *Traveller* in 1985. She later moved to Belfast for a number of years where she spent time in a women's aid centre before making up with her husband and moving to the Black Hills area. Here, she assembled a local group to fight for travellers' rights. 'It was always hard for me,' she said, 'because I was a traveller and then I was a woman, but I just fought my battle with the councillors and then they appreciated what I was doing.'

Nan successfully lobbied for new halting sites on the Glen Road, West Belfast, which were equipped with a fresh-water supply and toilets, as well as a playschool and a clinic for babies. She also visited schools in the area and explained to the teachers how important it was that traveller children learned about their own culture and heritage. As a result, schools ordered special jigsaws and toys with images of families living in caravans.

Nan Joyce remains the best-known traveller in Ireland. Through her pioneering work she has advanced the rights of travellers and created a cultural awareness of the problems faced by this minority group. The Travellers' Rights Committee has since spawned a number of groups and organisations dedicated to catering to the needs of the travelling community. Nan's autobiography *My Life on the Road* (first published as *Traveller*) has become one of the most important written documents on the life of the travelling community in Ireland. Nan continues to promote a sense of pride in a community that has been demoralised by many years of abuse. 'I'm a travelling woman and I'm very proud of my culture,' says Nan. 'I never hide it. I always tell the children, never be ashamed of who you are. We are the oldest group in Ireland.'

SISTER STANISLAUS KENNEDY

FOUNDRESS OF FOCUS IRELAND AND THE IMMIGRANT COUNCIL OF IRELAND

—— 1940– ——

Sister Stanislaus Kennedy is one of Ireland's best-known social innovators. A creative and dynamic thinker, she has set in place some of the country's most influential non-profit organisations. Known affectionately as Sister Stan, she was the first religious sister to receive an honorary doctorate in law from Trinity College, Dublin. She has been campaigning for the homeless since 1983 and has been instrumental in providing thousands of people with food, shelter and a safe refuge. Because of her pioneering work, the Irish government appointed her first chair of the National Committee to Combat Poverty, and she was later selected by the European Commission to co-ordinate projects on rural poverty within the European Union. Sister Stanislaus is best known for founding Focus Point, (now Focus Ireland) in 1985, an organisation whose mission is 'to advance the right of people out-of-home to live in a place they call home through quality services, research, and advocacy.'

Sister Stanislaus was born Treasa Kennedy in Lispole, Dingle, County Kerry, in 1940. Growing up on the family farm alongside her four siblings, the young Treasa was moved by stories she read and heard about the poorest areas of Ireland. She became aware of the distinct social differences between the 'haves' and the 'have-nots'. At the age of eighteen, she joined the Religious Sisters of Charity, an order founded by Mary Aikenhead in 1815, whose main priority was the plight of the poor.

In the 1960s Sister Stanislaus was sent to Kilkenny to work alongside Bishop Peter Birch in developing the town's social services. During this time, she studied for a degree in social science at UCD, before travelling to Manchester to undertake further training in social work.

Sister Stanislaus returned to Kilkenny with a better understanding of the roots of the problems faced by modern society, and began working towards helping families as a whole rather than concentrating on individual members. The successful partnership of Sister Stanislaus, Bishop Peter Birch and another Sister of Charity, Sister Campion, resulted in an innovative model of community care which became a blueprint for the rest of Ireland. In developing this model, Sister Stanislaus learned much about the governmental systems serving the most vulnerable members of society.

In 1983 Sister Stanislaus moved to Dublin and began her lifetime commitment to the homeless community. Her first move was to co-ordinate research into the number of homeless women living on the streets of Ireland. Irish society seemed to have turned a blind eye to the homeless, with many preferring to pretend that this growing sector of society simply didn't exist. However, after six months of research had been carried out by her team, Sister Stanislaus found that there were over 500 homeless women in Ireland. Her next step was to set about researching the effects of homelessness on women. With this in mind, she rented the top floor of a building in Dublin and spent a year living with eight homeless women between the ages of fifteen and twenty-five. What struck Sister Stanislaus most forcefully during this time was that, despite having no home, no place to wash or change their clothes and no door to lock behind them to keep them safe, the worst aspect of homelessness for these women was the derogatory way in which other people treated them. She realised that their sense of self-respect and dignity was more important to them than anything else, but it was being gradually eroded by the tide of mistreatment they suffered as a result of being homeless. Sister Stanislaus noted that they were perceived to be 'no good, lazy, or on drugs, and they became what they were perceived to be. In the deepest part of our being we all know a hidden beauty, a hidden dignity, and when that is not recognised by the other, it is soul destroying.'

During her research, Sister Stanislaus discovered that there was little being done to help the

WHAT STRUCK SISTER STANISLAUS MOST FORCEFULLY DURING THIS TIME WAS THAT THE WORST ASPECT OF HOMELESSNESS FOR THESE WOMEN WAS THE DEROGATORY WAY IN WHICH OTHER PEOPLE TREATED THEM

homeless. 'There was no one on the streets at night to reach out to young people, so they were open to all kinds of exploitation; no drop-in centre where the homeless could get information and advice; no restaurant where they could get good food at a reasonable price; nowhere they would be safe that was a nice place to be.' In response to this, Sister Stanislaus established Focus Point – the biggest national voluntary organisation in Ireland. Its objectives are: to respond to the needs of people out-of-home and those at risk of becoming homeless through a range of appropriate high-quality services; to provide emergency transitional and long-term accommodation for people out-of-home; and to campaign and lobby for the rights of people out-of-home and the prevention of homelessness. Having spent so much time with homeless women, Sister Stanislaus knew that the most important aspect of her new organisation would be the way in which each homeless individual was treated, and so she would always advocate to her staff members and volunteers the idea that 'how we do something is just as important as what we do'. She published her findings in the book *But Where Can I Go?* (1985), the first study carried out on homeless women in Ireland. This book gave readers an opportunity to uncover the real reasons behind homelessness; with many victims forced onto the streets because of family violence and abuse.

In 1997, because of her commendable work with the poor and vulnerable in society, Sister Stanislaus was appointed to the Council of State by President Mary McAleese. Two years later Sister Stanislaus opened a holistic spiritual meditation centre in Dublin city called The Sanctuary, which provides a secure refuge for people living in 'stressful situations'. In 2001 she launched Social Innovations Ireland, an organisation designed to respond efficiently to societal problems as they arise. Of the many projects that have resulted from this organisation, two in particular have brought significant change to Ireland: The Immigrant Council of Ireland and Young Social Innovators. The Immigrant Council of Ireland serves both as an independent law centre and human rights organisation for immigrants. It champions the rights of immigrants and their families, and acts as a catalyst for public debate and policy change. Young Social Innovators (YSI) was co-founded by Sister Stanislaus and Rachel Collier in 2001. After a successful pilot, the programme was launched nationwide in September 2004. YSI is now the largest programme of social-awareness education and action in Ireland. To date, over 25,000 people between the ages of fifteen and eighteen have taken part.

For almost fifty years, Sister Stanislaus has been evolving with the needs of her time. She has received many awards, including the University of New York Special Honour for Commitment to the Disadvantaged in Ireland (1993), as well as the Meteor Humanitarian of the Year Award (2004). Sister Stanislaus has opened doors for those who have experienced the most debilitating effects of exclusion and has embraced the dawning of a new generation of social innovators. Today, Focus Ireland, the Immigrant Council of Ireland and Young Social Innovators continue to restore a sense of dignity and confidence to thousands of people.

DELIA LARKIN

LEADER OF THE IRISH WOMEN WORKERS' UNION

— 1878–1949 —

Alongside Cissy Cahalan, Mai Clifford, Sheila Conroy and Mary Galway, Delia Larkin was one of the great trade unionists. The younger sister of trade union giant James Larkin, Delia fought long and hard to establish a place for women in the trade union movement. Although the fact that she was a woman prevented her from being taken as seriously as her brother, Delia was pivotal in the development of the Irish Women Workers' Union, and during her lifetime she worked hard to earn equal pay and the right to vote for women. A true leader, she took charge of Liberty Hall during the lockout of 1913 and arranged for 3,000 children to be fed every morning. Afterwards, when many of the women involved in the lockout were not reinstated in their jobs, she turned them into a theatrical troupe and took them on a tour around Europe. It is fair to say that Delia Larkin proved to be one of the most resourceful leaders ever to have worked for the Irish trade union movement.

Born on 27 February 1878 in the slums of Liverpool, Delia was the fifth child of Mary Ann McNulty and James Larkin, poor Irish emigrants from County Down. When Delia was nine years old, her father died of tuberculosis and her two eldest brothers, Hugh and James, were sent out to work to provide for the family. James was only eleven at the time. Delia spent some years working as a nurse in Liverpool before following James to Belfast where she ran a hotel, and then to Dublin where she helped establish a trade union for women in 1911 called the Irish Women Workers' Union (IWWU). This was to be a branch of the Irish Transport and General Workers' Union (ITGWU) which had been founded by her brother in 1909. Serving as the first general secretary, Delia had her work cut out for her, as women in industry had never been organised in this way before in Ireland.

She placed her first advertisement looking for members in the *Irish Worker* on 12 August 1911 and in a subsequent column she defined the main aims of the new organisation: 'All we ask for is just shorter hours, better pay than the scandalous limit now existing and conditions of labour befitting a human being.' In the first six months of the union, £172 was paid out in strike fees and they won as much as a £70-a-week increase in wages. Although largely based in Dublin, the IWWU soon had branches in Belfast, Wexford and Cork. By 1912 the union had 1,000 members and was seeking independence of any affiliation with the ITGWU. Members came to Delia with problems ranging from high rents and poor working conditions to requiring assistance finding suitable marriage partners and decent housing.

Delia began representing women on Ireland's first trade boards which had been set up to regulate wages within the badly paid manufacturing sectors. Delia also represented the IWWU at the Irish Trades Union Conference three years in a row. As a suffragette, Delia attended a mass rally in Dublin on behalf of the union to demand women's suffrage in the Home Rule Bill, and she saw to it that suffrage meetings were well advertised in the *Irish Worker*, a labour movement newspaper she helped to edit.

Delia took it upon herself to organise mixed events for members of both the men's and women's unions, including socials, annual outings and concerts. She formed the Union Choir in 1912, and really came into her own when she set up and trained the Irish Workers' Dramatic Class, which made its stage debut on St Stephen's Night 1912, with four one-act plays, three of which starred Delia herself.

In 1913 the strength of the IWWU was tested when 310 women were locked out of the Jacobs' Biscuit Factory for wearing the IWWU badge. Paterson's Match Factory soon followed suit. While James 'Big Jim' Larkin went to England in search of support, Delia took charge of Liberty Hall and with the help of a band of determined women, including Constance Markievicz and Hanna Sheehy Skeffington, she provided daily breakfasts for the children and ran a soup kitchen for the starving locked-out workers. When the *Daily Herald* League instigated a plan to send strikers' children to England to be cared for until the end of the lockout, the London-based organisers approached Delia for help in implementing the idea. However, fearing that the children would end up in the homes of 'atheists and socialists', the Catholic Church stepped in and boycotted any attempt made by Delia to transport the children abroad.

In 1915 James Connolly took control of Liberty Hall during James Larkin's absence. It was clear from the start that Delia was unhappy with Connolly's presence. Growing increasingly frustrated with the lack of respect being shown to her at Liberty Hall, Delia returned to Liverpool where she worked as a nurse until 1918. She then returned to Dublin to rally support for the anti-conscription movement. She went back to work at Liberty Hall, this time in the insurance section. She began campaigning for the release of the Sydney Twelve, members of the Industrial Workers of the World who had been arrested on charges of arson, sedition and forgery – although it was widely believed that the real reason for their arrest was their opposition to conscription. Because of her connections with the Communist Party of Ireland, Delia was refused re-entry into the IWWU – an organisation she had been instrumental in founding.

On 8 February 1921, at the age of forty-three, Delia Larkin married Patrick Colgan, a member of the Irish Citizen Army. They moved to a flat at 17 Gardiner Street before later settling in Ballsbridge, where Delia's brother James joined them and lived out the remainder of his years. In the final years of Delia's life, she suffered frequently from ill health, resulting in 'a very quiet life, quite against my inclination', as she wrote in a letter to R.M. Fox shortly after her brother's death. She continued to maintain an interest in theatre and supported her brother Peter's founding of the left-wing Workers' Union of Ireland. Delia died at her home at 41 Wellington Road, Dublin, on 26 October 1949. She is remembered as one of the great trade unionists.

DOCTOR
KATHLEEN LYNN

FOUNDRESS OF THE FIRST HOSPITAL
FOR INFANTS IN IRELAND

—— 1874–1955 ——

K athleen Lynn was one of the first generation of Irish women to graduate with a degree in medicine. In her lifetime she was a dedicated suffragette, chief medical officer and captain of the Irish Citizen Army, a pioneering doctor and a saviour of children. During the Easter Rising in 1916, Kathleen bravely stepped up to take the place of a fallen comrade and senior officer, and held City Hall throughout a night of heavy artillery.

Kathleen Florence Lynn was born in Ballysakeery, County Mayo, on 28

January 1874, to Robert Young Lynn and Kathleen Marian Lynn, née Wynne. Both her father and grandfather were Anglican clergymen. Growing up in one of the hardest-hit areas during the Famine, Kathleen was deeply affected by the poverty, malnutrition, disease and ignorance that continued to destroy lives. At the age of sixteen she decided that she wanted to become a doctor, a highly unusual choice of vocation for a woman at the time, not least because the Royal University had only recently begun conferring medical degrees on women in 1884. Having studied for some time in England and Germany, Kathleen completed her schooling at Alexandra College, Dublin, and entered the Royal University of Ireland. In 1899 she graduated in medicine. She completed her postgraduate degree in America, and in 1909 became a fellow of the Royal College of Surgeons in Ireland.

When it came to securing employment, Kathleen found that she was discriminated against because of her sex. When the Adelaide Hospital refused to appoint her to house staff on the basis that they did not have suitable quarters for female doctors, Kathleen was forced to build up her experience working as an intern at the Royal Victoria Eye and Ear Hospital and the Rotunda Hospital. She then opened up a general practice in her home at 9 Belgrave Road, Rathmines, where her next-door neighbour was prominent Irish suffragette, Hanna Sheehy Skeffington.

Having experienced gender discrimination first-hand, Kathleen was inspired by the work of both her distant cousin Constance Markievicz and her next-door neighbour, Hanna Sheehy Skeffington, who championed the ideals of freeing Ireland from England and freeing women from subjugation. In 1912 Kathleen tended to the medical needs of suffragists who had been arrested and were on hunger strike, and in 1913 she came to the aid of those affected by the Dublin city lockout strike. When her good friend James Connolly formed the Irish Citizen Army (ICA) that same year, he elected Kathleen as chief medical officer. Over the next few years Kathleen provided first-aid classes to recruits of the ICA and Cumann na mBan and was active in smuggling arms in preparation for the uprising.

When the day of the 1916 Rising finally arrived, Kathleen followed her orders to deliver medical supplies to various stations. When Seán Connolly was shot and killed on the roof of City Hall, Kathleen, along with Seán's fiancée, labour rights activist Helena Molony, took over as senior officers and held City Hall through a night of heavy bombardment. They were overpowered by the British the following morning and Kathleen surrendered her weapon at gunpoint. For her part in the Rising, she was imprisoned in Kilmainham Jail alongside her cousin Constance.

Following her release a year later, Kathleen joined Sinn Féin, the political party led by Arthur Griffith, which now served as an umbrella organisation for all branches of the nationalist cause. Kathleen was later elected to the Sinn Féin executive. She was arrested for her work with Sinn Féin and threatened with deportation, but by this time the Spanish Flu had invaded Dublin, killing more than 18,000 people in the space of a few months. Dead bodies lined the streets and doctors were in short supply – especially doctors of Kathleen's level of efficiency and intuition. Dublin's lord mayor headed the petition to save Kathleen from deportation, calling her as 'innocent as a new-born babe'. In return for her freedom, Kathleen swore never to involve herself in politics again. She failed to keep this promise but her release saved the lives of hundreds, if not thousands, of people as she worked twenty-four hours a day to save those who had been infected.

The infant mortality rate in Ireland during the spread of the Spanish Flu was amongst the highest worldwide, at 165 deaths per 1,000 children. This was also a time when Irish soldiers were returning to Ireland after the First World War and many of them were infected with syphilis. Kathleen started a national campaign to insist on the testing of soldiers for syphilis before re-entering the country, but the British authorities refused to take action. As a result, thousands of syphilitic babies were born, adding to the high percentage of sick and ailing infants in Ireland. Kathleen felt that there was an urgent need for a hospital that cared exclusively for infants. She also wanted to provide classes for mothers to combat the ignorance that contributed to so many infant deaths. She organised a meeting with a group of her most capable and trusted friends, including Maud Gonne and fellow ICA member, Madeleine ffrench-Mullen, to discuss her ideas.

In 1919, following several months of fundraising, St Ultan's hospital was opened at 37 Charlemont Street in Dublin on Ascension Thursday. It was the first hospital in Ireland to care exclusively for infants. The hospital was named after the bishop of Meath who had cared for orphans in his monastery during the Yellow Plague in the sixth century. St Ultan's opened with only two cots and £70 in the bank. Kathleen travelled to America to raise more funds, and two goats called Bluebell and Lady Carson were donated to the hospital to provide a source of unspoiled milk.

When the Irish Free State was established in 1922, Kathleen refused to attend the celebrations. By this point she felt alienated from politics for a number of reasons: she was disappointed with the Anglo-Irish Treaty, frustrated by male nationalists' refusal to take the fight for women's suffrage seriously and angered by their failure to implement any of the social changes for which she had campaigned.

By 1929 St Ultan's had thirty-five cots and an outpatients' department that was funded by the Countess Markievicz Memorial Committee. That same year, St Ultan's began to benefit from the founding of the Irish Hospitals Sweepstakes. In time, this resourceful way of making money for a hospital badly in need of funding was eventually halted by the Irish government. However, St Ultan's flourished under Doctor Kathleen's ever-watchful eye. By 1932 an X-ray department had been installed, and in 1936 Dr Maria Montessori visited the hospital and spoke with Kathleen at length about children's capacity for self-education. Soon afterwards, Kathleen opened the first Montessori ward in a hospital.

In the late 1930s Dorothy Stopford Price, pioneer of the BCG vaccine that minimised the contagious and deadly threat of tuberculosis, began using the modern form of the vaccine at St Ultan's, ten years before it was used throughout the rest of Ireland. Kathleen was later instrumental in implementing a scheme that introduced the BCG vaccine to the rest of Ireland and helped to finally eradicate the disease. In May 1945 an official TB unit was opened in St Ultan's. That same year, Kathleen was elected vice-chairperson of the Save the German Children Society which was set up to find homes for war-stricken children.

Kathleen continued to work up until six months before her death at the age of eighty-one on 14 September 1955. By this time, St Ultan's had 90 cots, 444 recorded admittances and 15,000 outpatients. The hospital remained open until 1975 when a lack of funding caused it to close and reopen as a private clinic.

During her lifetime, Kathleen Lynn was a conscientious, politically minded campaigner for reform. Although she fought in the Easter Rising, she also led prayer rallies for peace during the War of Independence. As the founder and backbone of St Ultan's Hospital, she was forced to wage lengthy battles against the government to ensure that the infants of Ireland were cared for to the best of her abilities. Like many nationalist women of her day, Kathleen Lynn left the political world disheartened by the way in which Irish women, having fought side by side with the men, were ultimately cast aside, their contributions for the most part forgotten. However, Kathleen Lynn's legacy lives on today in the many lives she saved at St Ultan's Hospital.

MARY MCALEESE

FIRST IRISH PRESIDENT FROM NORTHERN IRELAND

— 1951– —

Mary McAleese grew up in Northern Ireland during the Troubles. Her memories of the 1960s are dominated by violence as members of her family were frequently badly beaten and intimidated, forcing them to become refugees in their own homeland. Since then, Mary McAleese has become a champion of the oppressed, fighting for the rights of women and minority groups. She is the eighth president of Ireland and the first Irish president to have been born in Northern Ireland. She is also the first woman in the world to succeed another woman as an elected head of state.

Mary Patricia Leneghan was born in Ardoyne, Belfast, on 27 June 1951. She was the eldest of nine children born to Paddy Leneghan, a barman from Roscommon who would later own The Long Bar on the Falls Road, and

Claire McManus, an apprentice hairdresser from County Down. Mary was educated at St Dominic's High School, where she set up a St Vincent de Paul society that is still in operation today. Through the society, Mary worked in a local hostel for the homeless and paid home visits to the sick and elderly. She also worked in the No Name Club for young adults with intellectual disabilities at Muckamore Hospital, and was 'a very minor minion' in the setting up of the first credit union in Ardoyne in the 1960s. At the age of fourteen, Mary decided that she wanted to study law when she left school. This was partly due to the influence of her favourite television show, *Perry Mason*, and partly due to the location of her school, which was sandwiched between a courthouse and a jailhouse. As a result, Mary remembers a pervading sense of 'things legal in the ether and the atmosphere'.

Living in a predominantly Protestant area, Mary's family home came under threat many times. On one occasion, her sixteen-year-old deaf brother John was viciously attacked. Another time, Mary had a nightmare about a gunman standing at their living-room window. Terrified, she begged her mother to stay with relatives the following night as she and her sister Nora had been invited to a party at Queen's University. When the family returned to their home on the Crumlin Road the following day, they were horrified to find that it had been riddled with bullets overnight. It was clear that if any member of their family had remained at home that night, they would have been murdered.

Mary's parents and her eight brothers and sisters eventually moved to the village of Rostrevor in County Down, but by this time Mary had already moved away from home and was studying at Queen's University in Belfast. She graduated in 1973 with an honours degree in law. During her time at Queen's, Mary was president of the college law society. She was also involved in setting up the first Women's Aid group in Belfast. One of Mary's most unusual accolades during this period is that of 'Man of the Match' following a controversial GAA game between Queen's University and UCD, in which UCD supplied the referee. When Mary's future husband Martin McAleese was fouled by a rival player, Mary ran on to the pitch with her umbrella protesting angrily at the unfairness of the situation.

In 1975 Mary succeeded Mary Robinson as Reid Professor of Criminal Law, Criminology and Penology at Trinity College Dublin. At twenty-four,

Mary McAleese was the youngest person ever appointed to this post. She also co-founded the Campaign for Homosexual Law Reform with Senator David Norris. Her awareness of the plight of gay men and lesbians had developed during her twenty-first summer which she spent in America working for a company that produced food for airlines. Here, she befriended the first openly gay person she had ever known, who shared with her his experiences of being excluded from society. From that point on, Mary was committed to ending the exclusion of gay men and lesbians. In an address she made at the 2007 International Association for Suicide Prevention, she urged listeners to fight against the 'undercurrent of both bias and hostility which young gay people must find deeply hurtful and inhibiting'.

In 1976 Mary married Martin McAleese, an accountant who later became a dentist. They had originally planned to hold their wedding reception at the Golden Pheasant in Lisburn, which was owned by two brothers from Ardoyne, Tony and Myles O'Reilly, friends of the family. But as the guest list grew, they were forced to book a bigger venue at the Ardmore Hotel in Newry. Sadly, Mary and Martin later found out that on the day of their wedding, three Ulster Volunteer Force gunmen entered the Golden Pheasant restaurant and killed the two brothers before detonating two bombs and demolishing the building.

In 1979 Mary went to work for RTÉ as a presenter and reporter in television current affairs, initially working on the programme *Frontline* and later on *Today Tonight*. However, this was to prove one of the most difficult periods of her life: 'I was a Catholic, a northerner, a nationalist and a woman – a quadruple deviant in the eyes of many influential people in RTÉ.' In 1981 Mary returned to the Reid professorship at Trinity, but continued to work part-time for RTÉ for a further four years. In 1982 she gave birth to her first child, Emma, and three years later she gave birth to twins, Justin and Sara Mai. In 1984 Mary was a member of the Catholic Church Episcopal Delegation to the New Ireland Forum.

In 1987 Mary returned to her alma mater, Queen's University, where she was appointed director of the Institute of Professional Legal Studies. In 1994 she became the first female to be appointed pro-vice chancellor of the Queen's University of Belfast.

By the time Mary Robinson announced in 1997 that she would not be standing for a second term in the presidency, Mary McAleese had been working as a conscientious objector against violence and discrimination for over twenty years. Although the idea of running for president had never crossed her mind before then, she soon heard her name being circulated by members of the Fianna Fáil Party who felt she would be perfect for the job. In 1997, after a challenging and controversial campaign battle in which she found herself running against three other women – Fine Gael candidate Mary Banotti, Labour candidate Adi Roche and independent candidate Dana Rosemary Scallon – as well as Derek Nally, Mary McAleese was elected the eighth president of Ireland, with 45.2 per cent of first-preference votes. In 2004 she stood unopposed for a second term of office.

The theme of Mary's presidency, 'Building Bridges', has been one she has consistently held fast to despite the repercussions. In 1998 she announced that she would officially celebrate 12 July as a mark of respect for the traditions of Northern Irish unionists, an action that was criticised by the more ardent nationalists. She also incurred some criticism from the Irish Roman Catholic hierarchy for receiving communion in a Church of Ireland cathedral in Dublin. However, Mary's reconciliatory work in both the north and south of Ireland has revealed her dedication to principles of peace and anti-sectarianism.

Mary's journey from a working-class family in a war-torn community to that of leader of the country shows sheer determination and a belief in a better world. Having grown up in a climate of fear and intimidation, Mary has since committed herself to ensuring that future generations in Northern Ireland will never have to endure the same terror. She continues to be a president who promotes a more inclusive society for all of her people, regardless of gender, religion, race, sexuality or political beliefs.

NELL MCCAFFERTY

GROUND-BREAKING JOURNALIST

— 1944- —

Nell McCafferty was a guiding light during the feminist revolution of the 1970s. One of the founding members of the Irish Women's Liberation Movement, she campaigned for the right of women to contraception and equal pay. Through her ground-breaking newspaper columns she also highlighted the plight of working-class Catholics in her native Derry and the horrors of Dublin's children's courts.

Nell was born on 28 March 1944 in the Bogside, a nationalist area of Derry. From a young age she observed the demeaning effects of gender inequality on her mother Lily, who depended on Nell's father for money:

[He would] give a certain amount to my mother, while concealing how much he kept back for himself. My father never told his full wages on the patriarchal

principle that my mother should not worry about debt because he would always have something left by for emergencies. He was better than most men, by his stern principles. However, he abused his power on the Friday nights when they weren't speaking by withholding her portion of the wages until she asked – while tradesmen were knocking at the door.

Nell won a scholarship to study arts at Queen's University, making her the first member of her family to continue on to third-level education. She concedes that the most 'sustained political gesture' she made at Queen's University was to attend lunches held by Oxfam in support of famine relief in Third World countries. After graduating, Nell took on part-time work as a teacher in various schools in Ireland and France.

In 1965 Nell got her first taste of politics when she participated in a protest against the Stormont Government alongside fellow teacher John Hume. In 1967 she travelled to a kibbutz in Tel Aviv and explored life in a collective. While there, she witnessed Israel's six-day war against the neighbouring states of Egypt, Jordan and Syria. Although Nell sent first-hand accounts of the conflict back to local Derry newspapers, the Irish press didn't seem interested in publishing them.

When Nell returned to Northern Ireland, she visited Eamonn McCann at Derry's Labour Party headquarters, where she helped with preparations for the upcoming general election. She took short-term teaching posts, signed on for unemployment benefit for two years and became an active member in the civil rights movement for equal votes, homes and jobs for Catholics. She campaigned on behalf of republican women in jail, while proudly acknowledging the fact that her mother, on finding her nest empty, had come into her own and become involved in local politics, even opening a political salon in her house during the Troubles.

Nell was instrumental in co-founding the Irish Women's Liberation Movement (IWLM) in 1970 with a band of influential female journalists and political activists, including, amongst others, Máirín de Burca, Mary Maher, Moira Woods and Mary Kenny. These women met every Monday night at Gaj's Restaurant on Baggot Street and compiled a charter of demands called 'Chains or Change' in which they outlined to the public the aims of the movement: they demanded equal pay, equality before the law, equal education, contraception, and justice for deserted wives, unmarried mothers and widows. They shocked Irish women into an awareness of their disadvantaged situation and encouraged them to demand change. At the time, working women were

treated as cheap labour, earning less than 55 per cent of men's wages, and were forced to resign from their jobs if they married. There were no financial safeguards for single mothers, widows and deserted wives. To promote the charter, Nell appeared on *The Late Late Show*, where she stirred up a heated debate on the inequalities experienced in the day-to-day lives of Irish women.

In 1970 Nell moved to Dublin to work as a journalist in the women's section of *The Irish Times*. She took up her post alongside the likes of Maeve Binchy, Mary Maher and Mary Cummins. She made a name for herself by writing a series of articles about Dublin's children's courts, where the age of criminal responsibility was seven and children were sent to reform schools for playing truant or stealing sweets.

In May 1971 Nell and the IWLM brought the issue of contraception to the public's attention when forty-seven women travelled by train to Belfast and returned to Connolly station carrying a supply of various contraceptives. They challenged the customs officers to arrest them for illegal importation of contraceptives, which was considered a crime in the eyes of the government and was punishable by a prison sentence. The embarrassed customs officers allowed the women to pass. Nell later revealed that the pills were in fact aspirin as the band of passionate reformers had arrived in Belfast only to discover that a doctor's prescription was needed before the contraceptive pill could be given out. However, they had done their job, as the next day a national debate on contraception raged across the country, inspiring women who had never before questioned their lot in life to come forward and support the IWLM.

Another famous incident saw the IWLM challenge the archaic law that forbade women to order pints as it was deemed 'unladylike'. Nell and a group of women went into a Dublin city-centre bar and ordered forty brandies. They waited for these to be served and then ordered one pint of Guinness. When the barman refused to serve the pint, the women drank their brandies and walked out of the pub without paying.

ANOTHER FAMOUS INCIDENT SAW THE IWLM CHALLENGE THE ARCHAIC LAW THAT FORBADE WOMEN FROM ORDERING PINTS AS IT WAS DEEMED 'UNLADYLIKE'

By the summer of 1971, the IWLM had disbanded as its members went about forming other organisations to achieve their goals. These included Nuala Fennell's AIM, which campaigned for the reform of laws relating to women and the family; Adapt, which was a support group for deserted wives; Irish Women's Aid which provided a refuge for women and children suffering from abuse; and Cherish, a support group for single parents.

Equal pay, contraception, divorce and the right of married women to continue to work in state jobs were all eventually legalised and in no small part due to the work of Nell McCafferty and the IWLM. Speaking of her motivations in an interview, Nell said:

We enjoyed the struggle, at least at the beginning. It was like shooting fish in a barrel. The obstacles to women were incredible, ludicrous, and stood out like a sore thumb. Ireland was full of men in suits who never had to deal with the likes of us before, and to see them challenged by someone as formidable as Mary Robinson – it was great. It is terrific if you are a revolutionary and you can achieve the revolution in a short time.

Nell continued her work as a journalist and a campaigner for civil rights. She was in Derry on Bloody Sunday in 1972 when British soldiers opened fire and killed thirteen civil rights protesters. She wrote a number of works that focused on women republicans, including a book about Peggy Deery, a mother of fourteen from Derry who was shot on Bloody Sunday and whose son was killed by his own IRA bomb, as well as a book on the 'dirty protest' carried out by republican women in Armagh jail. Nell left *The Irish Times* in 1977 and subsequently worked for the *Irish Press*, the *Sunday Tribune*, *Hot Press*, *In Dublin*, *Magill* and the *Irish Daily Mail*.

In 2004 she published her autobiography, *Nell*, which featured a detailed account of her fifteen-year relationship with distinguished Irish writer Nuala O'Faolain. She followed this with an appearance on *The Late Late Show* during which she accused the pope of inciting homophobia and implored all parents of gay children to let their children know they were loved. In 2008, at the age of sixty-four, Nell caused further controversy when she posed naked for American artist Daniel Mark Duffy's exhibition of portraits of older women, in order 'to confront prejudice against older people, and my own inhibitions about growing old.'

In over forty years as a journalist, feminist and civil rights campaigner, Nell McCafferty has become one of Ireland's most controversial and respected social commentators. Through her work highlighting the plight of children at the criminal courts, women in society, Catholics in Derry and gay men and lesbians in Ireland, Nell McCafferty has continued to ask the questions that have provoked positive changes in society with their answers.

CATHERINE McAULEY

FOUNDRESS OF THE SISTERS OF MERCY

— 1778–1841 —

When Catherine McAuley first found herself called to the aid of homeless and abused women and children, she had no intention of starting a religious organisation. 'I only wanted to help the poor – as I thought this was what God was asking of me,' she said. Her compassionate work in caring for and educating the most vulnerable members of society was met with resistance by those who accused her of meddling in the work of the clergy. Although she was a devout Catholic, Catherine did not want to let the rigidity of a religious congregation prevent her from reaching out to those most in need of help. She eventually founded the religious Sisters of Mercy to ensure that her works of mercy would continue long after she was gone. She remained throughout her life a true pioneer in the areas of social work, social innovation and education.

Catherine was born at Stormanstown House, Drumcondra, County Dublin, on 29 September 1778, to James McGauley, a wealthy upper-class Catholic who had acquired his fortune from the building trade, and his young wife Elinor McGauley, née Conway. Catherine had one older sister, Mary, and a younger brother, James. When Catherine's father died in 1783, Elinor, an extravagant woman thirty years his junior, changed the family name to McAuley and began to rapidly spend her way through the family fortune. By the time of Elinor's death, Catherine and her siblings were left without an inheritance and were fostered out to the care of various Protestant relatives. Having lived for a time with their uncle Owen Conway, a surgeon, and later with a kind Protestant family by the name of Armstrong, both of Catherine's siblings became Protestants. Catherine, on the other hand, continued to become more passionate about the Catholic faith.

When Catherine Callaghan, a distant relative of Catherine's mother, returned from India in 1803 with her husband William and purchased Coolock House, a twenty-two-acre estate a few miles north-west of Dublin, she asked Catherine to come and live with them as their adopted daughter. Here, Catherine remained as a companion and household manager for the elderly childless Quaker couple for the next twenty-five years. She engaged in charitable works and daily prayer, and became such a strong influence on the couple that they both converted to Catholicism on their death beds; Catherine Callaghan in 1818 and William in 1822. For her years of loving devotion to the couple, Catherine inherited their entire fortune, which was estimated to be £25,000 – a sizeable amount at the time.

Catherine remained at the estate for the next six years, devoting herself to helping the poor, feeding the hungry, visiting the sick, clothing the cold and teaching the illiterate. During this time, she came into contact with many abused women, unemployed servant girls and orphans who had been pushed out into the cold by a neglectful society. In 1824 Catherine decided to use her inheritance to open a building especially for the care and education of vulnerable women and children, located on the corner of Baggot Street and Herbert Street in Dublin. Catherine was soon joined in her mission by a community of like-minded secular women. On 24 September 1827, on the feast of Our Lady of Mercy, the first residents came to live in the House of Mercy, which had several classrooms, a chapel, a dormitory for the homeless and unemployed women, and accommodation for Catherine and her co-workers.

Catherine's sister Mary died of consumption in August 1827, leaving her husband Dr William Macauley, a surgeon at the Royal Hospital in Kilmainham, to rear five children between the ages of six and sixteen. To help out, Catherine often stayed with the family on Military Road, and would bring the children along with her to Baggot Street every morning. When Dr Macauley died suddenly of fever in January 1829, Catherine became the legal guardian of eight children, including her six-year-old cousin Teresa Byrn and two orphans who had been left in her care at Coolock. In September 1829 Catherine sold Coolock House and placed her nephews in Carlow College as boarders, while she moved to Baggot Street permanently with her adopted girls.

CATHERINE WAS ACCUSED OF LURING AWAY WOMEN WHO MIGHT OTHERWISE HAVE JOINED RECOGNISED RELIGIOUS COMMUNITIES

It wasn't long before Catherine and her co-workers came under criticism for operating a lay institution in the manner of a pious organisation and for imitating a congregation without abiding by any religious rules. Catherine was accused of luring away women who might otherwise have joined recognised religious communities. Catherine's clerical mentors advised her to pay heed to the criticism and to reorganise as a religious congregation. She eventually agreed on the condition that she could form a non-enclosed order, unlike the many female religious orders of the day.

In 1830, at fifty-two years of age, Catherine McAuley entered the formation programme of the Presentation Sisters in George's Hill, Dublin, alongside Anna Maria Doyle and Elizabeth Harley, to formally prepare for her new congregation. On 12 December 1831, Catherine professed her vows as a Sister of Mercy, and the Mercy Congregation was launched. She returned to the House of Mercy as Sister Mary Catherine and continued her work educating young children, visiting the sick and imprisoned, and caring for distressed and abused women. Her 'meals on feet' programme for feeding the sick in their homes paved the way for the present-day Meals on Wheels. In her application for papal approval of her new order, Catherine declared: 'The principal purpose of this Congregation is to educate poor little girls, to lodge and maintain poor young ladies who are in danger, that they may be provided for in a proper manner, and to visit the sick poor'.

Seven more women received the habit of the Sisters of Mercy on 23 January 1832, including Catherine's niece Mary Teresa Macauley. By the following spring, 300 girls were attending the school on Baggot Street and thousands of women and girls had been welcomed into the shelter. A second convent was opened shortly afterwards in Dún Laoghaire.

THE GRIEVING SISTERS GATHERED AROUND HER BED WERE 'TO GET A GOOD CUP OF TEA ... WHEN I AM GONE'

When the cholera epidemic of 1832 hit Dublin, Catherine agreed to staff a cholera hospital on Townsend Street where for the next seven months the Sisters of Mercy nursed in shifts from 8 a.m. to 8 p.m., earning themselves a reputation as the hardest-working women in Ireland. Because of long hours and close proximity to contagious diseases, thirteen sisters died within a six-year period. Through the hard times Catherine is said to have meditated on the words of the 'Universal Prayer': 'Discover to me, O my God, the nothingness of this world, the greatness of heaven, the shortness of time, and the length of eternity.'

Over the next ten years Catherine travelled around the country overseeing the establishment of new convents. She always used the cheapest modes of transport available and often slept on the cold, hard floors of convents where beds were not yet available. Eventually, her years of hard work amongst the sick and vulnerable took their toll. On 11 November 1841, Catherine McAuley died of tuberculosis. Her last requests as she lay dying were that the Sisters of Mercy 'preserve union and peace amongst each other – that if they

did they would enjoy great happiness such that they would wonder where it came from', and also that the grieving sisters gathered around her bed were 'to get a good cup of tea ... when I am gone'.

Catherine spent only ten years as a Sister of Mercy but in that time she established twelve convents in Ireland and two in England. At the time of her death there were 150 Sisters of Mercy. By 1936 there were as many as 20,000 Sisters of Mercy in over 1,500 convents, and Catherine McAuley, declared Venerable by Pope John Paul II in 1990, is now believed to be the foundress of the largest congregation of women in the English-speaking world.

Catherine could have lived a charmed life of prosperity, but instead she chose to sacrifice her own needs for the needs of others, most especially for the 'protection and instruction of poor females'. Through her self-sacrifice and generosity of heart and spirit, as well as her legacy of a thriving congregation, she continues to inspire millions of people around the world today.

Máiread Corrigan Maguire and Betty Williams

Nobel Peace Prize winners

—·— 1944– AND 1943– —·—

Máiread Corrigan Maguire and Betty Williams co-founded the Community of Peace People in 1976 and were responsible for mobilising 35,000 people in Northern Ireland to take to the streets in a protest for peace. As a result of their efforts, both women won the

Nobel Peace Prize in 1977. Máiread was thirty-two years of age when she won the prize, making her the youngest recipient of the Nobel Peace Prize to date.

Máiread Corrigan was born into a Roman Catholic family in Belfast on 27 January 1944, the second child of five sisters and two brothers. Her father Andrew Corrigan was a window-cleaning contractor. Máiread was educated at St Vincent's primary school on the Falls Road before attending Miss Gordon's Commercial School for one year. Both of Máiread's parents were involved in Church and parish affairs in the local community. From a young age, Máiread was socially active as a member of the Legion of Mary, working with prisoners and elderly citizens. She also helped to start the first pre-school playgroup and a club for physically challenged teenagers in her home area of Andersonstown. From the age of sixteen, Máiread worked in various companies as a shorthand typist. She was employed as confidential secretary to the managing director of Arthur Guinness & Co. at the time of the founding of the Community of Peace People.

Betty Williams, née Smyth, was born in Belfast on 22 May 1943. Her mother Margaret was a Catholic and her father, George Smyth, was Church of Ireland, and so it was a mixed marriage – a rarity in Andersonstown in those days. When Betty was thirteen years old, her mother suffered a massive stroke and Betty dropped out of school to take on the role of caring for her mother and her younger sister. Betty's family, like most families in Northern Ireland at the time, had been deeply affected by sectarian violence. Her protestant grandfather, a riveter in a Belfast shipyard, had once been thrown into the hold of a ship that was under construction simply because his son was marrying a Catholic woman. Betty's cousin Daniel had been shot and killed by loyalist extremists as he stood at the front door of his house. His killers embossed the shape of a cross on his back with their machine-guns. Another of Betty's cousins was killed in an IRA car-bomb attack. 'So the Protestants killed one of my cousins, and the Catholics killed the other,' she later said.

In 1961 Betty married Ralph Williams in Bermuda. They had a son Paul and a daughter Deborah. In 1976 Betty was driving home from her mother's house when she witnessed the tragic death of three children. IRA fugitive Danny Lennon had been shot while attempting to flee the British authorities, causing him to lose control of his car and collide with the three children, Joanne, John and Andrew, who had been out walking with their mother Anne Maguire. Anne was also critically injured and later committed suicide in 1980. After witnessing these senseless killings, Betty immediately began to circulate a petition for peace and in less than forty-eight hours she had gathered over 6,000 signatures. When Máiread Corrigan, the deceased children's aunt, heard what Betty Williams had done, she invited her to the children's funeral.

Máiread, Betty and Ciaran McKeown went on to co-found the Community of Peace People. They organised a march for peace which was attended by 10,000 people, both Protestant and Catholic. 'It's very hard to gauge the effect our movement had when one is standing as close to it as I was,' says Betty. 'But of one thing I am certain. I witnessed a miracle on Finaghy Road North on August 10, 1976. What a beautiful memory it is, as I close my eyes and witness the first rally where 10,000 women ran from the buses they had hired to get to the rally and into each other's arms, and with tears in their eyes in one powerful act of love wiped out over 800 years of divided history.' Members of the IRA attempted to disrupt the march, accusing the marchers of being 'dupes for the British'.

The following week, Máiread and Betty led a second march – this time with 35,000 people. These marches are amongst the largest peace demonstrations ever held in the history of Northern Ireland. 'The second rally to Ormeau Park was phenomenal,' says Betty. 'You ask what it was like marching with 35,000 women? There are no words to describe how much emotion I felt. All 35,000 of us had only one common goal. Stop killing, start talking. It was a womb thing. We women, the givers of life, were becoming the protectors of life.'

The Community of Peace People mobilised thousands of people to become active for peace and to take part in six months of weekly rallies, resulting in a marked decrease in the rate of violence in Northern Ireland. One of the main ideas behind the Community of Peace People was that true peace could be achieved by integrating Catholic and Protestant institutions, such as schools and recreation centres, as well as residential areas. Although it was not a woman's movement, 90 per cent of the marchers were indeed women. The emotional rallies and protests soon made world headlines, prompting folk-singer Joan Baez to later write in her autobiography, 'And God bless the brave women of Ireland who, for a brief but exceptional moment in time, waged mass non-violent warfare in one of the most violent countries in the world.'

In 1977 Máiread and Betty were awarded the Nobel Peace Prize for their work. During their acceptance speech they declared:

> We are for life and creation, and we are against war and destruction, and in our rage, we screamed that the violence had to stop. But we also began to do something about it besides shouting. As far as we are concerned, every single death in the last eight years, and every death in every war that was ever fought, represents life needlessly wasted, a mother's labour spurned.

Since accepting the Nobel Peace Prize, both women have been working tirelessly for civil rights around the world. They are both involved in Peacejam, an American youth-education programme. In 2006 Máiread and Betty founded the Nobel Women's Initiative along with their fellow Nobel Peace laureates Shirin Ebadi, Wangari Maathai, Jody Williams and Rigoberta Menchu Tum, to reinforce the work already being done to achieve women's rights. In 1993 Máiread and Betty travelled to Thailand with six other Nobel Peace laureates in a failed effort to enter Myanmar (Burma) to protest against the detention of fellow Nobel Peace Prize-winner Aung San Suu Kyi, who had been leading peaceful protests against a military dictatorship.

Máiread co-founded the Committee on the Administration of Justice, a non-sectarian organisation in Northern Ireland which defends human rights and advocates a repeal of the government's emergency laws. She has since become involved in the Israeli/Palestinian conflict. In April 2007, while participating in a protest in the Palestinian village of Bil'in, Israeli security forces intervened and Máiread was hit by a rubber-coated steel bullet. Undeterred by this incident, she continues to campaign for Gaza's liberation.

Betty currently serves as the president of the World Centers of Compassion for Children, whose mission is to provide a strong political voice for children in areas afflicted by social, economic or political upheaval, and to respond to their material and emotional needs by creating safe and nurturing environments. As a result of many years of work, they have built the first City of Compassion for children in southern Italy. The Community of Peace People continues to work from its headquarters in 'Fredheim' Belfast, promoting a culture of peace both locally and internationally.

CATHERINE MAHON

FIRST FEMALE PRESIDENT OF THE IRISH NATIONAL TEACHERS' ORGANISATION

— 1869–1948 —

Catherine Mahon was a woman of great determination. She became the first female president of the Irish National Teachers' Organisation (INTO) and the first president to be re-elected for a second term. Catherine was a driving force behind the expansion of the INTO from a male-dominated boys' club that focused predominantly on the needs of male teachers to a progressive organisation in which women could become executive members, receive equal pay and finally have their say in matters regarding their employment. Remembered as an inspirational speaker who never held back when it came to fighting injustice, Catherine Mahon ignited in her fellow female teachers a burning desire to be treated with the fairness and equality they deserved; and this fire still burns at the heart of the INTO today.

Catherine was born on 15 May 1869, in Laccah, North Tipperary. She was the first child born to nineteen-year-old former shopkeeper Winifred O'Meara and her thirty-seven-year-old husband James Mahon, an agricultural labourer. For many years the Mahons lived in a cottage in the small farming town of Ballykinash, North Tipperary. Catherine was educated at Carrig national school, before continuing on to secondary education at the Birr Convent of Mercy. In October 1884, at the age of fifteen, Catherine was appointed school monitor. Convents were the major training centres for female Catholic national school teachers at the time, and monitorships were a form of scholarship promoted by the convents. Catherine sat her final examination in 1890 and went to work shortly afterwards as a recognised teacher at two schools run by the Sisters of Mercy. In September 1891 she was appointed principal of Glenculloo national school in County Tipperary, but left this post seven months later to take on the role of principal in her native Carrig national school.

The winter before Catherine was appointed principal of Carrig national school, two of the pupils had died of typhus and the school had subsequently been boycotted. When Catherine arrived only a handful of pupils were still attending the school but as she was a well-known and respected member of the community she soon gained the confidence of local parents and attendance levels began to rise.

At the end of her first year in Carrig, Catherine was promoted to the second level of the pay scale. However, she could progress no higher on this scale due to a commissioner's rule that prohibited teachers appointed after 1 August 1887 from qualifying as first-class teachers unless they had attended a training college. In 1898, to qualify for promotion, Catherine entered a one-year teachers' training course at Our Lady of Mercy Training College on Baggot Street, Dublin. Upon graduating, she was frustrated to find that changes had again been made to the salary scales and she was no longer entitled to a raise.

In the early 1900s Catherine became highly motivated in her political contributions. She became a member of several suffrage societies and a fervent Home Ruler. She also became a member of the INTO, an organisation that had been established in 1868 to gather Irish teachers together and en-sure that their opinions on matters affecting the interests of education and the teaching profession would be heard. However, the concerns of women teachers were for the most part relegated to second place. The INTO published a weekly journal called *The Irish School Weekly* (ISW), and in 1906 the first step towards addressing the interests of women teachers was taken when the ISW began publishing the 'Lady Teachers' Own Page', written under the pseudonym Kathleen Roche. The 'Lady Teachers' Own Page', and indeed its insightful feminist writer, were huge influences on Catherine, who later stated that before Kathleen Roche no one had ever 'arisen to point out our duty to us, or rather, to disabuse our minds of the idea that, like children, imbeciles, and all such, we should be good and keep silent, and ask no questions'.

Catherine first became involved with the INTO following the introduction of Rule 127(b) by the commissioners of national education in 1905, which stated that 'boys under eight years of age are ineligible for enrolment in a boys' school where there is not an assistant mistress, unless there is no suitable school under a mistress available in the locality'. As a result of this rule the idea of amalgamation was proposed, under which nearby schools for both boys and girls would be joined together as one. They would come under the guidance of a male principal and his female assistant, thus demoting many women from their role as principal. This meant that more women teachers would be employed as assistants, and as women were paid less than men for doing the same job, the whole affair was seen as a cost-saving measure. Catherine campaigned vigorously against this move, urging more female teachers to become members of the INTO. She was passionate about equal pay and often quoted the philosopher Herbert Spencer in saying, 'Equity knows no difference of sex'. It soon became clear to Catherine that before they could hope for equal pay, women first needed to make it onto the INTO executive to ensure that their voices would be heard. Catherine looked to England, which had a number of women on the executive of its teachers' union, and to Scotland where the vice-president of the Educational Institute of Scotland was female.

In September 1906 Catherine wrote to the ISW proclaiming that the time had come for women teachers to take their deserved places on the Central Executive Committee (CEC). She encouraged women to join their local associations and to nominate female representatives for pivotal roles. Despite this, when the vacancy for an assistants' representative was announced by the CEC, no female candidates were nominated. However, when the position of vice-president came up a few

AS WOMEN WERE PAID LESS THAN MEN FOR DOING THE SAME JOB, THE WHOLE AFFAIR WAS SEEN AS A COST-SAVING MEASURE

months later, Catherine was nominated by Kathleen Roche, who described her as having 'extraordinary enthusiasm. Her almost superhuman energy are traits seldom met with in one individual, and render her an ideal candidate for the position of vice-president of INTO.'

Together, Catherine and Kathleen succeeded in attracting thousands of new female members to the INTO, who had previously believed the organisation to be for the exclusive promotion of the interests of male teachers. The result was that in 1907 women were nominated for positions on the CEC for the first time. Out of fourteen teachers nominated for the office of vice-president, Catherine ranked fifth. Although she lost out on the vice-presidency, she won the right to special representation for women on the CEC, resulting in the creation of two new positions for women. Catherine was elected to represent female principals. During her first year she worked hard to recruit the 50 per cent of teachers who remained outside the realm of the INTO. She travelled around the country during weekends delivering riveting speeches, and she wrote to over 6,000 women, trying to 'awaken them to a sense of honour and duty'. She was a staunch campaigner for the civil rights of all teachers and fought against the rule that forbade teachers from taking an active part in politics, as well as the rule that prevented the spouses of public-house owners from being recognised as national school teachers. Catherine helped establish a court of appeal for teachers who were charged with 'inefficiency' by inspectors. She also sought support for the INTO Benevolent Fund 'to provide temporary relief to needy members, and to widows and orphans of members'. By the end of 1907, nearly half of the INTO's membership was made up of women.

In 1908 Catherine was instrumental in the equal distribution of the Birrell Education Grant. It had originally been intended that the grant would not cover wage increases and bonuses for teachers with an average attendance of less than thirty-five students. These teachers came mostly from rural communities and were already the most vulnerable members of the teaching world as low attendance figures meant they couldn't benefit from large results fees, fees earned by teachers for each pupil who passed their annual examination. The Birrell Grant was a landmark for Irish women teachers as it was distributed evenly amongst the sexes and set a precedent for the awarding of equal war bonuses in 1916, later followed by an equal pension scheme.

In 1909 Catherine campaigned against the enforcement of cookery and laundry classes on women teachers. She also fought for the provision of grants to cover the costs of cookery utensils and equipment. Female teachers had previously been expected to provide this equipment at their own expense.

In April 1911 Catherine was elected vice-president of the INTO and in 1912 she became president. She had such a positive impact on the organisation that the rules prohibiting a president from running for a second term were revoked. During this time, Catherine battled against the rule that obliged female teachers to take three months' maternity leave and to employ qualified substitutes at their own expense. When a principal was dismissed from his position after publicly calling for the removal of a senior inspector, Catherine fought for the replacement of the National Board of Education with an elected board.

Following her resignation from the CEC in 1915, Catherine became an active member of Fianna Fáil and was the first woman to be elected to the North Tipperary County Council. In 1937 she moved with her mother and her two widowed sisters, Mary Daly and Margaret Barry, to a house in Balbriggan, County Dublin. She died here on 27 February 1948.

In a tribute published in the *Midlands Tribune*, Catherine Mahon was remembered as being 'a great and true-hearted woman, who gave all for the welfare of others. Miss Mahon's life's work remains a monument to her memory.'

CONSTANCE MARKIEVICZ

FIRST WOMAN TO BE ELECTED TO THE BRITISH HOUSE OF COMMONS

— 1868–1927 —

C onstance Markievicz was the first woman to be elected to the British House of Commons, though she did not take her seat. She was also the first woman in Europe to hold a cabinet position as minister for labour in the Irish Republic from 1919 to 1922. She remained the only female cabinet minister in Irish history until 1979 when Máire Geoghegan-Quinn was appointed to the post of minister for the Gaeltacht.

Constance was born with a silver spoon in her mouth, but she would soon spit it out in repulsion at the ill-treatment of the Irish by the British,

and of women by men. Her constant frustration with the restrictions placed on women in Victorian society led to her joining the suffrage movement. Constance also challenged the perceived pacifism of her sex when she founded Fianna Éireann (Soldiers of Ireland), an organisation similar to the boy scouts, except that instead of learning how to tie knots and read maps, Constance taught young men how to use guns. During the 1916 Rising, Constance was one of the few women to fight as a soldier. As a member of

James Connolly's Irish Citizen Army, for whom she had designed uniforms and composed the army's anthem from an old Polish song, Constance was the only one of seventy women imprisoned after the Rising to be placed in solitary confinement. Despite her views on the necessity of force in ridding Ireland of British rule, she was strongly opposed to Irish involvement in the Great War and co-founded the Irish Neutrality League in 1914. An empathetic but pragmatic woman, during the lockout of 1913 Constance sold all of her jewellery and took out many loans to feed the starving workers and their families. In the end, she gave away all of her worldly possessions in her fight to help the poor and to liberate Ireland.

Constance Georgine Gore-Booth was born at Buckingham Gate in London on 4 February 1868. She was the eldest of three daughters and two sons born to Arctic-explorer Sir Henry Gore-Booth and Lady Georgina, née Hill. Her sister Eva Gore-Booth later became an important poet and campaigner for women's suffrage. Not long after her birth, Constance and her family moved to the forty-eight-room Lissadell House in Sligo, where her father had been born. Sir Henry was a compassionate landlord and during the famine of 1879–88 he provided free food for the tenants on his estate. Constance learned much from his example. In 1887 when Constance and Eva were presented at the court of Queen Victoria, Constance was described by many as 'the new Irish beauty'. However, she had no intentions of becoming a society queen.

In 1893 Constance went to study at the Slade School of Art in London and it was around this time that she first became a member of the National Union of Women's Suffrage Societies (NUWSS). She continued her studies at the Académie Julian in Paris where she met her future husband, Casimir Dunin-Markievicz, a Ukrainian aristocrat of Polish descent. In 1900 the pair wed and shortly after the marriage, Constance, now Countess Markievicz, gave birth to a baby girl called Maeve Alyss, who was raised by her grandparents in Lissadell. In 1903 the newlyweds moved to Dublin where they regularly attended salons at artist Sarah Purser's house. Here, Constance met Nathaniel Hone and John Butler Yeats, with whom she was instrumental in founding the United Artists' Club, with the intention of bringing all those with an artistic leaning together. It was in this setting that Constance also first met revolutionaries Michael Davitt and Maud Gonne.

In 1906 Constance became frustrated with her life, believing it held little meaning. She felt that 'nature should provide me with something to live for, something to die for'. She rented a small cottage in the Dublin countryside in which she found copies of nationalist publications left behind by the previous tenant, Padraic Colum. Constance read these publications from cover to cover and by the time she had left the cottage she felt she had found her calling. In 1908, at the age of forty, Markievicz went directly from a function at Dublin Castle, wearing a satin ball gown and a tiara, to her first meeting of Maud Gonne's revolutionary women's movement, Inghinidhe na hÉireann (Daughters of Erin). What Maud and the other women thought of this sparkly arrival is anyone's guess. Through these meetings, Constance began to realise that the struggle for women's equality needed to be connected to the movement for Irish independence. 'There can be no free women in an enslaved nation,' she declared.

'NATURE SHOULD PROVIDE ME WITH SOMETHING TO LIVE FOR, SOMETHING TO DIE FOR'

In 1909 Constance founded Fianna Éireann, a paramilitary organisation that Pádraig Pearse later described as being as important as the creation of the Irish Volunteers in 1913. In 1911 Constance was jailed for the first time for speaking out at a demonstration attended by 30,000 people, against George V's visit to Ireland. In 1913 Markievicz's work in helping to organise the ITGWU and to run the soup kitchens during the lockout earned her honorary membership of the union, not to mention a severe beating from the Dublin police. Undeterred, Constance continued to fight for the causes she believed in.

During the Easter Rising of 1916, having held out against the British for six days, Lieutenant Markievicz famously kissed her beloved revolver before surrendering to the British. At her court-martial, Constance told the court, 'I did what was right and I stand by it.' She was originally sentenced to death but General Maxwell converted this to life in prison on 'account of the prisoner's sex'. Upon hearing this, the staunch feminist replied, 'I do wish your lot had the decency to shoot me'. In her prison cell on 29 December 1916, Constance was philosophical about the circumstances which had led to her arrest, writing: 'All my life, in a funny way, seems to have led up to the past year, and it's all been such a hurry-scurry of a life. Now I feel that I have done what I was born to do.'

The rebel countess was released from prison in 1917 as part of a general amnesty. She returned to Sligo where she was welcomed with the Freedom of the City. On arriving in Dublin, she discovered that her home had been wrecked by the British and so she went to stay with her cousin Dr Kathleen Lynn for a while, during which time she was received into the Catholic Church.

In 1919 Constance joined her colleagues at the first incarnation of Dáil Éireann, but she left government again in 1922 in opposition to the Anglo-Irish Treaty. She fought in the Irish Civil War for the republican side, and joined Fianna Fáil when it was founded in 1926.

After the Civil War, Constance regained her seat in the Dáil, but her republican politics ran afoul of the Free State government

> HAVING DONATED ALL HER EARTHLY POSSESSIONS TO THE POOR, CONSTANCE MARKIEVICZ DIED PENNILESS IN A PUBLIC WARD AT SIR PATRICK DUNN'S HOSPITAL

and she found herself imprisoned once again. Along with ninety-two other women prisoners, she went on hunger strike and was released a month later.

A few weeks after her release, on 15 July 1927, having donated all of her earthly possessions to the poor, Constance Markievicz died penniless in a public ward at Sir Patrick Dunn's Hospital. She was fifty-nine years of age.

Denied the recognition of a state funeral by the Free State government, it is said that when Constance's coffin was being taken to the republican plot at Glasnevin Cemetery, as many as 30,000 people turned up to say goodbye. Countess Constance Markievicz remains to this day the most celebrated woman of the Irish republican movement.

To C.M. on her prison birthday, February 1917:

What has time to do with thee,
Who hast found the victors' way
To be rich in poverty,
Without sunshine to be gay,
To be free in a prison cell?
Nay, on that undreamed judgement day,
When, on the old-world's scrap-heap flung,
Powers and empires pass away,
Radiant and unconquerable
Thou shalt be young.

Eva Gore-Booth

QUEEN MEDB

LEGENDARY QUEEN OF CONNACHT

Queen Medb is considered both a historical and mythological queen as there are no clear indications as to where fact ends and myth begins. Believed to have been born in Rathcrogan, County Roscommon, around the same time as the birth of Christ, most of what is known of her comes from the seventh-century epic, *An Táin Bó Cuailnge* (*The Cattle Raid of Cooley*), in which she led the forces of Connacht against Ulster.

Medb is one of the few women to have actively partaken in war in the early legends. Reputed to have had a voracious sexual appetite, she often bragged about taking thirty lovers a day. Upon taking a husband, she demanded of him three things – that he be without fear, meanness or jealousy; the last trait being particularly important as Medb was known to have had regular affairs throughout her marriages to a series of powerful men, including Conchobar Mac Nessa of Ulster, a Connacht chieftain called Ailill, and finally Ailill Mac Ross, son of the king of Leinster.

Medb's father, Eochaid Feidlich, the king of Connacht, arranged for her

to be married to Conchobar Mac Nessa, king of Ulster, as an apology for killing Conchobar's father in battle. But after giving birth to a son, whom she called Glaisne, Medb grew tired of Conchobar and left him. To make up for this, Eochaid then arranged for his other daughter Clothra to wed Conchobar.

When Eochaid died, leaving instructions for Clothra to be made queen of Connacht, Medb was furious. She killed her pregnant sister and took the crown by force. Clothra's son Furbaid was cut from his mother's womb after Medb had killed her. In retaliation for the murder of his wife, Conchobar raped Medb and a war between Ulster and Connacht ensued. During this war, warrior Eochaid Dála proved such a loyal subject to Medb that she took him as her husband and the new king of Connacht. While married to Eochaid, Medb also took seventeen-year-old Ailill Mac Máta, chief of her royal bodyguard, as her lover. When Eochaid discovered the affair he challenged Ailill to single combat but lost. Medb then married Ailill under the

> ## MEDB IS SAID TO BE BURIED STANDING UPRIGHT IN A FORTY-FOOT-HIGH STONE CAIRN IN KNOCKNAREA, FACING HER ENEMIES IN ULSTER

Brehon marriage contract, called Lánamnas fir for bantinacur, where the man brings less property to the marriage than the woman. They had seven sons: Fedlimid, Cairbre, Eochaid, Fergus, Cet, Sin and Dáire, whose names were later all changed to Maine when Medb learned from a druid that her son Maine would kill Conchobar. Her son Eochaid, now called Maine, was the one to kill him. They also had a daughter, Findabair.

In the *Cattle Raid of Cooley*, Queen Medb calculated both the sum of her own belongings and those of her husband Ailill and discovered that he had one more powerful stud bull than her, thus making her the less equal of the pair. Medb found a better bull owned by Dáire Mac Fiachna in Ulster and when he refused to sell it to her she declared war. Medb enlisted the help of her army as well as that of her lover Fergus Mac Roich, foster-father of Cúchulainn. It was said that Medb seduced Fergus into turning against

Ulster 'because he preferred the buttocks of a woman to his own people'. As the Ulster warriors were under a divine curse at the time, the only warrior left to fight was the young Cúchulainn, who demanded single combat. Medb offered her daughter Findabair in marriage to a series of warriors as payment for fighting Cúchulainn, but they were all defeated. Nevertheless, Medb secured the bull, which then fought Ailill's bull. Both bulls died as a result.

According to legend, Medb lived to be one hundred and twenty. In her later years, she took her daily bath at a spring near her home at Inis Clothran. She was bathing there one day when her nephew Furbaid killed her to avenge his mother Clothra's murder. Medb is said to be buried standing upright in a forty-foot-high stone cairn in Knocknarea, facing her enemies in Ulster.

JOAN DENISE MORIARTY

FOUNDRESS OF THE IRISH NATIONAL BALLET

— *c.* 1920–1992 —

The name Joan Denise Moriarty is synonymous with ballet in Ireland, and for good reason. She is responsible for demystifying the dance form and making it possible for thousands of young people in Ireland to receive ballet training. Many of Joan Denise's dance students were later given the option of a career at her professional ballet company, the Irish National Ballet, which was the first professional ballet company to be established in Ireland.

The details of Joan Denise's early life are obscure. It is believed that her parents were from Mallow, County Cork, but moved to Liverpool around 1907. There is another widely held belief that Joan was the grand-daughter of a Lord Chief Justice of Appeal for Ireland, and that she spent some time in an orphanage in north England before being fostered by relatives in Mallow. Regardless of her parentage, Joan Denise Moriarty was born *c.*1920 and spent her early years in Liverpool. She started dancing at the age of six and later became the champion Irish step dancer of England in 1931. She was also a member of the Gaelic League and won many awards for her talent as a war-pipe player.

Joan Denise studied ballet in London from a young age under the tutelage of Dame Marie Rambert, who was one of the biggest influences on British ballet. However, at the age of fourteen she was forced to spend months away from rehearsals while recovering from a nasty bout of scarlet fever. During these months she experienced a growth spurt and when she returned to the studio Madame Rambert dismissed her as being 'too big' to be a dancer, adding that if Joan Denise was to appear on stage 'there'd be no more room for anyone else'. As there was a tradition of small male dancers in England and France, Joan Denise was now ineligible to perform in any of the classical ballets. For a time she considered moving to America where the male dancers were taller. But Marie Rambert had seen a great deal of talent in her young pupil and she urged Joan Denise to channel it into teaching other dancers. Joan Denise was further inspired to teach after a chance meeting in Cork:

My mother and myself were talking to some friends on Patrick's Bridge and the friends turned around to me and said 'What are you doing?' and I explained I was a dancer and was hoping to continue my career and so on. And a man there said, 'Oh ballet, I can't stand it! What is it … a man chasing a woman around the stage?' Well I was a very young person at the time but I was furious. I remember my face getting redder. I wanted to burst out in temper, but I made a vow that day standing on that bridge that I would then come back and start a ballet school, and that we would have a ballet company in Cork and a ballet company in Ireland. Very high falutin' ideas but you know what youth is, nothing stands in your way. I wanted to make him eat his words.

With this in mind, Joan Denise became a distinguished teacher of ballet, registering with the Royal Academy of Dance. The Moriarty family returned to Mallow and Joan Denise set up her first ballet school there in 1934. After the death of her mother in 1940, Joan Denise moved to a little studio on Patrick Street, then to Emmett Place, where she would spend the majority of her professional career. In 1945 she met composer Aloys Fleischmann, professor of music at UCC, who asked her to play the war pipes in his new work *Clare's Dragoons*. This was the start of a successful lifelong collaboration between the pair. In combining an amateur ballet company with an amateur orchestra company, they produced some of the most innovative productions ever seen in the world of ballet, including *The Golden Bell of Ko*, *Macha Ruadh*, *An Coitin Dearg* and *The Planting Stick*.

In 1954 Joan Denise upheld the vow she had made to herself that fateful day on Patrick's Bridge by setting up Cork Ballet Group, the city's first ballet company. In 1959 she launched the first Irish professional ballet company, the Irish Theatre Ballet, which employed a number of dancers Joan Denise had personally trained in the Cork Ballet Group. When the company went into administration due to lack of funding, Joan Denise refused to give up. After ten years of lobbying, she was finally awarded £40,000 by the Arts Council and she set about establishing the Irish Ballet Company, known afterwards as the Irish National Ballet. When Ninette de Valois, founder of The Royal Ballet and creator of modern British ballet, arrived unannounced to see the first performance of Joan Denise's new professional company, she was so impressed with what she saw that she donated half of the Erasmus

Award she had just received from the Dutch government to the fledgling professional ballet group.

Joan Denise was now in a position to pioneer many exciting new productions that brought ballet in line with the more traditional heritage of Ireland. In the late 1960s she choreographed thirteen one-act folk ballets for the RTÉ television programme *An Damhsa*. She choreographed many ballets set to the music of Seán O'Riada, including *Billy the Music*. Her first full-length work, a dance version of Synge's *Playboy of the Western World*, premiered at the Dublin Theatre Festival in 1978, and later went on tour to New York. It was revived with music by the Chieftains at the Sadler's Wells Theatre, London, in 1980, where it received rave reviews. In 1981 Joan Denise received an award of $10,000 from the Irish American Cultural Institute to assist the production of her second full-length work, *The Táin*, at the Dublin Theatre festival, with music composed by Aloys Fleischmann and performed by the Radio Éireann Symphony Orchestra.

The Irish National Ballet continued to develop and perform under Joan Denise's guidance until 1985 when, following a change of policy by the Arts Council which stipulated that the artistic director of the Irish National Ballet have no other work commitments, Joan Denise resigned, but she continued to work with the amateur Cork Ballet Company until her death on 24 January 1992.

Joan Denise Moriarty started a ballet company in Ireland at a time when ballet was seen as an elitist art form with no place in Irish culture. She was to prove her critics wrong by pioneering a new form of dance which combined the more fluid elements of Irish dance with the elegance of ballet against a backdrop of Irish myth and lore. She choreographed over 100 original works for her companies, and by the time of her death in 1992 she had created a strong ballet culture that had become one of the most prevalent art forms in modern Ireland.

AGNES MORROGH BERNARD

FOUNDRESS OF THE FOXFORD WOOLLEN MILLS

—— 1842–1932 ——

Agnes Morrogh Bernard was the driving force behind the restoration of the famine-stricken Mayo town of Foxford. An extremely practical and resourceful woman, Agnes provided the inhabitants of first Ballaghaderreen and later Foxford with a means of making a living. She not only saw to it that the dispirited inhabitants had food and clothing, but in building the Foxford Woollen Mills she went one step further by enabling the locals to become self-sufficient.

Agnes was born in Cheltenham, Gloucestershire, England, on 24 February 1842. The eldest of ten children born to a wealthy Catholic family, the Morroghs of Glanmire, Agnes returned with her family to Cork shortly after her birth. She remained there until her father John Morrogh inherited the Bernard Estates at Sheheree, Killarney, County Kerry, as well as the Bernard name.

In Killarney, Agnes witnessed first-hand the devastation that the potato blight was wreaking on the lives of rural dwellers. She later recalled how moved she was when as a young child she witnessed a starving woman enter her father's kitchen and beg to be allowed eat the nettles that were being boiled, such was the extent of poverty at the time. Agnes's father was a fair landlord. He was conscious of the double prejudice of being both poor and a woman in those times and so he always made sure to provide work for the women tenants on his land. It was in this early setting that Agnes learned the importance of providing people with an opportunity to make their own living.

Agnes was educated at home by her mother Frances Blount, a devoted Catholic, before being sent to the Laurel Hill Convent in Limerick for three years and then on to the Dames Anglaises Convent in Paris for a further two years. It was during this time that Agnes realised she wanted to enter the religious life. Despite her father's protestations, a few days after attending a ball held in honour of her twenty-first birthday, Agnes Morrogh Bernard exchanged a life of privilege for one of self-sacrifice when she entered the novitiate of the Sisters of Charity. This order had been founded by Mary Aikenhead in 1815 and appealed especially to Agnes because of its fourth vow of service to the poor. On 16 January 1866, Agnes was professed Sister Mary Joseph Arsenius, and over the next couple of years she worked as a teacher in various Dublin schools including the Gardiner Street School.

In April 1876 Agnes was sent to the poor town of Ballaghaderreen in County Mayo, where she was to spend the next fourteen years as superior of a new convent. During this time she established a successful laundry, bakery, pharmacy, lending library, industrial school and national school. In a bid to empower the women of the area, she established a textile business and saw to it that the local girls were taught the arts of spinning, weaving, knitting, dress-making, lace-making and crochet. In 1891, having implemented huge changes in the town of Ballaghaderreen, Agnes was sent to the neighbouring 'God-forsaken town of Foxford', which was one of the poorest districts in the west of Ireland. Agnes arrived with four of her sisters and they immediately set to work, taking over the running of the national school and providing the starving children with a daily hot breakfast. Agnes established a technical school that offered training in different farming methods and, in an effort to generate a sense of pride in their locality, she also initiated a competition for the best-kept garden.

> **AGNES ARRIVED WITH FOUR OF HER SISTERS AND THEY IMMEDIATELY SET TO WORK, TAKING OVER THE RUNNING OF THE NATIONAL SCHOOL AND PROVIDING THE STARVING CHILDREN WITH A DAILY HOT BREAKFAST**

Agnes's most important challenge was to establish an industry that would enable the people of Foxford to earn their own living. She looked to the neighbouring River Moy and the surrounding fields that were filled with sheep, and realised that it was the perfect place in which to run a woollen mill. With this in mind, she travelled to County Tyrone to speak with established woollen-mill owners, only to be told to 'go home and say your prayers'. Undaunted, Agnes contacted John Smith, owner of the Caledon Mills in County Tyrone, whose initial response was 'a pack of untrained women, secluded from the world, knowing nothing of machinery or business, how could they succeed where man failed?' However, Smith was soon won over by Agnes's determination and he began drawing up plans for the new mill.

He loaned Agnes his manager to oversee operations and his accountant to train in one of the sisters. Agnes applied to the Congested Districts Board that had recently been set up to provide loans to projects aimed at alleviating poverty in the west of Ireland. She was given a loan of £7,000 and a grant of £1,500 for training. The loan was guaranteed by Agnes's superior general who mortgaged the head house of the congregation in Milltown – such was her belief in the work of Sister Arsenius.

In 1892 Foxford Woollen Mills opened with only two hand looms. By 1905 the mills were employing over 150 people and turning a profit; their flannels, tweeds, shawls, blankets and clerical cloths could be purchased from Brown Thomas and Arnotts. As the mill became more successful, Agnes had comfortable houses built for the employees and set about lifting the spirits of the downtrodden Foxford community. Her early efforts saw her set up a Brass and Reed Band in 1897 which is still going strong today. She opened a music school, started a dramatic society and held parties and concerts. She also encouraged sporting activities and was instrumental in the building of a handball alley in Foxford in 1901. One of Agnes's last major undertakings was the opening of a teachers' training unit in Milltown for nuns of her own order who were not allowed to leave their convents to attend Catholic teacher-training colleges.

Agnes Morrogh Bernard continued to work for the betterment of Foxford until her death on 21 April 1932. She was ninety years of age. At the time, the success of the Foxford Woollen Mills was at its peak, employing 230 workers. Agnes left behind her a successful industry which provided work, hope and dignity to generations of Foxford men and women.

NANO NAGLE

PIONEERING EDUCATOR AND FOUNDRESS OF THE PRESENTATION SISTERS

— 1718–1784 —

The education of women has always been a pressing issue for feminists, who recognise a strong link between ignorance and oppression. In Ireland, many women have carried the torch for this cause, from Anna Haslam to Anne Jellicoe, and from Catherine Mahon to Katherine Zappone and Ann Louise Gilligan. However, long before any of these women set their sights on the education of women, Nano Nagle was pacing the streets of Cork city teaching young girls how to read, write, count and pray. Nano knew that without education, no permanent change in society could ever occur. She provided young girls with skills they would never have

otherwise acquired, setting in motion a chain of events that later led to the emancipation of women from their role as second-class citizens. Long before Catherine McAuley and Mary Aikenhead founded their congregations, or Agnes Morrogh Bernard and Sister Stanislaus Kennedy began working with the poor, Nano Nagle was the first woman in Ireland to set up a women's religious group dedicated to alleviating the suffering of poor Irish women.

Nano was born Honora Nagle in Ballygriffin, County Cork, in 1718, to Garrett and Ann Nagle, née Matthew. Nano was the eldest of six children and her father was one of the wealthiest Catholic landowners in the country. At the time, the Penal Laws were in place, suppressing Irish nationalism and stifling Catholics through poverty and oppression. Catholics were not allowed to vote, hold public office, buy land, practice law, own weapons or provide education; all of which were punishable by death. In this dangerous climate, Nano received her early education at a hedge school in the ruins of Monanimy Castle near her home. However, as the climate became more hostile and Catholic teachers and priests were being killed for operating these hedge schools, Nano and her sister Ann were smuggled abroad to France in the hold of a cargo ship. Here, they continued their education in luxury, surrounded by the most prominent members of the Irish *émigré* community.

Nano remained in Paris for many years after the end of her schooling, enjoying the hectic social life of a girl about town. But her life was to change forever when, at the age of twenty-two, while returning home in the early hours of the morning from an all-night ball, she saw Paris' poor huddling outside the gates of a church waiting to hear mass. As Nano watched these cold and hungry people who had woken early, fasting even though many had a long working day ahead, she was instantly filled with shame over her own life which seemed to her empty of reason. A few

> CATHOLICS WERE NOT ALLOWED TO VOTE, HOLD PUBLIC OFFICE, BUY LAND, PRACTICE LAW, OWN WEAPONS OR PROVIDE EDUCATION; ALL OF WHICH WERE PUNISHABLE BY DEATH

years later when Nano's father died, she returned to Ireland to be with her family. Having been away from Ireland for so many years, she now saw the country with fresh eyes and was horrified by the rising number of children living in poverty. She was moved when on one occasion she went to look for some expensive material that she had brought home from Paris only to find that her sister Ann had sold it to feed a poor family in distress. Her sister's kindness and concern for the poor had a profound effect on Nano.

When Nano's sister Ann and their mother died in quick succession, Nano returned to France where she decided to enter the Ursuline Convent. But she couldn't get the image of Ireland's impoverished children out of her mind and, upon talking with her advisor, she decided that her energies would be of better use in Ireland where Catholics were being denied the human right of education. Nano believed that she had received a divine calling from God. However, the decision to leave the safety and security of the French convent in order to return to Ireland where she would be risking her life, was not an easy one.

In 1749 Nano returned to Cork and moved in with her brother Joseph and his family. While pretending to attend church, Nano set about opening a school for young girls in a two-roomed mud shack on Cove Lane. She soon had thirty pupils and within a year this figure had risen to 200. By 1769 Nano had opened five schools for girls and two for boys. These schools were illegal and with stories abounding of Catholic teachers being hung from trees and rolled through the streets in fire-engulfed barrels, Nano did her best to keep her work secret, hiding it even from her brother. However, when a man called to Joseph's house to enquire about enrolling his daughter in Ms Nagle's school, the secret was out. At first Joseph was horrified by the risk Nano was taking but he was soon won over and even helped to finance the schools when he could.

Sparing no thought for her own safety, Nano educated children during the day and visited and nursed the poverty-ridden sick and elderly by night. She became known as the 'Lady with the Lantern' because she was often to be seen roaming through the streets of Cork at night holding a lantern in her hand.

As Nano's number of pupils grew, she decided to extend her educational work through an order of religious women. In 1771 she invited a group of

Ursulines to Ireland to take over the running of the schools. However, she soon learned that the Ursulines' rules would not permit her and the other nuns to go outside the convent, a freedom that they needed to carry out their work. She was also disappointed to learn that they were mainly interested in educating middle-class girls, when Nano had established the schools primarily for the education of the poor. Nano decided that to continue with her important work she would have to develop a new order of religious women. In 1775 she established a community known as the Sisters of Charitable Instruction of the Sacred Heart of Jesus – a religious association of celibate women who took vows and religious names and dressed in caps and shawls. While taking her vows, Nano chose the name Sister Saint John of God. Pope Pius VII elevated their group to a religious order in 1805 and they were named the Union of Sisters of the Presentation of the Blessed Virgin Mary, but became better known as the

NANO CELEBRATED BY INVITING LOCAL PAUPERS TO A MEAL SERVED BY HERSELF AND HER SISTERS

Presentation Sisters. The first convent in Ireland was opened on Christmas Day, 1777, and Nano celebrated by inviting local paupers to a meal served by herself and her sisters.

Nano continued to work every day in each of her schools while visiting the sick at home by night. In 1783 she opened a home for destitute elderly women in Cork. Suffering from poor eyesight and a weak chest, she was frequently ill but rarely let it be known, believing that 'she who makes a sacrifice for the good of souls will have the fortitude to make light of discomforts'.

On 26 April 1784, Nano began feeling ill, but dismissing any concerns for her own health, she decided to 'walk it off as I am used to doing'. While walking, she collapsed on Cross Street and died shortly afterwards of tuberculosis. She was sixty-five years of age. Her last recorded words were, 'Spend yourselves for the poor'. While preparing her body, Nano's sisters discovered that her knees were riddled with large ulcers and her feet were badly inflamed. Her body bore the scars of a lifetime spent kneeling on cold floors to teach children and walking miles to visit the sick in their homes.

Since her death, Nano's legacy continues in the education of girls and women across Ireland and the world. In 1995, the extent of Nano's influence was revealed when she was voted 'Ireland's Greatest Woman' in a phone-in poll conducted by Marian Finucane on RTÉ radio. She remains the original champion of women's education.

ROSEMARY NELSON

HUMAN RIGHTS LAWYER

— 1958–1999 —

Rosemary Nelson was an internationally respected human rights lawyer who took on cases of persecution, false accusation and harassment in Northern Ireland. She was the first female solicitor to open a legal practice in Lurgan, County Armagh, and was indiscriminate in representing clients from both the nationalist and unionist sides of the community. Throughout her career, she worked tirelessly on behalf of victims of domestic abuse and members of the travelling community. But it was her work on a number of high-profile republican cases, including that of the Drumcree marching dispute, and her determination to persevere with these cases in spite of the hostile intimidation she often faced, that revealed Rosemary to be a true champion of justice.

Rosemary Nelson, née Magee, was born on 4 September 1958 in Lurgan, County Armagh, to Tommy and Sheila Magee. She was the middle child of five daughters and two sons. Born with a strawberry birthmark on one side of her face, from the age of ten through to her mid-teens, Rosemary spent periods of up to fifteen weeks at a time in a Scottish hospital undergoing skin-graft surgery. The facial scarring that resulted from these painful operations was later used in loyalist propaganda to promote the idea of Rosemary as a republican bomber.

Educated at St Michael's Grammar School, Rosemary was passionate about the Irish language and spent most of her teenage summers in the Gaeltacht areas of County Donegal. She often spoke Irish with her brother Eunan when they didn't want anyone else to know what they were talking about. Rosemary studied law at Queen's University, Belfast, and graduated in 1981. She then worked for two established legal firms before helping to set up an advice and health centre in a Lurgan housing estate where she offered help to vulnerable women, particularly the elderly, those on state benefits and members of the travelling community.

In 1989 Rosemary opened her own legal firm in Lurgan. Her work at the advice centre meant she was already well known and she became an agony aunt of sorts to many in the area who came to her seeking advice on marital difficulties.

Based as she was in the mid-Ulster area, Rosemary soon became involved in some of the most controversial republican cases of the time. One such case was that of the Drumcree marching dispute. Rosemary became the legal representative for the Garvaghy Road Residents' Coalition in Portadown, a nationalist community group contesting Orange Order parades that were passing through the Catholic Garvaghy area on their way from Drumcree church. By the late 1990s the Drumcree dispute had escalated and became the focus of mass protests and murderous violence. In another case, Rosemary represented the family of Portadown Catholic father-of-two Robert Hamill, who had been killed in a sectarian attack in 1997 while an armed RUC patrol at the scene refused to intervene and made no attempt to arrest the killers. Rosemary also successfully appealed against the conviction of prominent republican Colin Duffy for killing two members of the RUC, and represented Mícheál Caraher, one of the south Armagh snipers thought to have been involved in a sniping campaign against British security forces.

By this time, Rosemary was being labelled a 'bomber' in loyalist leaflets and was receiving death threats. She was at home one evening when her ten-year-old son handed her the phone and the voice on the other end informed her, 'You're dead.' In

THE TRAGIC MURDER OF ONE OF NORTHERN IRELAND'S BRAVEST SOLICITORS SENT SHOCKWAVES THROUGH-OUT THE WESTERN WORLD

another incident, Rosemary was shopping in her local supermarket when a man came up to her and told her to 'stop representing IRA scum' or she would be killed. But Rosemary was dedicated to her work as a solicitor and refused to let such intimidation deter her. She strongly believed that everyone was entitled to justice. When her sister Bernie cautioned her about getting involved in such controversial cases, Rosemary replied, 'How would you like it if your daughter went in to a shop one day and somebody accused her of shoplifting and no solicitor would defend her?'

In July 1998 the Independent Commission for Police Complaints (ICPC), which monitored internal RUC inquiries, raised concerns about the RUC's handling of the investigation into alleged threats against Rosemary Nelson. The RUC team was withdrawn from the investigation and replaced by the London Metropolitan Police. In September of that year, Rosemary told a hearing at the US Congress in Washington that she was being intimidated by the RUC and by loyalist paramilitaries. The United Nations special rapporteur on the Independence of Judges and Lawyers, Param Curamaswamy, noted these threats and announced in a televised interview that he believed the life of Rosemary Nelson to be in danger.

A few weeks before her death, Rosemary spearheaded demands for an inquiry into an alleged collusion between British security forces and loyalist paramilitaries that had led to the killing of nationalist lawyer Pat Finucane. On 15 March 1999, a week after the ten-year celebration of her law practice, Rosemary was driving past Tannaghmore primary school, where her eight-year-old daughter Sarah was a pupil, when she halted at a junction. As the car came to a stop, a bomb was activated and it ripped up through the floor of her vehicle. Rosemary's sister Bernie rushed to the scene and held Rosemary's hand as she was cut from the car. Rosemary died later that day following hours of intensive surgery to save her life. A loyalist paramilitary splinter group called the Red Hand Defenders later claimed responsibility for the killing. However, no one has ever been charged in connection with Rosemary's murder.

The tragic murder of one of Northern Ireland's bravest solicitors sent shockwaves throughout the western world. At home in Armagh, all of those who had been touched by her life, including the many women who had sought her help and members of the travelling community whom she helped battle against prejudice, had lost their most beloved defender.

CHRISTINA NOBLE

INSPIRATIONAL HUMANITARIAN

— 1944- —

Christina Noble has lived a life of unimaginable suffering and generosity. Having endured years of violent abuse at the hands of both relations and strangers, she has used these experiences to help her reach out to the abandoned children of Vietnam and Mongolia, where her foundation has helped over 500,000 children.

Christina Byrne was born on 23 December 1944 in the Liberties district of inner-city Dublin. She was the eldest girl of eight children born to Tom Byrne, a bare-knuckle fighter and alcoholic, and Annie Gross, a woman known to all as 'The Lady' because of her soft-spoken voice and gentle ways. Christina was only ten when her beloved mother died. She and her siblings were subsequently split up and sent to different Church-run industrial schools where they suffered various forms of abuse. Christina

was even told at one point that her brothers and sisters had died.

While trying to escape from the first home she was sent to, Christina jumped out of a window and broke both an arm and a leg in the fall. Despite her injuries she managed to crawl to Dublin's city centre where she spent the next two years sleeping rough in various coal sheds near to her family home in Marrowbone Lane in the Liberties. She was eventually found and sent to the infamous St Joseph's Industrial School at Letterfrack near Clifden, County Galway, where she spent the next four years. At the age of sixteen, Christina was released from St Joseph's and sent back to Dublin with a single £5 note. Her father, who was by now homeless, met her at the train station. On the pretence of buying two tickets for them to leave the city together, Christina's father took the only money she had, went to the pub and slipped out the back door, leaving Christina alone and destitute in Dublin. Christina ended up spending her nights in a hole she dug in the ground in Phoenix Park. As she had no money, she was reduced to eating warm candle drippings from the church as well as crab apples that made her sick. During this time she gave birth to a baby boy called Thomas but was forced to put him up for adoption.

> **WHILE TRYING TO ESCAPE FROM THE FIRST HOME SHE WAS SENT TO, CHRISTINA JUMPED OUT OF A WINDOW AND BROKE BOTH AN ARM AND A LEG IN THE FALL**

At the age of eighteen, Christina travelled to Birmingham where her brother Andy was now living. In Birmingham, she met and married Mario, a Greek Cypriot, with whom she had three children: Helenita, Nicolas and Androula. Christina's new husband regularly beat her. The years of abuse finally took their toll on Christina. She suffered a nervous breakdown and was forced to undergo shock treatment. It was during this low point in her life that she had a very vivid dream about Vietnam:

> In the dream, naked Vietnamese children were running down a dirt road fleeing from a napalm bombing. The ground under the children was cracked and coming

apart and the children were reaching to me. One of the girls had a look in her eyes that implored me to pick her up and protect her and take her to safety. Above the escaping children was a brilliant white light that contained the word 'Vietnam'.

Over the next twenty years, Christina married and divorced again, and opened a successful catering business in Surrey. During the union strikes in England in the 1970s she used her catering supplies to help feed needy families in her neighbourhood. But throughout this time Christina was still haunted by her dream about the poor Vietnamese children. In 1989, when she was forty-four years of age, she gave up her home, closed her successful catering business in Surrey and booked an aeroplane ticket to Vietnam. With no backing, no training in childcare, no knowledge of the country or its language, and only £2,000 in her pocket, Christina arrived in Vietnam, determined to try and help some of the 50,000 street children who had either been abandoned by their families or orphaned during the twenty years of war:

> **WITH NO BACKING, NO TRAINING IN CHILDCARE, NO KNOWLEDGE OF THE COUNTRY OR ITS LANGUAGE, AND ONLY £2,000 IN HER POCKET, CHRISTINA ARRIVED IN VIETNAM**

My decision was made. Here, my dream, my destiny, would be fulfilled. Here, the pain and the sorrow and the anger of my childhood in Ireland would be resolved. I would work with the street children of Ho Chi Minh City. I would work with the ill and the unwanted, with the lonely and the misbegotten, with the throwaway children of this war-torn country. I would work with the children who were living as I had lived so long ago in Dublin.

With plans to open an orphanage, Christina took to the streets after dark, chasing leads, following word of mouth, looking for isolated children and kicking down doors to save children from paedophiles.

Christina's first major breakthrough came months later when Enterprise Oil, then based in Vietnam, gave her £14,000. Needing a further £34,000 to set up an orphanage, Christina returned to Britain to sell off most of her possessions. Through raffles, auctions and car-boot sales she managed to raise the extra cash. In July 1991 she finally realised her dream when she opened the Christina Noble Children's Foundation in Ho Chi Minh City with forty-two staff and six volunteers. Since then, her foundation has rescued more than 500,000 children from a life of poverty and abuse. Christina has established in excess of seventy projects, including a social and medical centre that provides an integrated care programme for abandoned babies, street children and sick or malnourished infants. On average each month, the centre provides medical care for between 400 and 600 outpatients, and residential care and treatment for 80 inpatients. Christina's Sunshine School provides free education to over 350 street children aged between six and sixteen years old. Her boys' and girls' shelters provide residential care, nutritional meals, clean clothing, education and social activities. In addition, Christina has established dental programmes, vocational and job-placement schemes, English classes, art projects and physiotherapy clinics.

CHRISTINA TOOK TO THE STREETS AFTER DARK, CHASING LEADS, FOLLOWING WORD OF MOUTH, LOOKING FOR ISOLATED CHILDREN AND KICKING DOWN DOORS TO SAVE CHILDREN FROM PAEDOPHILES

In 1997 Christina expanded her work to Mongolia where thousands of children roam the streets, seeking shelter from the bitterly cold winter temperatures in manholes and pipes below the street surfaces. Here, Christina established a programme of providing education to children as young as eight who are incarcerated in the country's jails. At the Ger Village, she provides residential care for fifty orphaned or abandoned children who would otherwise most likely be preyed upon by gangs and sex traffickers.

In boldly and bravely following a dream, Christina Noble has saved the lives of thousands of innocent children. Her inspirational work has won her many awards, including the OBE from Prince Charles in 2003. But the greatest reward that Christina continues to receive is the love and affection of the children of Vietnam and Mongolia, to whom she is better known as 'Mama Tina'.

EDNA O'BRIEN

IRISH WRITER WHOSE BOOKS WERE BANNED IN IRELAND

— 1930– —

Edna O'Brien has been alternatively described as 'the most gifted woman now writing in English' by the Pulitzer Prize-winning American novelist Philip Roth, and as 'a smear on Irish womanhood' by the Irish government censor. Edna has spent the greater part of her life battling Church and state for the right to write honestly about her experiences as an Irish woman. Closer to home, Edna's own mother kept an eraser close at hand when reading her books, to blot out any words or passages she considered offensive. Edna later regretfully remarked that her mother had a dread of the written word, believing it led to sin.

When Edna's first novel *The Country Girls* was published in 1960, its rich depictions of young convent girls provoked instant outrage amongst a largely conservative Catholic nation and it was quickly banned. Book burnings were organised in Edna's parish, during which women reportedly fainted upon overhearing mere snippets of the provocative prose. For the next twenty years, Edna's name would be synonymous with sex, and not always in a good way.

Edna's next five novels were also banned, but despite all this controversy she continued to write. At a time when young women were supposed to be seen but not heard, Edna's early semi-autobiographical works became a lifeline for a generation of repressed young Irish girls who were overjoyed to find a literary reflection of their own lives.

Edna O'Brien was born on 15 December 1930, in the farming community of Tuamgraney, County Clare. Her father Michael, a volatile man, was a great raconteur and was passionate about horses. Edna's mother Lena had worked as a maid in New York for many years before returning to Ireland to raise a family. Edna was the youngest of five siblings.

WHILE HER BOOKS CONTINUED TO BE BANNED IN IRELAND UNTIL THE LATE 1970S, THEY MET WITH GREAT SUCCESS IN OTHER COUNTRIES AND SHE WON NUMEROUS AWARDS

Following her education at the Convent of Mercy in Loughrea, Edna went on to study at the Pharmaceutical College in Dublin by night while working in a pharmacy on Cabra Road during the day. Around this time she became interested in the works of James Joyce. She purchased a copy of T.S. Eliot's *Introducing James Joyce* for four pence, which included excerpts from Joyce's *A Portrait of the Artist as a Young Man*. At this point, Edna had written a few articles for the *Irish Press* and had fledgling aspirations of becoming a fiction writer, but had always felt encumbered by her adjective-heavy approach. Joyce was to change all this. As she read the Christmas dinner scene in *A Portrait of the Artist as a Young Man* she realised, 'I need go no further than my own interior, my own experience, for whatever I wanted to write'.

One of Edna's regular customers at the pharmacy was the fiery Czech writer Ernest Gébler, who was twenty years her senior, married and a communist when they first met. The couple later married in 1954, despite the protestations of Edna's parents. They had two sons, Carlo and Sasha, but divorced a decade later.

In 1960 Edna published her first novel, *The Country Girls*. It took her just three weeks to write, and turned her world upside down. Banned and burned in Ireland for its frank portrayal of the sexual awakenings of teenage girls, *The Country Girls* was the first book in a trilogy, followed by *The Lonely Girl* in 1962 and *Girls in their Married Bliss* in 1964. These books traced the lives of characters Kate and Baba, from their strict convent-school days in the Irish countryside through to their failed marriages in London; the city Edna would move to in order to escape the persecution she faced in her home country. While her books continued to be banned in Ireland until the late 1970s, they met with great success in other countries and she won numerous awards, including the Kingsley Amis Fiction Award for her debut novel in 1962.

Edna also went on to write for the stage. In 1981 her first play, *Virginia*, based on the letters of Virginia Woolf to her husband Leonard and her lover Vita Sackville-West, opened at the Stratford Festival in Ontario. Since then, many of her plays have been produced, including *Our Father*, the complicated story of a family reunion in 1970s rural Ireland, which opened at the Almeida Theatre in 1999, and *Triptych*, a one-act drama about three women vying for the affections of one man, which opened at the Magic Theatre in San Francisco in 2003. She has also written children's books and, as a short-story writer, has been regularly published in *The New Yorker*.

In 1997 Edna came under attack once again when her book *Down by the River* was published. Inspired by the 1992 'Miss X' case in which a fourteen-year-old girl became the centre of a nationwide debate on abortion, Edna's fictionalised account contrasts the heavy-handed dealings of Church and state with the moral repercussions and conflicted feelings of a young girl who has been raped by her father.

Refusing to heed the advice of her critics, who pointed out the potentially exploitative nature of using recent real-life situations as the basis for her fiction, Edna published *In the Forest* in 2002. This book was based on the 1994 abduction and murder of a young mother, her infant son and a priest in Cregg Woods, County Clare, by a youth on remand from prison. However, not all critics disapproved of her technique of using real-life as a springboard for fiction, with the *Irish Independent* describing it as 'her best book and a modern masterpiece'.

EDNA O'BRIEN'S VOLUMINOUS BODY OF WORK CHARTS THE HOPES AND DREAMS OF A GENERATION OF FEMALE READERS ON THE VERGE OF BREAKING FREE FROM THEIR SHACKLES

Edna O'Brien's voluminous body of work reflects the hopes and dreams of a generation of female readers on the verge of breaking free from the various inequalities they were living with. Edna's work also establishes the former pharmacist as one of the great free thinkers of her time.

Having written more than twenty novels, Edna continues to provoke and enrich the public imagination, whether it is through writing about the IRA or about the relationship between James Joyce and Nora Barnacle. Edna uses her books to explore the murkiest waters of the human psyche, reaching out to her readers with unflinching poetic prose.

In 2006, the woman who once penned film scripts for Elizabeth Taylor and was described by *Vanity Fair* magazine as the 'Playgirl of the Western World', was appointed adjunct professor of English literature in University College, Dublin. Here, she was awarded the Ulysses Medal for her work and she continues to inspire a new generation of country girls.

SINÉAD O'CONNOR

MUSICIAN AND INFLUENTIAL NON-CONFORMIST

—— 1966– ——

S inéad O'Connor has been surrounded by controversy throughout her career. A passionate and courageous artist, she has openly questioned life's many building blocks, angering the old Ireland of blind faith in the process, but inspiring younger generations of Irish men and women who are seeking a way back to some form of spirituality.

A firm believer in remaining true to personal ideologies, Sinéad has never been afraid to stand by her convictions, regardless of public opinion. In 1990 she refused to set foot on a stage in New Jersey if officials played a recording of the American national anthem before her concert. She explained that she was against national anthems being played at public gatherings as, since most of these songs were composed during wars, she saw them as nationalist tirades. The officials reluctantly gave in to Sinéad's request but later banned her from singing there again. As a result of this personal stance, Frank Sinatra declared that he would like to 'kick her ass' and Sinéad's music was banned from many American radio stations.

In 1991 Sinéad, one of the few female Irish singers to conquer America, refused her Grammy Award for Best Alternative Album on the basis that she believed the awards to be a reflection of commercial success rather than artistic merit. In a letter outlining her beliefs on the matter to Mike Greene, president of the National Academy of Recording Arts and Science, Sinéad wrote, 'As artists, I believe that our function is to express the feelings of the human race … It is my opinion that the various art establishments do not recognise this.'

HER RECORDS WERE DESTROYED BY CATHOLICS AROUND THE WORLD, MORE RADIO STATIONS REFUSED TO PLAY HER SONGS AND SINÉAD WAS BOOED AND HECKLED BY ANGRY AUDIENCES

A woman often said to be ahead of her time, Sinéad brought the issue of child sex abuse within the Roman Catholic Church to the attention of a world not yet ready to listen. In 1992, while singing an *a capella* version of Bob Marley's song 'War', Sinéad tore up a picture of Pope John Paul II on the American television show *Saturday Night Live* in protest against the Catholic Church for covering up these abuses. She then implored viewers to 'fight the real enemy'. In the resulting media frenzy, Sinéad was vilified, with journalists neglecting to report the reasons behind her actions. Her records were destroyed by Catholics around the world, more radio stations refused to play her songs and Sinéad was booed and heckled by angry audiences. In attempting to highlight the abuse being carried out by many Catholic priests, Sinéad was the one who suffered, and not the men behind the atrocities she was decrying. It was seven long years before allegations of abuse became recurring headlines in national Irish newspapers.

Surprisingly, this incident did not signal Sinéad's departure from the Catholic faith. Instead, in 1999, rather than waiting for the Catholic Church to change its policies on female participation, she became a priest and was ordained by Bishop Michael Cox, a member of the Latin Tridentine Church. By this time, Sinéad had become the living embodiment of a generation's frustrated relationship with its religion.

Sinéad was born in Dublin on 8 December 1966 to Seán O'Connor, a structural engineer who later became a barrister, and dressmaker Marie O'Connor. She has four siblings. When she was eight, her parents separated and she lived for a while with her mother, at whose hands she reportedly suffered years of frequent physical abuse, the effects of which she later wrote about in her song 'Fire on Babylon'. While trying to secure custody of his children, Sinéad's father became chairman of the Divorce Action Group and later became the second man in Ireland to win sole custody of his children.

When Sinéad was fourteen she was caught shoplifting and was sentenced to two years incarceration in a juvenile detention home. Here, she met a music teacher who changed her life by giving her a guitar and a book of Bob Dylan songs. In music, Sinéad found the ultimate form of expression. Her ascent to fame began when she was discovered singing Barbra Streisand's 'Evergreen' by the sister of Paul Byrne, drummer for the band An Tua Nua, who asked her to co-write and record a song with them called 'Take My Hand'.

In 1983 Sinéad was sent to a Quaker boarding school in Waterford. At sixteen she left to study voice and piano at Dublin's College of Music, paying her way by waitressing and delivering 'kiss-o-grams' in a French-maid costume. In 1984, after placing an advert in *Hot Press*, Sinéad met Columb Farrelly and formed a band called Ton Ton Macoute. A year later she moved to London and it was here that she came to the attention of manager Fachtna Ó Ceallaigh, former head of U2's Mother Records. Ensign Records promptly signed her up, allowing the twenty-year-old musician to produce her own album.

In 1987 her first album *The Lion and the Cobra* was released. It achieved gold-record status and earned her a Best Female Rock Vocal Performance Grammy nomination for the song 'Madinka'. In 1990 she followed this up with *I Do Not Want What I Haven't Got*. This album sold five million copies worldwide and included the song 'Nothing Compares 2 U', which became a number one single in numerous countries around the world, including the UK, Germany, Australia, America and Ireland, where it became the eighth most successful single of the decade. The song's accompanying music video won the 1990 MTV Video Music Award, making it the first time a woman had ever won that category. Sinéad was also named artist of the year by *Rolling Stone* magazine. Since then, Sinéad has released ten further albums selling over fifteen million copies.

SHE HAS STUDIED OPERA AND THEOLOGY AND, FOR MANY YEARS, HAS BATTLED WITH THE DEBILITATING EFFECTS OF BI-POLAR DISORDER

In 1993 Sinéad played Ophelia in *Hamlet* at Dublin's Project Arts Centre and in 1997 she appeared as the Virgin Mary in Neil Jordan's *The Butcher Boy*. She has studied opera and theology and, for many years, has battled with the debilitating effects of bi-polar disorder, which she was diagnosed with in 2007.

Sinéad was cited by the *All Music Guide* as 'the first and in many ways the most influential of the numerous female performers whose music dominated airwaves' throughout the 1990s. Her staunch rejection of female stereotypes paved the way for a new movement of female musicians, from P.J. Harvey to Alanis Morissette. Sinéad's music is a reflection of her own spiritual journey and reveals a woman who openly and honestly uses her art to explore the deeper meaning of life.

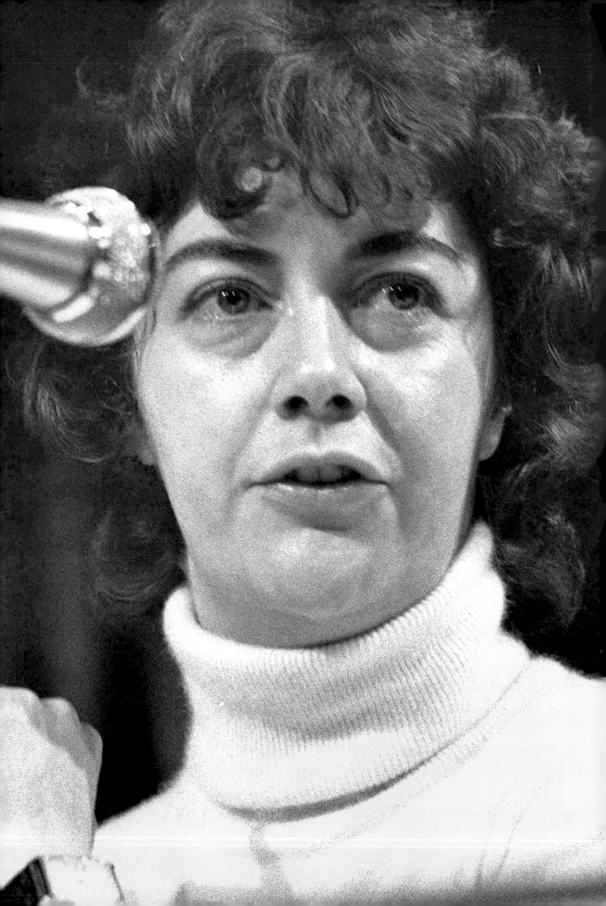

NUALA O'FAOLAIN

MEMOIRIST AND JOURNALIST

—— 1940–2008 ——

Nuala O'Faolain first captured the public imagination during the 1980s when she began writing a series of columns for *The Irish Times*. However, it was a 200-page memoir, written as an introduction to a publication of her collected newspaper columns in 1996, which made her a household name. A frank and honest account of the complexities involved in being not just a woman, but an Irish woman, *Are You Somebody?* touched a raw public nerve. It became a bestseller in Ireland and went on to top *The New York Times* bestseller list within a year, prompting *The New York Times Book Review* to declare, 'This book has to be read'.

Nuala O'Faolain was born in Dublin on 1 March 1940, at the beginning of a decade she later described as 'a living tomb for women'. She was the second of nine children born to Thomas and Catherine O'Faolain. Catherine was disappointed in married life by her adulterous husband. Thomas was a teacher-turned-soldier-turned-journalist. He wrote a social column for the *Dublin Evening Press* under the pen-name Terry O'Sullivan and was rarely at home to tend to his growing family. The strain of thirteen pregnancies and a philandering husband eventually caused Nuala's mother to buckle and she drowned her sorrows in books and alcohol. Her only source of pride was the few book reviews she had written that were published. Nuala later remarked that her father 'treated the family as if he had met them at a cocktail party' while her mother had been 'in the wrong job'.

NUALA HAD A BOHEMIAN CHILDHOOD IN MANY WAYS, WITH LITTLE MONEY AND PLENTY OF BOOKS

Nuala had a bohemian childhood in many ways, with little money and plenty of books. She later commented that her siblings were neglected by her parents to the point that one of her younger sisters suffered from tuberculosis for over a year without anyone noticing. From her mother, Nuala inherited a love of books and, later on, a love of alcohol. She was able to read by the age of four and was soon ploughing her way through *Anne of Green Gables*, *Heidi* and the 'easy bits of Ulysses'.

At the age of fourteen Nuala began stealing money from her mother to attend dance-halls where she met older men. She later admitted that 'for the sake of those bouts of devouring each other – I would do anything'. When a nun reported Nuala's affair with a married man to her parents, Nuala's father, in an unusually pro-active move, sold the family car to pay for her enrolment in a remote boarding school. Here, with no other distractions, Nuala excelled academically.

On completing her Leaving Certificate at the age of seventeen, Nuala secretly hoped that she wouldn't get a scholarship for university as she wanted to work in Clery's in Dublin, where the shopkeepers 'had the best fun'. She took a summer job in the hire-purchase office of a furniture shop on Grafton Street and went through a devoutly religious period during which she joined the Legion of Mary and attended mass daily.

However, a life in Clery's was not to be as Nuala won a scholarship to study English at UCD. Here, she discovered left-wing politics and alcohol, and skipped her first-year exams as she was too busy canvassing for Noel Browne's socialist group in a by-election. She eventually dropped out of college and went to England to work at various unskilled jobs, including stints as a canteen assistant at a water-softener factory near Heathrow Airport and as a domestic in a London hospital. Unable to save the fare for the boat ride back to Ireland, Nuala stayed in London until a friend of hers became pregnant and sent Nuala on ahead of her to break the news to the girl's parents.

Back in Dublin, writer Mary Lavin offered to give Nuala an allowance to pay for a room in Pembroke Street while she studied and re-took her UCD exams. Shaped by the experience of working in jobs that she found monotonous and uninteresting, Nuala was determined not to let academic opportunities bypass her a second time. Over the next few years she received a scholarship to the University of Hull in England where she studied medieval literature, as well as a travelling student scholarship to the University of Oxford where she completed a postgraduate degree in nineteenth-century literature. At Oxford, she became the first woman to direct an Oxford University dramatic society play in over forty years when she directed Oscar Wilde's *The Importance of Being Earnest*.

Having lectured for a time in the English Department at UCD, Nuala moved to London and became a producer with the BBC, initially making television and radio programmes for the first years of the Open University's arts faculty. She then moved to the BBC Open Door unit where she made community-access documentaries on such topics as transsexuals, religious cults and the Troubles in Northern Ireland. When she wasn't busy working or travelling, Nuala spent her free time in London sitting in a chair drinking cheap white wine and reading books, just like her mother had done before her. She sought help from a psychiatrist who warned her 'you are going to great trouble and flying in the face of the facts of your life, to recreate your mother's life'.

In 1977, having realised that the place she liked best in London was London Airport, Nuala returned to Ireland and went to work for RTÉ in the current affairs section. After reading that women aged fifty-five or over accounted for less than 3 per cent of human faces seen on television in a year, Nuala decided to make a series called *Plain Tales* where older women told the stories of their lives while looking directly at the camera. The series won the Jacob's Award for Television Programme of the Year, leading to Nuala being interviewed on Gay Byrne's radio show. After hearing this interview, Conor Brady, then editor of *The Irish Times*, invited Nuala to write a weekly opinion column for the newspaper, making her one of the first female Irish columnists. Her columns on abortion, divorce, emigration, Dublin's first gay B&B, the traveller community and the class system attracted a large following and won her the annual award for Journalist of the Year in 1986.

Ten years later, an Irish publishing company called New Island Books offered to publish a selection of Nuala's columns in a book. Nuala was asked to write an introduction, but on putting pen to paper she found herself unable to stop writing and ended up handing in a 200-page introduction, or an 'accidental memoir'. The book initially had a small print run and was released quietly without any advertising. But when Nuala began talking about it in television interviews, it quickly became a bestseller, with bookshops selling copies directly from boxes as their staff didn't have time to put them on the shelves.

> IT QUICKLY BECAME A BESTSELLER, WITH BOOKSHOPS SELLING COPIES DIRECTLY FROM BOXES AS THEIR STAFF DIDN'T HAVE TIME TO PUT THEM ON THE SHELVES

In one particular interview about her memoir, the first question Nuala recalls being asked was: 'So, you've slept with a lot of people. How many?' Her response to this was that only three of her lovers had really counted, and with that 'we were off and running. It seems the next day the world became unhinged.' The introduction, which was later reprinted as a book on its own, *Are You Somebody? The Accidental Memoir of a Dublin Woman*, was one of the first of its kind to deal with a middle-aged Irish woman's thoughts on love, sex and marriage. Filled with memories of Nuala's negligent parents, the sexual urges of her youth, the lack of a language to deal with male dominance, her ascent in the world of academia, her broken relationships and her regret for the life unlived, *Are You Somebody?* became a worldwide success and gave a much-needed voice to Irish women.

In 1999 Nuala accepted a scholarship to Yaddo, the artists' colony in New York. Here, she wrote her first fictional novel called *My Dream of You* in which she addressed the hopes and fears of middle-aged single women. In 2003 *Almost There*, a sequel to her first memoir, was published. She followed this up with *The Story of Chicago May*, the fictionalised account of an Irish-born prostitute and criminal known as the Queen of Crooks, which won the 2006 Prix Femina prize.

In her later years, Nuala lived with Brooklyn-based attorney John Low-Beer and his daughter Anna. They registered as domestic partners in 2003 but Nuala later decided to live by herself again. In February 2008 she was covering the US presidential election for the *Sunday Tribune* newspaper when she was diagnosed with metastatic cancer. Deciding against chemotherapy, Nuala embarked on a final visit to her favourite cities, including Paris, Madrid, Berlin and Sicily. On 12 April 2008, she was interviewed about her reaction to the diagnosis on Marian Finucane's radio show on RTÉ Radio One. During the interview she said, 'Even if I gained time through the chemotherapy, it isn't time I want. Because as soon as I knew I was going to die soon, the goodness went out of life.' She also paid tribute in the interview to journalist Nell McCafferty with whom she had lived and enjoyed a fifteen-year relationship. She revealed that her years with Nell were 'the greatest fun and I owe so much to them. And in fact as far as I am concerned Irish women owe so much to Nell and I was dead lucky to live with her.' Nuala died in the Blackrock Hospice in Dublin just before midnight on 9 May 2008. She was sixty-eight years of age.

In the last year of her life, Nuala struck a chord in her homeland when she spoke in a characteristically open manner about her reaction to being diagnosed with terminal cancer. Her brave, emotional and honest radio interview instigated a national conversation about death and the indescribable fear experienced by people who are diagnosed with a terminal illness.

MAUREEN O'HARA

HOLLYWOOD ACTRESS

—✦— 1920– —✦—

Maureen O'Hara is the best-known Irish actress to grace the big screen and is regarded as the most beautiful woman of her day. The 'Queen of Technicolor', as she was to be later called, Maureen's striking colouring found its greatest fan in Herbert T. Kalmus, inventor of the Technicolor process, who used her image to summon in a new era of cinema.

At seventeen, Maureen signed her first Hollywood film contract under the watchful eye of her parents and the parish priest. She would go on to appear in fifty-nine feature films, including *Miracle on 34th Street* (1947), *Lady Godiva* (1955) and *The Parent Trap* (1961), in a career spanning over sixty years from 1938 to 2000. During this time she became famous as the woman tough enough to stand up to John Wayne in the five films they made together. Outside of the acting world, Maureen has also had the distinction of becoming the first woman president of a scheduled airline in the USA following the death of her husband Charles Blair in 1978. Her awards range from the Irish Film Institute's Lifetime Achievement Award for her work as an actress, to the Amelia Earhart Award by the Zonta Club of New York for her achievements in the airline industry, to the coveted Most Beautiful Legs in America Award from the National Hosiery Manufacturers.

MAUREEN HAS ALSO HAD THE DISTINCTION OF BECOMING THE FIRST WOMAN PRESIDENT OF A SCHEDULED AIRLINE IN THE USA

Maureen FitzSimons was born in Ranelagh, Dublin, on 17 August 1920. Her father Charles Stewart Parnell FitzSimons was a shopkeeper and part-owner of the Shamrock Rovers, a football team Maureen has passionately supported her entire life. Growing up, Maureen often pleaded with her father to form a soccer team for women but before he had a chance to, she was whisked off to Hollywood. Maureen's mother, Marguerita Lilburn, was a successful women's clothier and a former opera contralto and she passed on to her daughter a passion for singing. Later on, Maureen sang on many TV variety shows alongside the likes of Perry Como and Andy Williams. Maureen was the second of six FitzSimons children. Her eldest sister Peggy, a renowned soprano, later refused a scholarship to study at the La Scala Academy, considered the world's most prestigious opera school, in order to enter the convent of the Sisters of Charity.

During her youth, Maureen was known for organising backyard stage shows with her brothers and sisters. She was a regular prize-winner at the local and national *feiseanna*. When she was fourteen she began studying acting at the Abbey Theatre in Dublin but, aware of the pitfalls of pinning all her hopes on a theatrical career, Maureen's parents encouraged her to enrol in classes on secretarial skills, book-keeping and stenography.

Maureen had just landed her first leading stage role at the Abbey when she received a request from her agent to travel to London to do a screen test for Elstree Studios. The screen test was unsuccessful, but during her stay in London Maureen was introduced to actor Charles Laughton who owned a film company called Mayflower Pictures with his partner, Eric Pommer. Charles was looking for a young girl to cast in the new Alfred Hitchcock film *Jamaica Inn*. When Charles asked Maureen to read from the script, the serious Abbey-trained actress politely declined, stating that she couldn't possibly read from a script she knew nothing about. Charles asked if there was any film footage of her and she informed him of the screen test she had done earlier that day. He tracked down the show-reel and was at first unimpressed, but later realised that, try as he might, he couldn't get the image of Maureen's haunting eyes out of his mind. By the time Maureen arrived back in Dublin, a seven-year contract awaited her from Mayflower Pictures.

Having changed Maureen's surname from FitzSimons to O'Hara, Laughton and Pommer proceeded to introduce the young Dubliner in *Jamaica Inn*, followed by a role as Esmeralda in *The Hunchback of Notre Dame* (1939), a film that proved so successful Maureen's contract was bought out by RKO, one of the five big studios of Hollywood's Golden Age.

Maureen soon gained a reputation as a unique actress who was prepared to do anything the boys could do, and more. From fisticuffs to fencing, Maureen gave as good as she got when it came to sharing the screen with Hollywood heavyweights such as Tyrone Power, Douglas Fairbanks Jnr, Jimmy Stewart and Rex Harrison. Maureen endeared herself to a generation of female film fans who were bored of seeing women portrayed as passive and weak on the silver screen. However, Maureen's thirst for adventure often led to disagreements with the studio who thought 'I was crazy to perform all of my own fencing stunts, but I loved it'.

In 1941 Maureen was cast in *How Green Was My Valley*, the story of a poor mining family in Wales. This film was to mark the beginning of a long and complex relationship with American-Irish director John Ford who went on to cast Maureen in four more films: *The Quiet Man*, *Rio Grande*, *The Wings of Eagles* and *The Long Gray Line*.

Describing music as her first love, Maureen had the opportunity to combine her passion for theatre with singing when she starred in the Broadway musical *Christine* in 1960, which told the story of a woman who visits India and falls in love with her deceased daughter's husband. The musical was written by Nobel Prize-winner Pearl S. Buck. Maureen also released two successful albums: *Love Letters From Maureen O'Hara* and *Maureen O'Hara Sings Her Favourite Irish Songs*.

O'Hara married George Hanley Brown in 1938, but their marriage was annulled in 1941. Later that year, she wed director William Price. The couple had a daughter, Bronwyn, before Price's problems with alcohol led to a divorce in 1953.

In 1968 Maureen married Charles Blair, a former brigadier general in the Air Force and a famous aviator who, in 1951, flew the first solo flight over the North Pole. Charles had been a friend of Maureen's family for many years. Having finally found someone with whom she could 'live the adventures I'd only acted out on the Fox and Universal lots', Maureen decided it was time to retire from the world of acting. The couple turned their attention towards managing a commuter seaplane service in the Caribbean called Antilles Airboats. However, after ten happy years together, Charles died in a tragic accident when the engine of the plane he was flying exploded. Heartbroken, Maureen took over the running of the airline and later sold it.

Since 1991, Maureen has appeared in a handful of films, including *Only the Lonely* with John Candy, who she described as one of her all-time-favourite leading men, *The Christmas Box*, *Cab to Canada* and *The Last Dance*. In 2004 her memoir *'Tis Herself* was published and became an instant bestseller. Maureen is the only Irish actress to have a star dedicated to her on the Hollywood Walk of Fame, and she continues to be remembered by many, in the words of John Ford, as 'the best bloody actress in Hollywood'.

GRACE O'MALLEY

LEGENDARY PIRATE QUEEN

— C. 1530–1603 —

Grace O'Malley, otherwise known as Granuaile, was an ambitious pirate and rebel who was once described as the most 'notorious woman in all the coasts of Ireland'. Her fearless usurpation of male power and her legendary exploits during the time of Henry VIII and Queen Elizabeth have made her one of the most fascinating Irish women of all time.

Grace was born in County Mayo sometime around the year 1530. Her father Owen 'Black Oak' O'Malley was a powerful chieftain of the Umhall Uachtarach and her mother Margaret also hailed from this important clan. At the time of Grace's birth, Brehon Law had been governing Irish life for some 1,500 years. This set of laws empowered women, allowing them to fight in battle, drink alcohol and retain their property after marriage. They were also allowed to file for divorce within the first year of marriage; a law that Grace took full advantage of throughout her adult years.

Growing up, Grace had no interest in taking care of the household as was expected of women. Instead, she begged her father to take her fishing and sailing with him. When he initially objected because of her gender and the fact that her long hair would catch in the ship's ropes, Grace is said to have cut her hair short, earning her the nickname Gráinne Mhaol, or Bald Grace. Under her father's guidance, Grace studied the features and landmarks of the west coast and learned to predict the weather. She also paid close attention to her father's various negotiations with clan leaders and traders.

For centuries Grace's clan had ruled Clew Bay and its surrounding islands. But their land came under threat in the sixteenth century when King Henry VIII realised that England was vulnerable to attack through Ireland. He made an offer to the Gaelic chieftains that if they surrendered their land to the crown he would return it to them under his name and bestow the appropriate title upon each clan leader. While many Gaelic chiefs agreed to this, the O'Malleys held firm.

At the age of sixteen, Grace married Donal O'Flaherty and moved to the Cock's Castle in Bunowen, Connemara; a castle Donal had stolen from the Joyce clan. They had two sons, Owen and Murrough, and one daughter, Margaret. While Donal controlled large parts of Connacht, Grace maintained a proactive role in her husband's political and economic affairs, as well as leading trade expeditions to Scotland, Spain and Portugal. When her husband was killed by the Joyces in a bid to regain control of Bunowen, Grace defended the castle so fiercely that it was renamed the Hen's Castle in her honour.

After Donal's death, Grace returned to Clew Bay with 200 recruits. Taking her lead from Galway's imposition of taxes on ships trading in the area, Grace implemented a similar system. She levied a tax on all passengers sailing in the waters off her own land and, in exchange, the passengers were guaranteed safe passage. She also attacked cargo ships bound for Galway. As a result, the terror-stricken inhabitants of the city inscribed the words, 'From the ferocious O'Flaherties good Lord deliver us' above the city's west gates.

Grace next set her sights on Rockfleet Castle which stood on the northeastern side of Clew Bay and was owned by Richard-an-Iarainn Burke. In 1566 she married Richard under Brehon Law and, having taken over his castle, divorced him one year later.

It is believed that on their one-year anniversary Grace and her followers locked themselves in Rockfleet Castle and Grace called out to her husband, 'Richard Burke, I dismiss you!' And with that the union was dissolved. Grace had one son with Richard, whom they called Theobald. Legend suggests that Theobald was born at sea while Grace was engaged in battle with a Turkish ship.

> THE TERROR-STRICKEN INHABITANTS OF THE CITY INSCRIBED THE WORDS, 'FROM THE FEROCIOUS O'FLAHERTIES GOOD LORD DELIVER US' ABOVE THE CITY'S WEST GATES

In 1577 Grace began raiding the lands of the Earl of Desmond. She was soon captured and imprisoned for eighteen months in Limerick gaol and Dublin Castle. In 1583 Richard Burke died and Grace returned to Rockfleet where her pirating activities quickly attracted the attention of Sir Richard Bingham, the new governor of Connacht. Bingham eventually captured Grace and seized her possessions, including her fleet of ships, and took control of her sea lanes. By this time, Grace had amassed a great deal of wealth from her marriages and her pirating activities. However, as the chieftain of her clan she refused to surrender control to the British monarchy. She had worked long and hard to amass her wealth and power, and to safeguard it from the men in her life. There was no way she was now going to relinquish everything to another woman in a foreign country. Using the skills of diplomacy that she had learned from her father, Grace decided to appeal to the monarch as the queen of one clan to the queen of another. She sent a petition to Queen Elizabeth requesting that she be allowed to continue in 'free liberty during her life to invade with sword and fire all your highness' enemies'. In response, the queen sent Grace a list of eighteen questions regarding her life, heritage, property, marriages and children. Much of what is known about Grace today stems from the documents that she returned. Indeed, nearly all of what has been recorded about the life of the Irish pirate queen Grace O'Malley has been sourced in British documents and historical notes.

When Grace's half-brother Donal and her sons Theobald and Murrough were arrested by Bingham, Grace decided it was time to speak with Queen Elizabeth face to face. In July 1593 she set sail for Greenwich Castle in London. When the two leaders met they conversed in Latin, their only shared language.

> QUEEN ELIZABETH WAS SO TAKEN BY THE IRISH SEA-QUEEN THAT SHE GRANTED GRACE THE FREEDOM TO CONTINUE HER WAY OF LIFE AS AN INDEPENDENT CHIEF

Queen Elizabeth was so taken by the Irish sea-queen that she granted Grace the freedom to continue her way of life as an independent chief and she ordered that Grace's kin be released from prison. Queen Elizabeth also ordered that Grace's sons provide for their mother with rents deducted from their taxes.

On Grace's triumphant return from London she decided to pay a visit to Howth Castle only to find the gates locked as the inhabitants were eating dinner. Infuriated, Grace kidnapped the castle's heir and declared that she would release him only if the lord of Howth promised to always keep the gates of Howth open and to always have an extra place set for dinner; a promise that has been adhered to at Howth Castle ever since.

Grace lived out the rest of her years at sea. She died at Rockfleet in 1603, the same year that Queen Elizabeth died. She is thought to be buried in an abbey on Clare Island, on which the words 'Terra Mariq Potens O'Maille' are inscribed, meaning 'O'Malley: Strong on Land and Sea'.

In her lifetime, Grace O'Malley flouted convention and gender stereotypes. As one of her detractors aptly put it, she 'impudently passed the part of womanhood'. As an independent thinker ahead of her time, Grace was persecuted and hunted down for most of her adult life, but she persevered. Her reputation in Ireland was such that she was both followed and feared. In the centuries since her death, she has continued to fascinate generations of Irish women who are captivated by this fearless leader and warrior.

SONIA O'SULLIVAN

OLYMPIC MEDAL-WINNING ATHLETE

— 1969– —

S onia O'Sullivan is Ireland's most illustrious sportswoman. During a career that has seen many highs and lows, she has captured the hearts of the Irish nation. Sonia's country stood loyally by her while she wept over her defeat in Atlanta and rejoiced with her when she won the silver medal in the women's 5,000m at the Olympic Games.

Sonia was born on 28 November 1969, in Cobh, County Cork, to John and Mary O'Sullivan. Growing up in the harbour town, Sonia's father John was the goalkeeper for the Cobh Ramblers' football team; the same team that later launched Roy Keane in 1990. When Sonia was twelve she realised that by joining the local athletics club she would be able to attend discos and go away on weekend trips. With this in mind, along with a group of her friends, she quickly signed up. Sonia started out with the 100m and the long jump, but admits to being terrible at both. However, at the end of the first track season she ran a cross-country race and, despite taking a wrong turn during the race, Sonia won.

Sonia's teacher, Mr Jim Hennessy, saw her potential and encouraged her to enter more races. When he told Sonia before a race one day that she was going to beat her rival Anita Philpott, who would also go on to represent Ireland internationally, Sonia believed him and from that point on she never lost another race to Anita. Years later when Sonia ran the Dublin women's mini marathon, Mr Hennessy insisted on being wheeled outside of the hospital in which he was a patient, to wave at his former protégé as she passed by. Sonia remembers it as 'an extraordinary moment'.

While still in secondary school, Sonia decided she needed a training schedule so she contacted a coach she had heard great things about called Seán Kennedy. Seán began writing new training programmes for Sonia every two weeks and dropping them through her parents' letter-box.

As a result of her dedicated training and improved pace, Sonia became the

first Irish woman to be offered a sports scholarship to Villanova University in America, joining the ranks of male Irish Olympic and world champions Ronnie Delaney, Eamonn Coughlan and Marcus O'Sullivan. However, she suffered a training injury before her departure and arrived at the university on crutches. Disheartened by this unfortunate start to her time at Villanova, it took Sonia a while to settle in. But by the time she left in 1991, alongside her degree in accountancy, she had the honour of being a five-time National Collegiate Athletics Association champion over 3,000m, 5,000m and cross-country.

In 1990 Sonia entered her first major international competition at the European Championships in Split, where she finished eleventh in the 3,000m. Returning to Ireland in 1992, Sonia devoted all of her time and energies to running. In 1992 she competed at her first Olympic Games in Barcelona where she placed fourth in the 3,000m. That same year Sonia set six Irish national records in races of 1,500m to 5,000m; five of these records were set in the space of eleven days.

In 1993 Sonia really began to make her mark on the athletics world. By the time the World Championships came around, she was the clear favourite to win the 3,000m race, only to have her hopes dashed at the last hurdle by the performances of three Chinese athletes. Undeterred, Sonia returned later in the week to claim a silver medal over 1,500m. In 1994 she set the fastest time of the year in four events: the 1,500m, 1 mile, 2,000m and 3,000m. On 8 July that year she broke the 2,000m world record, setting a new time of 5:25:36 that has yet to be beaten. At the European Championships Sonia won her first international gold medal over 3,000m. In 1995 Sonia decided to temporarily relocate to Australia where she was able to train at a high level during the Australian summer. This led to an unbeaten year on the track, culminating in a World Championship gold-medal performance over 5,000m.

Sonia was to endure the biggest setback of her career at the 1996 Olympic Games in Atlanta where she was the favourite to win gold in the 5,000m. But the stress of an intense training schedule and a neglected illness took their toll and for the first time in her career Sonia was unable to finish the race. Devastated and defeated, she felt that she had let her country down and it took her a long time to put the incident behind her.

When she eventually did, it was with the help of a new coach, Alan Storey, who encouraged Sonia to focus on a variety of shorter races rather than investing everything in one race as she had done in Atlanta. Within two years Sonia was enjoying her new training regime and she surprised many people when she claimed victory over both 8,000m and 4,000m at the 1998 World Cross-Country Championships in Marrakech. Later in the year, she followed up these triumphs with a double victory in both 5,000m and 10,000m at the European Championships. Sonia concluded this successful comeback year with a victory over 5,000m while representing Europe at the World Cup in South Africa.

In 1999 Sonia took a break from competing to give birth to her daughter Ciara with her Australian partner Nick Bideau. She returned to her intense training schedule ten days after the birth to regain fitness and prepare for the upcoming Olympics which were just over a year away. In 2000 Sonia qualified to run the 1,500m, 5,000m and 10,000m at the Olympic Games in Sydney. She ran a determined

SHE RAN A DETERMINED RACE TO EARN A SILVER MEDAL OVER 5,000M, MUCH TO THE EXCITEMENT AND PRIDE OF A COUNTRY WHO HAD WATCHED HER PROGRESS FROM THE DISAPPOINTMENT OF ATLANTA TO THE TRIUMPH OF SYDNEY

race to earn a silver medal over 5,000m, much to the excitement and pride of a country who had watched her progress from the disappointment of Atlanta to the triumph of Sydney. 'It was the greatest sporting event many people can remember,' Sonia later said, 'and to be a part of that and win a silver medal in the 5,000m was incredible. We had our first daughter Ciara there – she was toddling around the track with my medal around her neck. Great, great memories.'

In December 2001, Sonia gave birth to the couple's second child, Sophie, but she quickly recovered from childbirth and in 2002 she claimed her place on the Irish team running in the World Cross-Country at the Leopardstown

Race Course in Dublin. It was to be a triumphant day for Sonia and the home team who came away with a bronze medal. In 2005 Sonia ran the London Marathon for the first time and finished with a personal best time of 2:29:01.

Sonia O'Sullivan is one of the few Irish athletes whose public appeal has crossed over into the non-sporting world. By dealing with her disappointment at Atlanta and bouncing back to win a silver medal at the Sydney Olympic Games, she has become a truly inspirational figure.

ANNA PARNELL

LEADER OF THE LADIES'
LAND LEAGUE

— 1852–1911 —

Although the name of her older brother, Charles Stewart Parnell, is well known and celebrated throughout Ireland and indeed the world, Anna Parnell has been largely forgotten despite her huge achievements in the Land League movement. During the eighteen-month lifespan of the Ladies' Land League, Anna worked tirelessly to achieve its aims, encouraging farmers to withhold their rents, and fundraising to provide specially made huts for the evicted families. A passionate and keen observer of the plights of the Irish tenant, Anna lived by her word. She was described by Andrew Kettle, one of the founders of the Irish Land League, as having 'a better knowledge of the social and political forces of Ireland than any person, man or woman, I have ever met. She would have worked the Land League revolution to a much better conclusion than her great brother'.

Anna Parnell was born on 13 May 1852 in Avondale, County Wicklow, the fifth daughter of an Anglo-Irish Protestant landowner, John Stewart Parnell, and his Irish-American wife Delia Tudor Stewart. Anna was only seven years of age when her father died in 1858. Her eldest brother Charles inherited the family estate but, as it came with heavy debts, it was put up for rent. Meanwhile, Anna, her ten siblings and her mother moved to a smaller residence in Dalkey, Dún Laoghaire, and later to Dublin city where they settled until the late 1870s.

Under the sole guidance of their mother, the Parnell girls thrived. Educated by a series of governesses, Anna developed an interest in political science, philosophy and Irish history, but most especially in art. While her sister Fanny, who was four years her senior and her best friend, was making a name for herself publishing patriotic poetry in the *Irish People*, Anna enrolled at the Royal Dublin Academy of Art. She then continued her studies at the Heatherley School of Art in London; the only art school that allowed women to paint the nude model. Anna was to prove a talented painter, with a number of her paintings going on display in a leading London gallery.

> SHE THEN CONTINUED HER STUDIES AT THE HEATHERLEY SCHOOL OF ART IN LONDON; THE ONLY ART SCHOOL THAT ALLOWED WOMEN TO PAINT THE NUDE MODEL

However, Anna's focus soon changed when her brother Charles arrived in London to take up his position in Westminster as the new MP for Meath. Anna watched from the ladies' gallery in Westminster as her brother, frustrated that the Home Rulers' requests were continuously being ignored, began to implement a successful policy of obstructionism. This policy made Parnell a legendary figure, and Anna documented this event in her first political report in the *Celtic Monthly*.

At the end of the parliamentary session of 1877, Anna travelled to Bordentown, New Jersey, to stay in a house her mother had inherited. During this time, a severe agricultural depression swept across Ireland. Unable to pay their rents, farmers were evicted in mass numbers. In response, a group of Mayo farmers banded together to fight the evictions, leading to the establishment of the Irish National Land League in 1879, of which Charles Stewart Parnell was elected president. The long-term aim of the league was to enable Irish tenant farmers to become owners of their own land by applying to the British government for interest-free loans. The short-term aim was to reduce rents so that farmers could avoid eviction and starvation.

Upon hearing about the plight of the tenant farmers, Anna and her sister Fanny left immediately for New York where they worked twelve-hour days in the offices of the Irish Land League Relief Fund. They received contributions amounting to £60,000 and ensured that this money was distributed amongst those who needed it most.

DAVITT WAS QUICK TO NOTICE ANNA'S INTELLIGENCE AND SKILLS

Anna also began to work alongside Michael Davitt in the United States Land League offices on Washington Square. Here, Davitt was quick to notice Anna's intelligence and skills as an administrator. Upon his return to Ireland, Davitt acknowledged that it was only a matter of time before the leaders of the land agitation were imprisoned. Reflecting on the successful work of both Anna and Fanny Parnell in America, Davitt decided to establish a women's land league in order to keep up a semblance of an organisation while its real leaders were imprisoned. Despite the protestations of her brother Charles, who believed that a women's league would bring ridicule upon the men, twenty-eight-year-old Anna agreed to head the new Ladies' Irish National Land League at a meeting on 31 January 1881. Three days later Davitt was imprisoned, followed soon after by the rest of the Land League leaders and over 1,000 of its members.

It was time for the Ladies' Land League to make their mark. Rather than confining themselves to functioning as a mere semblance of an organisation as Davitt had suggested, Anna went full-throttle into the revolution. She organised public meetings during which she urged country-people to take a stand by withholding rent, as well as boycotting and resisting evictions.

The Ladies' Land League raised funds to support the families of the Land League prisoners and they distributed special wooden huts to shelter the growing number of evictees, which amounted to 14,600 over the course of four years.

Anna overhauled the entire administrative system, ensuring the safekeeping of and easy access to thousands of documents detailing rents and evictions. The Ladies' Land League also continued publishing the Land League newspaper *United Ireland*, printing it in secret and smuggling it out in bundles under their skirts.

> **ANNA OVERHAULED THE ENTIRE ADMINISTRATIVE SYSTEM, ENSURING THE SAFEKEEPING OF AND EASY ACCESS TO THOUSANDS OF DOCUMENTS DETAILING RENTS AND EVICTIONS**

During this time, the Ladies' Land League continued to fight against prejudice and prison sentences. When thirteen of their members were imprisoned, they were not arrested under the Coercion Act but under a law designed to keep prostitutes off the streets. Decried by the press as 'patriots in petticoats' and 'the screaming sisterhood', patriarchal Irish society was clearly uncomfortable with the idea of women in politics. Despite the 'cold atmosphere of censure', at the beginning of 1882, when Charles Stewart Parnell was released from jail after signing the Kilmainham Treaty, the Ladies' Land League had over 500 branches and thousands of members.

Seeing no further use for the Ladies' Land League, Charles dissolved the organisation upon his release, and accused his sister of spending too much money on aid. But Anna had merely been following the instructions of the Irish-American Fenians whose money had helped avert a famine and had saved many lives; the instructions being that these funds were not to be used for parliamentary purposes. Charles, a dedicated parliamentarian, was not happy with this. Anna felt that her brother and some of the other Land League members secretly resented the efficiency of the Ladies' Land League:

I think now that, added to their natural resentment at our having done what they asked us to do, they soon acquired a much stronger ground for their annoyance in the discovery that we were taking the Land League seriously and thought that not paying rent was intended to mean not paying it.

That same year, Anna lost her sister and best friend Fanny who died from a heart attack at the age of thirty-three. When Charles, horrified at the idea of his beloved sister being embalmed and moved to Ireland, saw to it that Fanny was buried in the US, the rift between Charles and Anna intensified. Shortly afterwards, she suffered a nervous breakdown. With the demise of the Ladies' Land League under circumstances which caused irreparable damage between Charles and herself, Anna resumed her interest in painting, changed her name to Cerisa Palmer and moved to Cornwall, England. She briefly re-emerged in 1904 following the release of Davitt's *The Fall of Feudalism in Ireland* in which he accused the Ladies' Land League of encouraging farmers to engage in acts of violence. Devastated by these 'vicious lies' which described 'Irish girls as being a pack of murderers, mutilators, hysterical idiots and fools', Anna responded by writing her own account of the events of the Land War in *The Tale of a Great Sham*. Unfortunately, she failed to find a publisher. In fact, the book was only eventually published in 1986, long after Anna's death, and by which time the Ladies' Land League had for the most part been written out of Irish history.

Anna died in a swimming accident at Ilfracombe, Devon, in 1911. Having broken into the patriarchal tradition of power and defied the perception that women were unable to affect revolutionary change, Anna had suffered greatly in life. At a meeting held at the beginning of the Ladies' Land

ANNA PARNELL DROWNED.

Woman Who Perished at Ilfracombe Said to be Irish Leader's Sister.

LONDON, Sept. 23.—The Pall Mall Gazette states that the woman who was drowned on Wednesday at Ilfracombe, the fashionable bathing resort on the north coast of Devon, where she was known as Miss Palmer, was Anna Parnell, a sister of the great Irish leader. Though nearly 60 years of age, she was a powerful swimmer and accustomed to going out in the roughest weather. It is thought that she was seized with cramps.

The New York Times
Published: September 24, 1911
Copyright © The New York Times

League in March 1881, she acknowledged that her actions would never be appreciated in her lifetime but she hoped that 'perhaps when we are dead and gone and another generation grown up … they will point to us as having set a noble example to all the women of Ireland.'

Sadly, like many of the activities carried out by Irish women before the latter half of the twentieth century, the success of the first mainstream female political organisation in Ireland, and of its revolutionary leader Anna Parnell, have largely been forgotten.

EDEL QUINN

HEROIC MISSIONARY FOR THE LEGION OF MARY

— 1907–1944 —

E del Quinn lived a relatively short life, dying at the age of thirty-six. But she made such an impact in this brief time that she was declared Venerable by Pope John Paul II in 1994, fifty years after her death. For a person to be pronounced Venerable, the Roman Catholic Church must posthumously declare the person 'heroic in virtue' during an investigation leading up to their canonisation as a saint, and 'heroic in virtue' is exactly how Edel was remembered by those who knew her.

During her early years with the Legion of Mary, Edel took charge of the Sancta Maria Hostel for prostitutes in Dublin, where her kindness and empathy gradually endeared her to the hardest of hearts. During her eight

years as a missionary in Africa, all the while suffering from an aggressive form of tuberculosis, Edel disregarded fears for her safety. As a single white woman travelling in the most dangerous parts of the continent she carried only a rifle to ward off predatory animals. One of the greatest missionaries ever to leave Ireland, Edel established hundreds of Legion of Mary branches and councils in Tanzania, Kenya, Tanganyika, Malawi and Mauritius, amongst other places. Armed with a permanent smile and her beloved rosary beads, she overcame the scepticism of local missionary priests by insisting that they 'please try the Legion for Our Lady's sake'.

Throughout her adult life, Edel Quinn devoted her time and energies to the causes she most believed in, all the while maintaining that 'An idealist who does not try to put his ideals into practice is not worth much.' Later, Frank Duff, founder of the Legion of Mary, described her as a woman who 'saw a star and aimed for it and would cut her way through forest and mountain to reach it, ready to tackle anything, willing to endure anything'.

WHILE HER PEERS KNEW HER AS THE CELEBRATED CAPTAIN OF THE CRICKET TEAM, EDEL REGULARLY ATTENDED MASS AND SET ASIDE TIME FOR PRAYER EACH DAY

Born near Kanturk in County Cork on 14 September 1907, Edel Mary Quinn was the eldest of five children. Her father Charles Quinn was a manager in the National Bank, and her mother Louise Burke Browne was a devout Catholic who attended daily mass and exerted an early spiritual influence over her daughter.

With each new promotion Edel's father gained, the family were forced to relocate, and during Edel's formative years she lived in Clonmel, Cahir, Enniscorthy and Tralee. She was later sent to finish her education at an English boarding-school at Upton Hall, Cheshire, run by the Sisters of the Faithful Companions of Jesus. It was in this setting that Edel's spiritual side blossomed. While her peers knew her as the celebrated captain of the cricket team, Edel regularly attended mass and set aside time for prayer each day.

She was so impressed by the lives of the Sisters of the Faithful Companions of Jesus, and the spiritual atmosphere in which they lived, that she decided to enter the convent and devote her life to God upon her return to Ireland.

Her return came sooner than expected when in July 1924 Edel was informed that she would no longer be able to attend the school as her father could not afford to pay her fees. Edel's father had run up serious debts on horseracing and had even taken money from the bank he managed in Tralee to help pay them off. As a result, Charles was demoted and sent to work at a junior post in Dublin. Now seventeen years of age, Edel moved home to her family's rented flat in Monkstown and postponed her entrance to religious life to help support her family financially.

> **BUT WHEN PIERRE PROPOSED ... EDEL HAD TO POLITELY TURN HIM DOWN, EXPLAINING THAT SHE PLANNED TO ENTER THE POOR CLARES, AN ORDER OF CONTEMPLATIVE NUNS**

She enrolled in a shorthand and typing course and she soon obtained a secretarial position in a tobacconist's shop. After some time, Edel left this position to take up a better-paid job working for Pierre Landrin of the Chagny Tile Company. Pierre was a lapsed Catholic who was so inspired by Edel's faith that he began accompanying her to mass. The pair became close friends, playing tennis and attending social events together. To the outside world, it looked like this attractive young couple would marry. But when the twenty-six-year-old Pierre proposed in 1927, Edel had to politely turn him down, explaining that she planned to enter the Poor Clares, an order of contemplative nuns.

Around this time, Edel was involved in a Loreto Convent Sodality Social Club for poor children. During one particular meeting, Edel's life was to change forever when she was invited by a fellow member, Mona Tierney, to attend a meeting of the Legion of Mary, an organisation of Catholic lay people who met to pray and carry out apostolic work. Impressed by the aims and beliefs of this Roman Catholic Marian movement, Edel joined the legion and committed herself to carrying out all aspects of its mission, including visiting city slums and hospitals, where it is said that her cheerful disposition made her a favourite with the people. Edel's enthusiasm for her work soon came to the attention of the Legion's founder, Frank Duff. He was so impressed by Edel that he asked her to take over the presidency of the praesidium which worked for the moral rescue and rehabilitation of Dublin prostitutes. She accepted the position and worked hard at it, often forsaking meals to devote as much time as possible to her mission.

In 1932, with her family financially stable once again, Edel attended a series of successful interviews for admission into the Poor Clares. It was decided that she would enter the Belfast convent on 25 March of that year. However, Edel's dream was dealt a cruel blow when she was diagnosed with an advanced and incurable form of tuberculosis. She was sent to rest and recuperate at the Newcastle Sanatorium, close to the Wicklow Mountains.

After eighteen months, and with her condition largely unchanged, Edel decided that the financial cost of her stay in the sanatorium was too great a burden to place on her family. She left uncured, reasoning that she might as well devote what time she had left to helping others rather than wasting away on a hospital bed.

Edel resumed her work for the Legion, adopting less stressful roles. In 1936 a request was sent to the Dublin headquarters, asking for Edel to be deployed as the Legion's envoy to East Africa. Despite the protestations of many, who feared for Edel's health and safety, Frank Duff argued that a warmer climate might actually benefit her. Frank also recognised Edel's potential, saying, 'You can't keep a wild bird in a cage. She must be given her chance. Edel is going to make history – if she is let.' Edel later wrote to Frank, thanking him for his decision, and reassuring him that 'whatever the consequences may be, rejoice that you had the faith and courage to emulate Our Lord, in His choice of weak things.'

On 30 October 1936, Edel set sail from London on a three-week long journey to Mombassa. Upon arrival, she went straight to work, forming the first African Legion of Mary group within two weeks. For the next eight years, despite her precarious health, Edel travelled all over Africa, spreading the word, helping where she could and translating the Legion of Mary pamphlets into several languages. The approach of her car, which had been provided by the Legion of Mary, was said to have been a welcome sight to many a lonely missionary.

Time and again Edel was laid low with the ever-present tuberculosis, as well as regular bouts of malaria, pneumonia, dysentery and sheer exhaustion, all of which began to take their toll. In 1941, while being nursed back to health at a convent in Malawi, she told an attending sister that Our Lady had allowed her three more years of missionary work.

On 12 May 1944, following a series of heart attacks, Edel died in Nairobi where she was buried in a small cemetery reserved for missionaries. Since her death, many miracles have been attributed to her intercession, including her appearance on O'Connell Bridge to dissuade an old friend from committing suicide, the restoration of sight to a blind baby, the recovery of many from mental illnesses and the apparent miraculous healing of many ailments.

Edel's perseverance in extending the reach of a cause she believed in so resolutely, despite ill-health and prejudice, has inspired many people around the world. Her words of wisdom offer a continuing source of hope:

> Sometimes it is really hard to struggle on; everything seems against us. I think the great thing is not to get discouraged, no matter how much we will fail, but always be ready to begin again. In that way only, will we be sure to persevere.

MARY ROBINSON

FIRST FEMALE PRESIDENT
OF IRELAND

— 1944- —

The extent to which traditional gender roles were reinvented in Ireland during the twentieth century was revealed when Mayo-born barrister, academic, liberal campaigner and member of the Irish senate, Mary Robinson was elected the first woman president of Ireland on 9 November 1990. Just as Barack Obama's election to the US presidency in 2008 revealed America to be a country ready for positive change, Mary Robinson's election revealed Ireland to be a modern country, full of progressive individuals who were liberal enough to choose a female president.

Born Mary Therese Winifred Bourke in Ballina, County Mayo, in May 1944, Mary was the only daughter of Aubrey and Tessa Bourke. As a child, she attended Miss Ruddy's Private School, and had a loving relationship with

her nanny, Anna Coyne, whom Mary would later repay for her kindnesses by nursing her during her final days.

From the age of ten, Mary attended the elite Mount Anville, a girls' school run by the Sacred Heart nuns at Dundrum, County Dublin. Here she considered following the path of many of her relations by becoming a nun. Indeed, she was related to Mother Arsenius, the pioneering foundress of the Foxford Woolen Mills. For her post-school year, Mary travelled to Paris where she attended Mlle Anita Pojninska's – a finishing school for daughters of the wealthy. While in Paris, she could freely discuss philosophy, religion, political thought and science. She read Albert Camus' *The Outsider* and related to it in a profound way. For a time Mary though about becoming a writer, but eventually decided it wasn't for her. Growing up she had been strongly influenced by her grandfather, H.C. Bourke, a solicitor who was passionate about defending the rights of tenants against unfair landlords, so she decided to study law at Trinity College.

In February 1967, Mary was elected auditor of the Trinity Law Society, and in a speech entitled 'Law and Morality' she argued for the separation of Church and state, the removal of the ban on divorce from the constitution, the repeal of the law against contraceptives and a removal of the law that made suicide a crime. Despite being cautioned about openly criticising the Catholic Church, Mary would repeatedly question the role of Church and state in enforcing personal morality.

After continuing her legal studies at King's Inn, Dublin, Mary won a much sought-after fellowship to Harvard Law School. She graduated in 1968 during a time of great political upheaval in America that saw both Martin Luther King and Robert Kennedy assassinated in the same year. As Mary watched her fellow students at Harvard organise marches and rallies against the war in Vietnam and apartheid in America, she realised that young people could make a real difference. But the most important lesson Mary learned at Harvard was that international law could be used to influence national law, a lesson she would use time and again in her pursuit of equal rights for women, fathers and travellers. She returned to Ireland with a fresh perspective on change and progress.

At the age of twenty-four, Mary was appointed Reid Professor of Criminal Law, making her the youngest professor of law in Ireland. A year later she was elected to Seanad Éireann. In 1971 Senator Robinson prepared a bill to legalise contraception. Although unable to get the votes necessary to publish the bill, she still received a large amount of hate mail. Back in Ballina, her parents walked out of the church for the first time in their lives after Mary was denounced from the pulpit. Two years later, Mary introduced a second bill that made it through the preliminary stage. When the Dail passed the first bill limiting the sale of contraception to married couples in 1979, this was in no small part due to Mary's early pioneering work.

In the early 1970s Mary became involved with Cherish, the single mothers organisation. Mary was president of Cherish for seventeen years and during this time gave numerous talks and helped to raise funds. Politically, she won the eventual abolition of the cut-off period for paternity and maintenance claims. She brought the Johnston case to the European Court of Human Rights in Strasbourg, which forced the Irish government to introduce the Status of Children Bill and bring an end to the discrimination against illegitimate children. Mary stood for equal rights, not just for mothers and their children, but also for fathers. In the Keegan case, she represented a single father who hadn't been consulted before his child was placed for adoption. This case changed adoption practice and now efforts are made to consult the natural father before a child is placed for adoption.

Mary, who was raised a Catholic, experienced a very personal concern in her own family when in 1970 she married the Protestant lawyer, conservationist and authority on eighteenth-century caricature, Nicholas Robinson, resulting in a short-lived rift with her parents who refused to attend the wedding. Mary's parents did not approve of the marriage as, like many parents, they felt that their soon to be son-in-law was simply not good enough for their daughter. However, the rift was mended when Mary's ageing aunt, Mother Aquinas, wrote to the family telling them what 'nonsense' it was. The newlyweds went on to have three children – Tessa, William and Aubrey.

In the mid 1970s Mary joined the Labour Party, but resigned in 1982 in protest against the Anglo-Irish agreement which the Labour Party/Fine Gael coalition government had signed with the British government of Margaret Thatcher. Mary argued that unionist politicians in Northern Ireland should have been consulted as part of this deal.

For two decades Mary campaigned vigorously on issues such as civil rights, women's rights, illegitimacy, adoption, the rights of travellers and the right to free information regarding abortion and contraception. Again and again she brought the Irish state before the European Court of Justice and the European Court of Human Rights in order to achieve her aims. In 1979 Mary brought the case of Mrs Josie Airey – a Cork woman who couldn't afford a solicitor to represent her in procuring a legal separation from her violent husband – to the European Courts. As a result of this ground-breaking case, civil legal aid was established in the Republic of Ireland. Mary worked as legal advisor for the Campaign for Homosexual Law Reform with future Trinity College senator David Norris. She also fought at the Labour Courts to have the Irish parliament's pension scheme extended to spouses of female parliamentarians, and won. In 1980 Mary succeeded in winning an injunction that prevented Dublin City Council from evicting travellers Rosella McDonald, her sick husband and their ten children from their site on the Tallaght by-pass. As a result, the Supreme Court stipulated that alternative accommodation must be provided before evicting travellers. That same year she presented her first divorce bill to the Labour parliamentary party.

Although Mary had resigned from the Labour Party, she was approached by the party in 1990 to run as a nominee supported by the Labour Party for the presidency. Mary agreed, but was insistent that she would run as an independent candidate and not as a Labour Party candidate. She believed that if she was elected president, even though it was a non-executive role, she would be able to give a voice to all of the voiceless people in Ireland for whom she had campaigned extensively over the years. Mary's popularity was clear from the start. She was further bolstered by the enormous support of Irish women across the country who took to the polls en force. Many women contacted her to say that for the first time they had voted differently from their husbands. During her acceptance address in 1990, Mary made a special reference to this brave new breed of Irish women: '… and above all by the women of Ireland, Mná na hÉireann, who instead of rocking the cradle, rocked the system …'.

As president, Mary was restricted in how she could address the public and so she showed her priorities by attending Aids benefits, traveller's projects, parties for one-parent families, events for Rape Crisis Centres, Third World Development Agencies and children's charities. She attended mass in the Women's Prison in Mountjoy and helped foster a better understanding of prisoners by the media and the public. She was the first Irish president since the founding of the Irish state to visit Queen Elizabeth II at Buckingham Palace and improved relations with Northern Ireland during her eighteen visits there as president, bearing the brunt of heavy criticism after shaking the hand of Republican leader Gerry Adams during a visit to West Belfast.

Mary also used her position as president to focus global attention on the horrific atrocities taking place in the Third World. In 1992 she was the first head of state to visit famine-stricken Somalia, and in 1994 she was the first head of state to visit post-genocide Rwanda, where she brought to light the suffering of the country in the aftermath of its bloody civil war. During a press conference held after her visit, she became visibly emotional, moving everyone who saw her, including *Sunday Tribune* editor Vincent Browne, who passed her a note afterwards that read: 'You were brilliant.'

At the end of Mary's tenure as president in 1997, Mary resigned a few weeks early to take up the post of the United Nations High Commissioner for Human Rights, becoming one of the few women to hold such a senior international post. By the time she left office in 2002, human rights issues were being monitored for the first time in more than twenty countries, including Rwanda and Kosovo. Since leaving the United Nations, Mary has been working to extend her policy of giving a voice to the voiceless around the world. An honorary president of Oxfam International and a founding member and former chair of the Council of Women World Leaders, Mary is also a patron of the International Community of Women Living with AIDS (ICW). In 2007 she was invited by Nelson Mandela to become one of The Elders – a group of politically independent, internationally trusted leaders who work to affect positive changes in society and challenge injustices.

Mary is currently president of Realizing Rights: The Ethical Globalization Initiative, whose mission is to 'put human rights standards at the heart of global governance and policy-making and to ensure that the needs of the poorest and most vulnerable are addressed on the global stage.' In August 2009 Mary was awarded the Presidential Medal of Freedom by American President Barack Obama who described her as 'an advocate for the hungry and the hunted, the forgotten and the ignored'. She continues to be, in the words of former US vice-president Al Gore, 'one of Ireland's greatest gifts to the world'.

ADI ROCHE

FOUNDRESS OF THE CHERNOBYL CHILDREN'S PROJECT INTERNATIONAL

— 1955– —

In January 1991 Adi Roche received a fax message that was to change her life. Sent by Belarusian and Ukrainian doctors, the message read: 'SOS Appeal. For God's sake help us to get the children out.' The fax was referring to the children of Chernobyl whose growing bodies were being mutilated by their radioactive surroundings. This heartbreaking message elicited an immediate response from Adi who began arranging for a group of children to be brought to Ireland for rest and recuperation. Five years had already elapsed since those early hours of 26 April 1986 when a safety test being carried out at the Chernobyl Nuclear Power Plant in the

Ukraine went tragically wrong. A massive explosion at the number-four reactor caused 190 tons of radioactive materials and over 100 million curies of radiation to be released into the environment, 70 per cent of which was deposited in Belarus. In 1991 the effects of what was described by the UN as 'the greatest environmental catastrophe in the history of humanity' were indisputable; babies were being born with severe deformities, and thyroid cancer, diseases of the nervous system and heart disease had all increased dramatically. Children as young as six were suffering heart attacks and strokes.

Unwilling to just sit back and watch these horrors unfold, Adi founded the Chernobyl Children's Project International (CCPI) to provide critical medical and humanitarian aid and to give the children of Belarus, Russia and the Ukraine the chance of a better life. Adi was one of the first Irish women to set foot in Chernobyl in the aftermath of the disaster when, accompanied by Mary Aherne and Mary Murray, she travelled through the affected areas. She encountered children writhing in pain, with no access to painkillers or basic medicines, whose parents had abandoned them because they couldn't cope with their deformities. Determined to ease the pain of these forgotten victims, Adi immediately set to work.

Through a combination of sheer willpower and the help of countless volunteers and supporters, Adi has since delivered humanitarian and medical aid valued at over €76 million to the areas most affected by the Chernobyl nuclear disaster. This money has worked small miracles. Today's cardiac-surgery waiting lists for children suffering from the Chernobyl heart defect have been reduced from 7,000 to fewer than 2,000. Adi's rest and recuperation programme has enabled more than 18,000 children to come to Ireland for medical treatment over the past eighteen summers. Just one month away from contamination can add up to two years to a child's life. An adoption agreement brokered by Adi and CCPI patron Ali Hewson in 1995 resulted in dozens of children being adopted by Irish families.

As well as developing an internationally recognised Non-Governmental Organisation that provides sustainable and community-based medical, social, educational and humanitarian programmes, Adi has also been at the forefront of research into the effects of Chernobyl. In order to open the eyes of the world to this disaster, Adi researched, developed and co-ordinated the first English-language documentary about the effects of the nuclear catastrophe, called *Black Wind, White Land – Living with Chernobyl*. This documentary subsequently inspired 7,000 volunteers to join Adi in her mission. In 2003 the work of the CCPI was featured in the Academy Award-winning film *Chernobyl Heart*.

Adi has also consistently high-lighted the work of the liquidators – a group of 800,000 coal miners, firemen and soldiers who risked their lives to prevent a nuclear explosion that would have wiped out most of Europe. Exposed to horrific levels of radiation, 20 per cent of these unsung heroes have since committed suicide and 70 per cent have been left permanently disabled. In 1998, for her outstanding humanitarian efforts, Adi was awarded the two highest national honours in Belarus, the Liquidators' Medal and the Frantcysk Skyryana Order Medal.

800,000 COAL MINERS, FIREMEN AND SOLDIERS RISKED THEIR LIVES TO PREVENT A NUCLEAR EXPLOSION THAT WOULD HAVE WIPED OUT MOST OF EUROPE

Before Adi was ever called to work on the frontline of the Chernobyl crisis, she had already been personally affected by the devastating effects of radiation. While growing up in Clonmel, her best friend Ann Condon was diagnosed with leukaemia and died shortly afterwards, leaving the young Adi with many unanswered questions and a deeply embedded fear and distrust of anything associated with radiation. In 1978, when the Irish government revealed plans to build a nuclear power plant in the Carnsore Point area of County Wexford, Adi and her husband Seán joined the 25,000-strong crowd of protesters at the anti-nuclear rally. While listening to the many speeches made on the day, Adi became convinced that nuclear power, in all its manifestations, was an energy system to be opposed. In 1979, while Jane Fonda, Jack Lemmon and Michael Douglas were entertaining film fans around the world in *The China Syndrome*, the story of a nuclear meltdown at a US plant, an accident occurred at the Three Mile Island nuclear power plant in

Pennsylvania. Adi's older brother Donal was living there at the time and he was forced to evacuate along with his young family.

When the Irish government shelved its plans to build the nuclear reactor in County Wexford, Adi realised that people power had to make a difference.

As the Cold War intensified and superpowers competed with one another in a race to build the most destructive nuclear weapons, Adi felt called to act. She joined the Irish Campaign for Nuclear Disarmament (ICND) with a view to ridding the world of nuclear weapons. In 1982 she left her job as an office administrator with Aer Lingus and became a full-time voluntary worker for ICND, setting up an office in her home in Ballincollig, County Cork. Her parents, both members of the local St Vincent de Paul and Meals on Wheels societies, had instilled in their daughter the values of volunteerism from a young age, and Adi had worked as a volunteer for the Legion of Mary in the past.

AS THE SARCOPHAGUS ENCASING THE DAMAGED NUCLEAR REACTOR AT CHERNOBYL CONTINUES TO LEAK LETHAL DOSES OF RADIATION, ADI MAINTAINS HER RELENTLESS CAMPAIGN

From her home office, Adi devised a Peace Education Programme for schools and ran peace-education classes in over fifty schools in Ireland, addressing the fears of young people who were nervous about the prospect of a nuclear war. For three years Adi represented Ireland on the Great Peace Journey through more than ten European countries, and in 1990 she became the first Irish woman to be elected to the board of directors of the International Peace Bureau (IPB), based in Geneva. During the presidential elections of 1997, Adi was the first woman to be chosen by an alliance of broad-spectrum political parties to run for president of Ireland.

Following the Chernobyl explosion, the nine million people living in the stricken areas of Belarus, Ukraine and western Russia received the highest-known exposure to radiation in the history of the atomic age. More than 2,000 towns and villages had to be evacuated because the radiation levels were so high they were uninhabitable. In response to the crisis, Adi and the

Chernobyl Children's Project International continue to deliver programmes that meet the changing needs of the children, adults and communities in the Chernobyl regions; their work includes cardiac, community and hospice care, life-saving operations, a rest and recuperation programme and construction projects.

Despite working countless hours to achieve her aims, Adi has always refused to take a salary from the CCPI. Since 1991, she has been responsible for keeping the plight of children and families affected by the Chernobyl disaster alive in the hearts and minds of people across the world, most particularly in Ireland, where she remains a household name.

As the sarcophagus encasing the damaged nuclear reactor at Chernobyl continues to leak lethal doses of radiation, Adi maintains her relentless campaign, urging European leaders to complete the new containment shelter at Chernobyl before another catastrophe occurs.

PEIG SAYERS

QUEEN OF THE GAELIC STORYTELLERS

—— 1873–1958 ——

Peig Sayers, one of Ireland's great *seanachaí*, was regarded by scholars in universities across Europe and America as the world's greatest storyteller. Peig's extraordinary memory enabled her to dictate over 600 tales, ballads and anecdotes to her son Maidhc File (Mike the Poet), and to scholars such as Seosamh Ó Dálaigh of the Folklore Commission. One of her memorised tales was 36,000 words long – half the length of a regular novel. She learned many of these stories from her father, Tomás Sayers, who was also a gifted storyteller, and from neighbours she and her brother visited as children.

Unlettered but not unlearned, Peig had a vocabulary of 30,000 words, which is more than twice that of the average person today. When she dictated her autobiography *Peig* (1936) to her son, she told it in such an eloquent and structured way that it needed little editing before it was published. The opening lines reveal Peig's philosophical nature:

> I am an old woman now, with one foot in the grave and the other on its edge. I have experienced much ease and much hardship from the day I was born until this very day. Had I known in advance half, or even one-third, of what the future had in store for me, my heart wouldn't have been as gay or as courageous as it was in the beginning of my days.

Born in Dunquin, County Kerry, to Tomás Sayers and Peig Brosnan, Peig was the youngest of four surviving children out of a brood of thirteen. She attended the local school from the age of six but, out of financial necessity, she left when she was fourteen to begin work as a domestic servant for the Currens in Dingle town. The Currens treated Peig well, but after four years health difficulties forced her to leave her work and return home. Here, she was reunited with her best friend Cáit Jim Boland, who was on the verge of emigrating to America. Emigration was widespread at the time and Ireland was to become known as the land of the very young and the very old. Cáit Jim promised Peig that as soon as she was settled in America she would send her the price of the fare so that Peig could follow her over. However, Cáit Jim suffered a hand injury soon after her arrival in America and, unable to work, she couldn't send money home to her friend.

THEY TREATED HER LIKE A SLAVE, SOMETIMES REFUSING TO FEED HER FOR DAYS AT A TIME

Peig resumed work as a domestic servant, hoping to save up to pay for the fare to America herself. She wasn't as lucky with her employers this time around though, as they treated her like a slave, sometimes refusing to feed her for days at a time. Peig was eventually left with little choice but to quit and return to her family home.

At the time, single girls who didn't have a job were quickly partnered with an eligible husband in an arranged marriage. But while Peig was described as having 'the most beautiful eyes', the one thing she lacked was a dowry.

Knowing that islanders didn't expect a dowry from their wives, Peig's father found a match for her in the islander and fisherman Pádraig Ó Guithín, otherwise known as Peatsaí Flint, who was over ten years Peig's senior. Marriage at the time was primarily a social and economic contract, with love rarely getting a mention in the small print, but later in life Peig recalled: 'It was a love-match til the day he died. And why shouldn't it, for he was a fine big man.'

The day after their wedding, Peatsaí took Peig home to his parents' house on the Great Blasket Island, a place where heaven is believed to be so close to the earth that it is described as being 'a foot and a half above the height of a man'. Peig and Peatsaí lived in this house for the next twenty years, after which they moved to a house of their own.

Over the next forty years, the Blasket Islands were to shape the life of Peig Sayers as much as she was to shape them. From dawn to dusk, the small Irish-speaking community was chiefly concerned with making sure they had enough food to eat. To get to the shop, the church or the doctor on the mainland, Peig had to travel three miles across tumultuous waters in a fifteen-foot currach with a bottle of holy water tied to the prow.

In a small community that had few books, and before the advent of television, radio and film, Peig was one of the Blasket Islands' most revered storytellers. At night islanders gathered in Peig Mhór's

(Big Peig's) house to hear her stories. Peig would sit directly in front of the fire, which was an unusual practice at the time as the *bean an tí* (woman of the house) normally sat to the side of the fire. Talk of death, fairies, the weather and the crops abounded and Peig, with a pipe in her mouth, would interlace these topics with the rendition of a related story, poem or song. She often told the heart-breaking story of her son who had fallen over the side of a cliff, and how afterwards she had stroked and coaxed his damaged skull back into shape before the wake: 'Me who wouldn't look at a cut, I had to compel myself to wash my fine young boy and lay him out in death …'

During the Gaelic revival of the 1930s, many scholars visited the Blasket Islands and were impressed with Peig's storytelling abilities. Peig had a deep love of the Irish language, describing it as 'noble and precious', and she was envied for her clear enunciation. Scholars Robin Flower, Kenneth Jackson and George Thomson encouraged Peig to dictate her stories to her son Maidhc File. These stories were published in journals and subsequently released as a book called *Scéalta ón mBlascaod* (*Stories from the Blasket*). In 1936 Dublin teacher Máire Ní Chinnéide persuaded Peig to dictate her autobiography *Peig*.

> TALK OF DEATH, FAIRIES, THE WEATHER AND THE CROPS ABOUNDED AND PEIG, WITH A PIPE IN HER MOUTH, WOULD INTERLACE THESE TOPICS WITH THE RENDITION OF A RELATED STORY, POEM OR SONG

A year later it won the prestigious Douglas Hyde prize, and it went on to become one of the bestselling Irish books ever published. In 1939 Peig followed this up with *Machnamh Seanmhná* (*An Old Woman's Reflections*).

Approaching seventy and nearly blind, Peig moved back to her native Dunquin with Maidhc File, where she regularly received visitors from around the world who were interested in the Gaelic revival. Five years later, the government decided that it could no longer guarantee the safety of the remaining ageing population on the Great Blasket Islands and the inhabitants were evacuated to the mainland. Later, Peig moved to St Elizabeth's Hospital where she died on 8 December 1958, at the age of eighty-five. Having surrendered herself to the will of God throughout her life, when asked upon her deathbed if she was afraid, Peig replied in her usual composed tone: 'Why should there be worry or anxiety on me when I am soon going to meet my own people?'

During the latter half of her life, Peig was responsible for bridging the divide between the old Ireland and the new. Aided by the advent of radio, she ensured the preservation of thousands of years of inherited folklore. Peig also provided the world with a detailed account of a woman's life on the Blasket Islands, something that has never been written about before, or since, in such detail. Through her stories, Peig and the women of the Blasket Islands will be forever remembered.

HANNA SHEEHY SKEFFINGTON

MILITANT SUFFRAGIST

— 1877–1946 —

H anna Sheehy Skeffington was raised in a 'strongly political household'. While her paternal ancestors advocated nationalist values, her mother espoused female autonomy.

Johanna Mary Sheehy was born on 24 May 1877 in Kanturk, County Cork. She was the first of six children born to David Sheehy, a nationalist MP and mill-owner, and Elizabeth 'Bessie' McCoy, a large formidable woman from Limerick. During Hanna's early years her father was jailed six times for his part in the Land War. His brother, Fr Eugene Sheehy, otherwise known as the 'rebel priest' for his support of both the Land League and the Ladies'

Land League, was also imprisoned many times, and became a huge influence on his young niece.

Hanna's mother instilled in her young daughters the belief that education is equally important for both men and women. When the family moved to Drumcondra, Dublin, in 1887, Hanna was sent to be educated at the Dominican Convent on Eccles Street. She later recalled that the education she received from the nuns gave her 'great independence of thought and action'.

When the tuberculosis epidemic hit Dublin, Hanna moved to France and Germany to continue her education. She developed a love for languages while abroad and on her return to Dublin she enrolled in St Mary's University College, a third-level college for women, where she studied French and German. In 1899 Hanna became one of the first of a new generation of women to graduate from an Irish university, with a BA in languages.

As suspicion and prejudice still surrounded women's education when Hanna graduated, she decided to found the Women Graduates' Association in 1901 to promote the 'interests of women in any scheme of university education in Ireland and to ensure that all advantages of such education shall be open to women equally with men.' In 1902 she attained a first-class honours MA degree and began teaching at a school on Eccles Street. She later taught French and German at the Rathmines College of Commerce, as well as becoming an examiner in the Intermediate Certificate examinations.

In June 1903 Hanna married Cavan-born Francis 'Frank' Skeffington, a university registrar whose commitment to equality saw him use Hanna's surname, and from then on the couple became known as the Sheehy Skeffingtons. The newlyweds moved into a house in Rathmines, next door to

Dr Kathleen Lynn, founder of St Ultan's Hospital for Infants. In 1904 Frank resigned from his position at UCD in protest against women being banned from attending the college. Hanna was now the sole wage earner.

Hanna and Frank were both members of the Irish Women's Suffrage and Local Government Association, but inspired by the suffragette activities of the Pankhursts in England they decided that a more militant suffrage organisation was needed in Ireland. Aided by Margaret Cousins, they founded the Irish Women's Franchise League in 1908. A year later, Hanna nearly died giving birth to their first and only child, a son called Owen Lancelot. An avowed pagan, Hanna was widely condemned for refusing to allow her son be baptised. She would also later refuse to have a priest administer the last rites to her.

SHE TRAVELLED TO AMERICA IN 1918 AND BECAME THE FIRST IRISH SINN FÉINER TO ENTER THE WHITE HOUSE

As the Irish Women's Franchise League divided into those who prioritised Home Rule over the woman's right to vote, and those who prioritised suffrage over every other cause, Hanna began contributing articles on education and feminist issues to the *Nation* newspaper and the *Bean na hÉireann* journal. In 1912 Hanna and Frank founded their own newspaper, the *Irish Citizen*, to promote the rights and responsibilities of citizenship for both sexes.

In 1913 Hanna and Frank became more dependent on their income from journalism when Hanna lost her teaching job after she was twice imprisoned for suffrage activities; the first time for breaking windows at Dublin Castle in protest against the exclusion of women's suffrage from the 1912 Home Rule Bill, and the second time for assaulting a policeman while attempting to give a leaflet to the Conservative leader, Bonar Law, in Dublin. During both incarcerations Hanna went on hunger strike and was promptly released. Her lack of employment left her freer to assist her friend James Connolly during the Dublin strike and lockout of 1913 when she worked in the soup kitchens set up in Liberty Hall.

During the 1916 Easter Rising, Hanna and her husband carried out a lot of work behind the scenes. Hanna brought food and messages to the insurgents, while Frank assisted the injured and tried to prevent looting. On the second day of the rising Frank and two other unarmed newspaper editors were arrested; all three were shot without trial the following morning on the orders of Captain J.C. Bowen-Colthurst of the Royal Irish Rifles. Broken-hearted and outraged, Hanna immediately began to campaign for justice. She refused compensation of £10,000 from the British army and instead forced the Royal Commission to hold an inquiry, which led to the court-martial of her husband's killer. He was found 'guilty but insane', and was later released after eighteen months' imprisonment.

Hanna continued with her work promoting feminism and nationalism. In 1918 she joined Sinn Féin but refused to join Cumann na mBan as she saw them as an auxiliary group. She travelled to America in 1918 and became the first Irish Sinn Féiner to enter the White House. Here, she gave President Woodrow Wilson an uncensored petition for Irish freedom from Cumann na mBan and a copy of the proclamation of the 1916 Rising. On her return to Ireland, she was detained in Liverpool and sent to Holloway Prison in London for travelling to America without the government's permission.

Over the next few years, Hanna travelled extensively, raising funds and speaking at over 250 meetings on the right of women to vote and the right to a free Ireland. Her talk 'British Militarism as I Have Known It' was later published as a pamphlet and was banned in Ireland and England until after the First World War. Her tour raised $40,000, which she handed over to Michael Collins.

During the War of Independence, Hanna was anti-Treaty like her fellow nationalists Constance Markievicz, Maud Gonne and Dr Kathleen Lynn, and she served as a judge in the republican courts of law that were set up to usurp the British courts. When over 7,000 republicans were imprisoned as a result of the Civil War, Hanna helped establish the Women's Prisoners' Defence League with Maud Gonne and Charlotte Despard, to campaign for prisoners' rights and fundraise on behalf of their families.

Throughout the 1920s Hanna continued to campaign, lecture and fundraise on behalf of her various organisations. In January 1933 she defied a barring order, which forbade her to enter Northern Ireland, so that she could speak out on behalf of the republican women prisoners in Armagh jail. She was arrested and held for fifteen days. In 1935, as a speaker for the Women Graduates' Association, she called on women to protest against the Conditions of Employment Bill which restricted employment opportunities for women. When de Valera's constitution was passed in 1937, she became a founder member of the Women's Social and Progressive League which attempted to alert women to the implications of the anti-women legislation passing through the Dáil. In 1943, at the age of sixty-six, Hanna stood as an independent candidate demanding equality for women in the general election. She had hoped to form a women's party if elected, but this was not to be. With no pension, Hanna returned to teaching and continued to do so until the end of her days. She died on 20 April 1946. In her obituary, *The Irish Times* described her as 'the ablest woman in Ireland'.

From Hanna's birth in 1877 to her death in 1946, Ireland had changed greatly. There is no doubt that many of the civil rights granted to women during this time were due in part to the work of Hanna Sheehy Skeffington, who believed that 'it is the dreamers and the visionaries that keep hope alive and feed enthusiasm – not the statesmen and the politicians. Sometimes it is harder to live for a cause than to die for it.'

EDITH WILKINS

PIONEERING HUMANITARIAN

—— 1957– ——

'She is the Mother Teresa of Darjeeling and the Himalayas.' This is how Dr Dawa Bhutia describes Cork-born nurse and humanitarian Edith Wilkins. 'Ask any street child in Darjeeling who takes care of them and the spontaneous answer is Mom … Edith Wilkins,' adds *Hindustan Times* journalist Amit Banerjee who has also witnessed Edith Wilkins' powerful influence on her adopted home of Siliguri in Darjeeling, India. In the 1980s Edith answered a cry for help, one she could have ignored but chose not to. Since then, she has endured severe illness, injuries and threats to her life in her mission to save India's street children from trafficking, prostitution, degradation and suffering.

Edith Wilkins was born on 17 June 1957, in the suburb of Douglas in Cork city. She was one of two girls in a family of seven born to Bert and

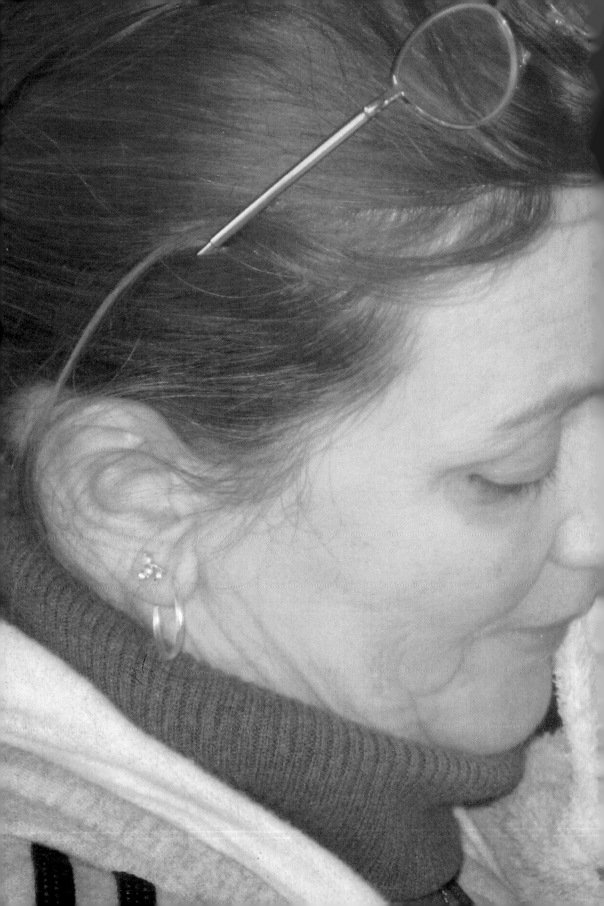

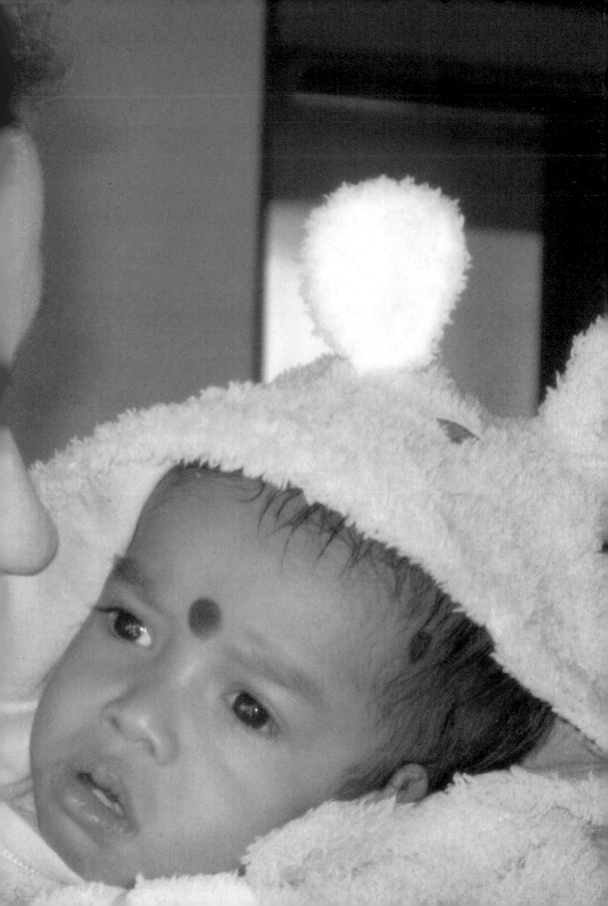

Imelda Wilkins, née Lordan. Edith's father Bert worked for many years in the marketing department of the ESB. Growing up, Edith attended Regina Mundi Secondary School. She spent her summer holidays each year in Lourdes with an organisation called the Christian Leadership Movement (CLM). Here, she helped care for the elderly and the sick who visited the Marian shrine.

WHEN EDITH FIRST ARRIVED IN THE HOT AND SWEATY OVERPOPULATED CITY OF KOLKATA, HER INITIAL REACTION WAS TO TURN AROUND AND RUN IN THE OPPOSITE DIRECTION TO ALL THE POVERTY AND DISEASE

After leaving school, Edith trained to become a nurse at the Cork Polio and General After-Care Association. She graduated with honours as a registered nurse for the intellectually disabled and went to work at the Royal Victoria Hospital in Kirkcaldy, near Edinburgh. In the early 1980s Edith returned to Cork and was offered a nursing position at St Finbarr's Hospital. Also working at the hospital at the time was an old school friend of Edith's, Rosaleen Somerson. Rosaleen had just returned from Kolkata, then Calcutta, where she had been working for the internationally renowned Irish organisation GOAL, which at that time was in its fledgling stages and had only two volunteers. On hearing about the suffering of thousands of abused children on the streets of India, Edith made a decision that was to change her life.

When Edith first arrived in the hot and sweaty overpopulated city of Kolkata, her initial reaction was to turn around and run in the opposite direction to all the poverty and disease. But she was soon won over by the countless street children who desperately needed to be loved and cared for.

Of the next twenty-one years, Edith spent eighteen in Kolkata, and three years in Khartoum, the capital of Sudan, where she directed operations for GOAL during a dangerous time of violence and unrest. Civil war had erupted in the southern capital of Juba and another war had broken out along the western border of Geneina. While Edith was working in

Geneina, a mass evacuation was ordered and she was given just one hour to get out. But when she couldn't find one of her volunteers she refused to leave. Having frantically searched the war-torn area, Edith eventually found the missing person and managed to escape just in time. As they left, soldiers opened fire on their vehicle, but thankfully Edith and her volunteers were unharmed.

Edith began her work in Kolkata at the Child in Need Institute. Here, she received an education, at a grass-roots level, on the lives of India's most poor and vulnerable who are subject to constant discrimination, poverty and abuse. She subsequently did a postgraduate course in counselling, with an emphasis on disturbed and abused children and young AIDS sufferers, and worked closely for many years with her good friend Mother Teresa. In 1984 Edith launched Amadir Bari, meaning Our Home, which was the first half-way house to be opened in India.

In January 2003 Edith was asked to come to Siliguri, Darjeeling, where drug addiction, the sexual and physical abuse of children, child trafficking and slave labour exist on a widespread scale. Thousands of children live on the streets in Siliguri and in the *bustees* (shanty towns) in Darjeeling because of both the closure of local tea-gardens, which were once a major source of employment in the area, and an inadequate amount of child services. As many as 2,000 children are being trafficked across the border every month and sold for use as sex workers, servants and child labourers, or used to smuggle drugs and other goods into the country.

When Edith arrived in 2003 these problems were not being addressed by any other non-governmental organisations. In response, Edith founded The Edith Wilkins Street Children's Foundation. This pioneering and hugely successful organisation has saved countless children from spending their lives foraging for food in rubbish dumps and fending off sexual predators. Instead, these vulnerable castaways are offered a home, somewhere to sleep without interruption, and the chance of an education that will hopefully empower them to rise out of the poverty cycle. Edith established a drop-in centre that children can call into during the day to eat a hot meal, play games, and most importantly to sleep, which is what most of these world-weary children do when they first arrive.

Edith established outreach clinics which are held in slum colonies and on railway platforms where most of these street children live. These clinics hire doctors to cater to the health needs of disadvantaged children, providing treatment of diseases, free medicine and counselling. They also offer a basic education to children between the ages of four and ten. Two of Edith's foster children, Dolly and Jamsed, run one of these clinics near a truck stand at Siliguri where the poverty is particularly severe.

Edith also opened a sickbay to take care of children suffering from mumps, tuberculosis and chickenpox, who would normally be left to lie uncared for on the side of the street. In her quest to end child trafficking, Edith has forged a working relationship with the Criminal Investigation Department (CID) of West Bengal as well as the border police. She has also been instrumental in pioneering a campaign to raise awareness amongst the 1,200 taxi drivers in Darjeeling who are perfectly placed to observe and report on any suspected child trafficking.

HER EYES WERE OPENED TO THE DARKEST AND MOST HORRIFIC ASPECTS OF HUMAN NATURE

Edith has endured much hardship while in India. She has been seriously ill with hepatitis, malaria, cholera, TB and typhoid, and her life has been threatened by the pimps who sell street children into prostitution. But the worst experiences Edith has endured is watching children die and having to bury their bodies herself.

In spite of all the abuse she has witnessed, Edith is continuously inspired by both the work of Gandhi and that of other voluntary workers in India including the GOAL leader John O'Shea; Noreen Dunne, founder of Hayden Hall, which provides poorer families with opportunities by empowering women; the Sisters of St Joseph of Cluny; and Sr Cyril Mooney from the Loreto Convent who has dedicated her life to India's street children.

Since arriving in India, Edith has fostered twenty children and adopted two, Omar and Karishma. She has spent three months sleeping on the streets observing the lives of street children. She speaks fluent Bengali and wears traditional Indian dress when necessary. While respecting the main religions in India – Hinduism, Islam and Buddhism – Edith maintains a strong Christian faith in 'the Man above'.

In over twenty-five years working in India, Edith Wilkins has changed the lives of thousands of children and families. She has provided the most vulnerable members of Indian society with much-needed care and encouragement, and has succeeded in seeing many of her foster children progress to third-level education.

When Edith gave up her life of relative comfort in the 1980s to tend to the needs of India's street children, her eyes were opened to the darkest and most horrific aspects of human nature. However, in the words of the Lord Mayor of Cork, Brian Bermingham, 'rather than simply be dismayed, Edith lit a candle rather than curse the darkness'. Edith's candle continues to light up the lives of many in Kolkata and Darjeeling today.

ACKNOWLEDGEMENTS

When I first approached Mercier Press with the idea of writing a book about inspirational Irish women, my idea was met with instant enthusiasm and support from both Commissioning Editor Eoin Purcell and Publisher Mary Feehan. I am forever indebted to them for giving me the opportunity to write my first book on a subject that I am passionate about. I would also like to thank my agent Julian Friedmann for his guidance and support.

While researching this book, I have had the pleasure and privilege of encountering many wonderful individuals who have been gracious with their time and assistance. For this I would like to thank: Councillor Paula Desmond, Pól Wilson from the Eileen Hickey Museum, Martina Malone, Moninne Griffith and Dawn Quinn from MarriagEquality, Lindie Naughton, Anna Farmer at A&A Farmar Book Publishers, Jacinta Kennedy-Ralph at Focus Ireland, Jennifer Doyle and Tom Desmond Jr at the National Library, Robert Mills at the Royal College of Physicians of Ireland, Sr Marie O'Leary, Sr Mary Christian, Sr Mary Kernan and Sr Rosemary McGowan from the Religious Sisters of Charity, Anne Dent, Sr Margaret Lythgoe and Sr Denise O'Brien from the La Sainte Union, Dr Sandra MacAvoy at the Women's Studies Centre UCC, Bride Rosney, Sr Claude Meagher at the Presentation Sisters in Limerick, Tony Heffernan from the Office of the Houses of the Oireachtas, Seán Brady at An Phoblacht, Jim Fitzpatrick, Br Lawrence Lew OP, Monica Gavin, Ann Rea at the Firkin Crane, Sinead Murphy, Roger Quail at Rubyworks, Fergal Tobin at Gill & Macmillan, Anne Chambers, Mairéad Lynch and Siobhán Colgan at the Abbey Theatre, Bobby Kalsi – VP Operations Lead, World Centers of Compassion for Children International, Brian Bergin at Independent Newspapers, Grace Keenan at *The Irish News*, Derek Speirs, Dr Katherine O'Donnell at the Women's Studies Centre UCD, Margaret Ó hÓgartaigh, Ruth Heneghan at O'Brien Press, Ruth Gordon at Druid Theatre, Mary O'Leary, Yvonne Kenny at INTO, Rosemary Cullen

Owens, Meda Ryan, Gráinne Mooney at Áras an Uachtaráin, Lee Guirreri, Attracta Tighe and Ethel M. Bignell at the Religious Sisters of Mercy; Roisin Gannon at the Nano Nagle Centre, Sr Bernadette at the Presentation Sisters in Nottingham, Maeve Meleady and David Caslin at the Christina Noble Foundation, Francis Devine and Deirdre Price at SIPTU, Charlie Campbell and Linda Van at Ed Victor, Fachtna O'Ceallaigh, Mary Baylis at Realizing Rights, Carolyn Murphy – PA to Maureen O'Hara, June Beck at the Maureen O'Hara Magazine, Catherine Murphy at the Legion of Mary, Anne Kearney at Examiner Publications, Áine Ní Chuaig at An Taibhdhearc, Byron Smith at Historical Aviation Ireland, Miriam Forde at the Chernobyl Children's Project International, Antoine Mac Gaoithín at the Royal Irish Academy, Micheal de Mordha at the Great Blasket Centre, Ann Warren and Bert Wilkins at the Edith Wilkins Foundation, and Wendy Logue, Catherine Twibill, Patrick Crowley, Sharon O'Donovan and the rest of the team at Mercier Press.

During the many months it has taken me to complete this book, I have spoken of nothing else and have forced everyone in my presence to listen to me rant and rave about the many inspiring feats of Irish women. For putting up with me over the past few months, I would like to thank my mother Dolores who makes the world a better place simply by being in it. Thanks also to my father Paul who continues to fight the fight for the rights of Irish workers. Thank you to my generous brother Paul who acted as my delivery man while I sat in my pyjamas writing, and to Stephanie O'Connell for bringing me sweets and passing on her enthusiasm for Anne Frank. Thank you to my sister Andrea who is growing up to be another inspirational Irish woman, and to my loving and supportive grandparents Ita and Paddy O'Mahony, whose courage and strength, despite the odds, inspires me on a day-to-day basis. Thanks also to my best pal Cian O'Mahony aka Accelerate and to Patrick, Ber and Alan O'Mahony. Thanks to Karen Cogan for reading bits and pieces of the book while in progress, and for her helpful advice and suggestions. Thank you to Rose Coughlan for all of my beautiful elephants. Thanks to my cousin Rachel, her lovely husband Eoin and their son Craig Ryan. Thank you to my caring godmother Marie Sweeney, her husband Tony and son Darren. Thank you also to my godfather Joe Depuis. For their hospitality and kindness in welcoming me into their home in Athy, thank you to Carmel, Willie, Liam and Ann Quinlan. For their hospitality and kindness in welcoming me into their home in Cloyne, thank you to Joanie and Rowan, Brownie and Blanket. For nurturing my love of the written word, I am forever grateful to my sixth-class teacher at Christ the King primary school, Catriona Horgan. For being great friends and housemates and for filling my time in London with happy memories, a sincere thank you to the Fraser Road girls: Shannon Perka, Marika Logan, Nardene Smith, Loren Welthagen, Nell & Adele, and my adopted baby sister, Ashley Ferguson. For helping to steady a very shaky glass, a big sincere thank you is due to Anne O'Malley.

Putting a list of inspirational Irish women together is a difficult process as there are so many to choose from. For contributing to the list in often passionate and rousing ways, I would like to thank: Joan McCarthy, Joanie Barron, Fiona O'Connell, Ailbhe NicGiolla Bhrighde, Trish Forde, Aisling Lynch, Claire Dooley, Julie Kelleher, Karen Kelleher, Katie Holly, Lisa Fingleton and Gill McCarthy, as well as Rosaleen Doyle and Pauline Mary Murray, whose fascinating conversation and warm, welcoming company on the train to Dublin reminded me of how truly special Irish women are.

Thanks also to the wonderful members of the Mná Mná choir, a group of brave, courageous and beautiful women, who have been a constant source of inspiration to me.

I would also like to make a special mention of my grandparents Bridie and Joe Depuis who unfortunately are no longer with us, but who encouraged me with their support by reading my newspaper articles religiously in their later years.

Last but not least, I would like to say a special and huge heartfelt thank you to my Evie, Evelyn Quinlan, for carefully reading the book as I wrote it and for keeping me fed and watered over the past few months, ensuring that I washed and maintained a semblance of sanity despite my cave-woman like tendencies. I am eternally grateful to you.

Thank you to everyone else who has shown me kindness during the writing of this book.

PICTURE CREDITS

Mary Aikenhead, Agnes Morrogh Bernard: *Courtesy of Religious Sisters of Charity*

Louie Bennett: *Courtesy of Rosemary Cullen Owens*

Eavan Boland: *Courtesy of Eavan Boland*

St Brigid of Kildare: *Courtesy of Brother Lawrence Lew Op*

Sr Sarah Clarke: *Courtesy of* The Irish News

Margaret Cousins: *Courtesy of the National Library of Ireland*

Eileen Desmond: *Courtesy of Councillor Paula Desmond*

Bernadette Devlin, Nan Joyce, Nell McCafferty, Nuala O'Faolain: *Courtesy of Derek Speirs*

Maire Drumm: *Courtesy of* An Phoblacht

Anne Louise Gilligan & Katherine Zappone: *Courtesy of Martina Malone*

Lady Augusta Gregory: *Lady Gregory painted by Antonio Mancini, Courtesy of Dublin City Council, The Hugh Lane Gallery*

Veronica Guerin: *Courtesy of Independent Newspapers*

Lady Mary Heath: *Courtesy of John Cussen*

Nora Herlihy: *Courtesy of Irish League of Credit Unions*

Garry Hynes: *Courtesy of Joe O'Shaughnessy*

Mother Jones: *Courtesy of David Mason*

Sr Stanislaus Kennedy: *Courtesy of Focus Ireland*

Delia Larkin: *Courtesy of SIPTU*

Dr Kathleen Lynn: *Courtesy of the Royal College of Physicians*

Mairead Corrigan Maguire: *Courtesy of Mairead Corrigan Maguire*

Betty Williams: *Courtesy of Bobby Kalsi, VP Operations Lead, World Center of Compassion for Children International*

Catherine Mahon: *Courtesy of INTO*

Constance Markievicz: *Courtesy of Lissadell House*

Mary McAleese: *Courtesy of Maxwell Photography*

Catherine McAuley: *Courtesy of Mercy International Association*

Queen Medb: *Courtesy of Jim Fitzpatrick*

Joan Denise Moriarty: *Photo taken by Roger Dann, Courtesy of The Joan Denise Moriarty School of Dance*

Rosemary Nelson: *Courtesy of the Eileen Hickey Irish Republican Museum, Belfast*

Christina Noble: *Courtesy of Christina Noble Children's Foundation*

Edna O'Brien: *Courtesy of Weidenfeld & Nicolson*

Sinead O'Connor: *Photographs taken by Kevin Abosch, Courtesy of Rubyworks*

Maureen O'Hara: *Photograph taken by Roddy McDowell, Courtesy of Maureen O'Hara*

Sonia O'Sullivan: *Courtesy of* The Evening Echo

Edel Quinn: *Courtesy of International Centre of the Legion of Mary*

Mary Robinson: *Courtesy of Áras an Uachtaráin na hÉireann*

Adi Roche: *Courtesy of Chernobyl Children's Project International*

Peig Sayers: *Courtesy of the Blasket Centre*

Edith Wilkins: *Courtesy of the Edith Wilkins Street Children Foundation*

BIBLIOGRAPHY

MARY AIKENHEAD
Aikenhead, Mary, *Letters of Mary Aikenhead* (M.H. Gill & Son, 1914)
Bayley Butler, Margaret, *A Candle was Lit: Life of Mother Mary Aikenhead* (Clonmore & Reynolds; Burns Oates & Washbourne, 1953)
Blake, Donal S., *Mary Aikenhead: Servant of the Poor* (Caritas, 2001)
Nethercott, Maria, *The Story of Mary Aikenhead: Foundress of the Irish Sisters of Charity* (Kessinger Publishing, 2009)
O Céirín, Cyril and Kit, *Women of Ireland: A Biographic Dictionary* (Tir Eolas, 1996)

http://multitext.ucc.ie/d/Mary_Aikenhead
http://www.sistersofcharity.org.au/story/mary.html
http://www.rsccaritas.ie/historybio.htm

DOCTOR JAMES BARRY
Bensusan, A.D., 'The Medical History of Dr. James Barry', *S.A. Medical Journal*, November 1965
Broderick, Marian, *Wild Irish Women: Extraordinary Lives from History* (O'Brien Press, 2002)
Duncker, Patricia, *James Miranda Barry* (Picador, 2000)
Holmes, Rachel, *Scanty Particulars* (Penguin, 2002)
O Céirín, Cyril and Kit, *Women of Ireland: A Biographic Dictionary* (Tir Eolas, 1996)
Oxford Dictionary of National Biography, *Barry, James (c.1799–1865)* (Oxford University Press, 2004)
Rose, June, *The Perfect Gentleman: The Remarkable Life of Dr. James Miranda Barry; the woman who served as an officer in the British Army from 1813 to 1859* (Hutchinson, 1977)

http://www.usmedicine.com/column.cfm?columnID=53&issueID=28
http://www.newscientist.com/article/mg19726462.000-histories-the-male-military-surgeon-who-wasnt.html
http://www.dailymail.co.uk/femail/article-528926/Dr-Barrys-deathbed-sex-secret-The-extraordinary-truth-great-war-hero-medical-pioneer.html

LOUIE BENNETT
Fox, Richard Michael, *Louie Bennett: her life and times* (Talbot Press, 1957)
Gallagher, John, *Courageous Irishwomen* (Fiona Books, 1995)
Jones, Mary, *These Obstreperous Lassies: A History of the Irish Women Workers' Union* (Gill & MacMillan, 1998)
Owens, Rosemary Cullen, *Louie Bennett* (Cork University Press, 2001)

EAVAN BOLAND
Boland, Eavan, *Collected Poems* (Carcanet Press, 1995)
Boland, Eavan, *New Territory* (Allen Figgis & Co., 1967)

Boland, Eavan, *Object Lessons: The Life of the Woman and the Poet in Our Time* (Carcanet, 1995)

http://www.poets.org/viewmedia.php/prmMID/15939
http://www.caffeinedestiny.com/boland.html
http://www.carcanet.co.uk/cgi-bin/scribe?showdoc=6;doctype=interview

SAINT BRIGID OF KILDARE
Broderick, Marian, *Wild Irish Women: Extraordinary Lives from History* (O'Brien Press, 2002)
Conlon, Val, *St. Brigid: Mary of the Gael* (Divine Mercy Publications, 1991)
O Céirín, Cyril and Kit, *Women of Ireland: A Biographic Dictionary* (Tir Eolas, 1996)
Smucker, Anna Egan, *The Life of Saint Brigid* (Appletree Press, 2007)
Wright, Brian, *Brigid: Goddess, Druidess and Saint* (The History Press Ltd, 2009)

http://en.wikipedia.org/wiki/Brigid_of_Ireland
http://www.newadvent.org/cathen/02784b.htm

SISTER SARAH CLARKE
Clarke, Sister Sarah, *No Faith in the System* (Mercier Press, 1995)
Manley, John, 'Irish-born nun presented with honour from Vatican', *The Irish News*, Monday 24 December, 2001
McFadyean, Melanie, 'Without Consent', *The Guardian*, Tuesday 14 February, 1995
McKay, Susan, 'Profile: Sister Sarah Clarke – A Wee Saint & A Major Security Risk', *Sunday Tribune*, 3 November, 1996
Ó Gadhra, Nollaig, 'A Nun who has lost no faith in the system', *The Irish Catholic*, Thursday 14 November, 1996
Russell, Mary, 'Mission Behind Bars', *The Irish Times*, Wednesday 7 June, 1995
Tierney, Ciaran, 'Death of Campaigning Galway Sister', *Connacht Tribune*, Friday 8 February, 2002

MARGARET COUSINS
Cousins, Margaret and James, *We Two Together* (Ganesh & Co., 1950)
Cullen, Mary and Luddy, Maria, *Female Activists: Irish Women and Change 1900-1960* (Woodfield Press, 2001)
O Céirín, Cyril and Kit, *Women of Ireland: A Biographic Dictionary* (Tir Eolas, 1996)

http://www.folkpark.com/childrens_corner/Emigrant_Stories/Margaret_Cousins/
http://pdfserve.informaworld.com/459685__751268155.pdf
http://www.hindu.com/2004/03/12/stories/2004031200330902.htm

EILEEN DESMOND
Duggan, Elaine, 'Eileen Desmond Laid to Rest in Crosshaven', *The Evening Echo*, 10 January, 2005
Duggan, Elaine, 'Eileen: A Trailblazer Politican', *The Evening Echo*, 12 January, 2005
Finlay, Fergus, 'We have Lost a Woman of Great Charm, Courage and Conviction; Tribute to the Late Eileen Desmond', *The Irish Examiner*, 11 January, 2005
Hollis, Daniel Webster, *The History of Ireland* (Greenwood Publishing, 2001)
'Obituaries – First Woman to get Top Cabinet Post', *The Irish Times*, 8 January, 2005
'Obituary: Mould-breaking Former Minister was a Lady to her Fingertips', *The Corkman*, 13 January, 2005

http://en.wikipedia.org/wiki/Eileen_Desmond
http://pb.rcpsych.org/cgi/reprint/10/6/130.pdf
http://www.qub.ac.uk/cawp/Irish%20bios/Irish_MEP.htm
'Graveside oration by Senator Michael McCarthy': http://www.labour.ie/press/listing/20050110122045.html

BERNADETTE DEVLIN MCALISKEY

Beresford, David, 'Devlin is 'very ill' after shooting', *The Guardian*, 17 January, 1981
'Bernadette McAliskey: Return of the Roaring Girl', *The Independent on Sunday*, 5 October, 2008
Devlin, Bernadette, *The Price of My Soul* (Pan Books, 1969)
Dooley, Brian, *Black and Green: the fight for civil rights in Northern Ireland & Black America* (Pluto Press, 1998)
English, Richard, *Bernadette: the story of Bernadette Devlin* (Hodder and Stoughton, 1975)
McAliskey, Bernadette Devlin, 'Interview', *Living Marxism*, Issue 70, August 1994
Standford, Peter, 'Bernadette Devlin: I'm uniquely qualified to bring lasting peace to Northern Ireland', *The Independent on Sunday*, 29 July, 2007
Target, G.W., *Armed Struggle: The History of the IRA* (Macmillan 2004)

Interview with Bernadette Devlin McAliskey: http://www.socialistworker.co.uk/art.php?id=6233
A Profile of Bernadette Devlin McAliskey by Chris Bambery: http://www.socialistworker.co.uk/art.php?id=6234
'I Don't Want to Wait Twenty-Six Years for Justice' Interview: http://www.solidarity-us.org/node/1852
http://news.bbc.co.uk/2/hi/uk_news/northern_ireland/6676049.stm
http://news.bbc.co.uk/2/hi/uk_news/northern_ireland/7109249.stm
http://www.stepni.org/

MAIRE DRUMM

Máire Drumm: Voice of a Risen People – A Commemorative Booklet (Sinn Fein Publications, 2006)
Moloney, Ed, *A Secret History of the IRA* (W.W. Norton & Company, 2003)
O Céirín, Cyril and Kit, *Women of Ireland: A Biographic Dictionary* (Tir Eolas, 1996)
Walsh, Rosaleen and Wilson, Pól, *A Rebel Heart: Máire Bn. Uí Dhroma* (Máire Drumm Commemoration Committee, 2001)

BIDDY EARLY

Gregory, Lady Augusta, *Visions and Beliefs in the West of Ireland* (Putnam's Sons, New York, 1920)
Lenihan, Edmund, *In Search of Biddy Early* (Mercier Press, 1987)
Mac Manus, Dermot, *The Middle Kingdom; the Faerie World of Ireland* (Colin Smythe Ltd, 1973)
Ryan, Meda, *Biddy Early: The Wise Woman of Clare* (Mercier Press, 1978)

ANN LOUISE GILLIGAN & KATHERINE ZAPPONE

Bracken, Ali, 'It's about Justice and Equality, But in the End, It Comes Down to Love', *Tribune*, 29 April, 2007
Cronin, Michael G., 'Two Lovers and Their Battle for a Better Future', *The Sunday Business Post*, 16 November, 2008
Dwyer, Ciara, 'Anne and Katherine Say It Loud', *Irish Independent*, 19 October, 2008
Gilligan, Ann Louise and Zappone, Katherine, *Our Lives Out Loud* (O'Brien Press, 2008)

http://www.kalcase.org

http://www.marriagequality.ie
http://www.ancosan.com

MAUD GONNE
Cardozo, Nancy, *Maud Gonne – Lucky Eyes & A High Heart* (Victor Gollancz Ltd, London, 1979)
Coxhead, Elizabeth, *Daughters of Erin: five women of the Irish Renaissance* (Smythe, 1979)
MacBride, Maud Gonne, *A Servant of the Queen: Reminiscences* (Gollancz, 1974)
Ward, Margaret, *Unmanageable Revolutionaries; Women and Irish nationalism* (Brandon, 1983)
Ward, Margaret, *Maud Gonne: Ireland's Joan of Arc* (Pandora, 1990)

LADY AUGUSTA GREGORY
Adams, Hazard, *Lady Gregory* (Bucknell University Press, 1973)
Coxhead, Elizabeth, *Lady Gregory: A Literary Portrait* (Secker & Warburg, 1966)
Gallagher, John, *Courageous Irishwomen* (Fiona Books, 1995)
Gregory, Lady Augusta, *Visions and Beliefs in the West of Ireland* (Putnam's Sons, New York, 1920)
Gregory, Lady Augusta, *Seventy Years: being the autobiography of Lady Gregory* (Smythe, 1974)
Hill, Judith, Lady Gregory: An Irish Life (Sutton, 2005)
O Céirín, Cyril and Kit, *Women of Ireland: A Biographic Dictionary* (Tir Eolas, 1996)

VERONICA GUERIN
Murdoch, Alan, 'Bullets that Ended a Quest for Justice', *The Independent,* 28 June, 1996
O' Reilly, Emily, *Veronica Guerin* (Vintage, 1997)
Sheridan, Michael, *A Letter to Veronica – The Last Days of Veronica Guerin, Crime Reporter* (Poolbeg, 1999)

http://www.encyclopedia.com
http://www.people.com/people/archive/article/0,,20148529,00.html
http://www.freemedia.at/Heroes_IPIReport2.00/20Guerin.htm

ANNA HASLAM
Cullen, Mary and Luddy, Maria, *Women, Power and Consciousness in 19th Century Ireland: Eight Biographical Studies* (Attic, 1995)
O Céirín, Cyril and Kit, *Women of Ireland: A Biographic Dictionary* (Tir Eolas, 1996)
Quinlan, Carmel, *Genteel Revolutionaries: Anna and Thomas Haslam & the Irish Women's Movement* (Cork University Press, 2005)

LADY MARY HEATH
Naughton, Lindie, *Lady Icarus: the life of Irish Aviator Lady Mary Heath* (Ashfield Press, 2004)
Traynor, Michael, *Iona: Ireland's First Commercial Airline* (IONA, 2004)

http://www.ladyicarus.blogspot.com/

NORA HERLIHY
Culloty, A.T., *Nora Herlihy: Irish Credit Union Pioneer* (Irish League of Credit Unions, 1990)

The Role of Women Entrepreneurs in the Irish Credit Union Movement by Olive McCarthy:
http://www.ucc.ie/ucc/depts/foodecon/CCS/DiscussionPapers/c_dp4_b.html
http://www.ilcu.ie/anniversary/index.jsp?pID=3472&nID=3475

http://www.creditunion.ie/files/2008/20080430125433_CUfocus_200804_founders.pdf

GARRY HYNES
Fay, Stephen, 'How She Broke the Abbey Habit', *The Independent on Sunday*, 6 September, 1992
Russell, Richard Rankin, *Martin McDonagh: A Casebook* (Routledge, 2007)

Recording of Professor Ciaran Benson's interview with Garry Hynes at the Theatre Forum Ireland Annual Conference, 2008: http://www.archive.org/details/AnnualConference2008 GarryHynes
http://www.celticcafe.com/celticcafe/Theatre/Shows/Juno/Juno_02.html
www.druid.ie
www.druidsynge.com

MOTHER MARY HARRIS JONES
Broderick, Marian, *Wild Irish Women: Extraordinary Lives from History* (O'Brien Press, 2002)
Foner, Philip S., *Mother Jones Speaks: Collected Writings and Speeches* (Monad Press, 1983)
Gorn, Elliott, *Mother Jones: The Most Dangerous Woman in America* (Hill and Wang, 2001)
Jones, Mary Harris, *The Autobiography of Mother Jones* (Kerr Publishing, 1990)

NAN JOYCE
Helleiner, Jane, *Irish Travellers: Racism and the Politics of Culture* (University of Toronto Press, 2003)
Joyce, Nan and Farmer, Anna, *My Life on the Road: A Traveller's Autobiography* (A. & A. Farmar, 2000)
'The Health Status Report' published by the Health Research Board, 1987
'Trocáire Human Rights Seminar in Galway', *The Irish Times*, 18 June, 1983

SR STANISLAUS KENNEDY
Battersby, Eileen, 'Friend of the Homeless & Invisible', *The Irish Times*, 24 December, 1998
Cleere, Ray, 'A man of action who helped the poor', *Kilkenny People*, 8 March, 2006
Dempsey, Anne, 'Sister Stan's Sanctuary', *The Irish Times*, 8 January, 2002
Kennedy, Sr Stanislaus, *One Million Poor? The Challenge of Irish Inequality* (Turoe Press, 1981)
Kennedy, Sr Stanislaus, *But Where Can I Go? Homeless Women in Dublin* (Arlen House, 1985)
Kennedy, Sr Stanislaus, *Streetwise: Homeless Among the Young in Ireland and Abroad* (Glendale, 1987)
Noble, Kenneth, 'A Contemplative in Action: Sister Stanislaus Kennedy', *For A Change*, Feb-March 2002

www.focusireland.ie
http://www.immigrantcouncil.ie
http://www.youngsocialinnovators.ie/

DELIA LARKIN
Broderick, Marian, *Wild Irish Women: Extraordinary Lives from History* (O'Brien Press, 2002)
Cody, Gabrielle H. and Spinchorn, Evert, *The Columbia Encyclopaedia of Modern Drama* (Columbia University Press, 2007)
Deane, Seamus, Bourke, Angela, Carpenter, Andrew and Williams, Jonathan, *The Field Day Anthology of Irish Writing* (NYU Press, 2002)

Dixon, Angi, 'Every Inch of her heart', *The Irish Post*, January 2003
O Céirín, Cyril and Kit, *Women of Ireland: A Biographic Dictionary* (Tir Eolas, 1996)

Save the Dublin Kiddies' Campaign: Clashes at the Port: http://multitext.ucc.ie/d/Save_the_Dublin_Kiddies_Campaign_Clashes_at_the_Port
One Big Union – The Revolutionary Years: http://www.anphoblacht.com/news/detail/36900
Organizing Informal Women Workers by Dan Gallin & Pat Horn: http://www.streetnet.org.za/english/GallinHornpaper.htm
http://ilhm.tripod.com/dlarkin.html

DR KATHLEEN LYNN
Gallagher, John, *Courageous Irishwomen* (Fiona Books, 1995)
Ó hÓgartaigh, Margaret, *Kathleen Lynn: Patriot, Irishwoman, Doctor* (Irish Academic Press, 2006)

Seven Women of the Labour Movement 1916, researched and written by Sinéad McCoole: www.labour.ie/.../seven_women_of_the_labour_movement1916.pdf

MARY MCALEESE
McGarry, Patsy, *First Citizen: Mary McAleese and the Irish Presidency* (O'Brien Press, 2008)
MacMánais, Ray, *The Road from Ardoyne: The Making of a President* (Brandon, 2004)

NELL MCCAFFERTY
Chrisafis, Angelique, 'Just Call me Nell', *The Guardian*, 22 November, 2004
Connolly, Linda, *The Irish Women's Movement: from Revolution to Devolution* (Palgrave Macmillan, 2002)
McCafferty, Nell, *Nell* (Penguin Ireland, 2004)
McCafferty, Nell (edited by Elgy Gillespie), *Vintage Nell: the McCafferty Reader* (Lilliput, 2005)
McGreevy, Ronan, 'RHA exhibition to include Nell McCafferty portrait', *The Irish Times*, 8 November, 2008
Sheehan, Maeve, 'Interview: Maeve Sheehan meets Nell McCafferty', *The Sunday Times*, 29 June, 2003

An Irish Life. Nell McCafferty in interview with Berit Haugen Keyes: http://www.threemonkeys online.com/als/_nell_mccafferty.html

CATHERINE MCAULEY
Bolster, Sister M. Angela (ed.), *The Correspondence of Catherine McAuley, 1827–1841* (The Congregation of the Sisters of Mercy, 1989)
Bolster, Sister M. Angela, *Catherine McAuley: Venerable for Mercy* (Dominican, 1990)
Broderick, Marian, *Wild Irish Women: Extraordinary Lives from History* (O'Brien Press, 2002)
Savage, Roland Burke, *Catherine McAuley: the First Sister of Mercy* (M.H. Gill & Son, 1949)

www.mercyworld.org

MAIREAD CORRIGAN MAGUIRE & BETTY WILLIAMS
Baez, Joan, *And A Voice to Sing With: The Autobiography of Joan Baez* (Arrow Books, 1987)
Buscher, Sarah and Lang, Bettina, *Mairead Corrigan and Betty Williams – Women Changing the World* (Feminist Press, The City University of New York, 1999)

Wells, Ronald, *People Behind the Peace: Community and Reconciliation in Northern Ireland* (William B. Eerdmans Publishing Co., 1999)

http://www.peacepeople.com
http://nobelprize.org
www.peacejam.org
http://cain.ulst.ac.uk/ni/security.htm
http://www.centersofcompassion.org
http://freegaza.org

CATHERINE MAHON
Chuinneagáin, Síle, *Catherine Mahon: First Woman President of the INTO* (INTO publication, 1998)
Fahey, T., *The Encyclopaedia of Ireland* (Gill & Macmillan, 2003)

The politics of equality: Catherine Mahon and the Irish national teachers' organisation, 1905–1916, Sile Chuinneagain: http://pdfserve.informaworld.com/877610__739098105.pdf
www.into.ie

CONSTANCE MARKIEVICZ
Coogan, Tim Pat, *The IRA: A History* (Robert Rinehart Publishers, 1993)
Coxhead, Elizabeth, *Daughters of Erin: five women of the Irish Renaissance* (Smythe, 1979)
De Rosa, Peter, *Rebels: The Irish Rising of 1916* (Bantam, 1990)
Haverty, Anne, *Constance Markievicz: An Independent Life* (Pandora, 1988)
Markievicz, Constance, *Prison Letters of Countess Markievicz 1868–1927* (Virago, 1987)
Moriarty, Mary and Sweeney, Catherine, *Markievicz: The Rebel Countess* (O'Brien Press, 1991)
Ward, Margaret, *Unmanageable Revolutionaries; Women and Irish nationalism* (Brandon, 1983)

QUEEN MEDB
Benard, Elizabeth and Moon, Beverly, *Goddesses Who Rule* (Oxford University Press, 2000)
Broderick, Marian, *Wild Irish Women: Extraordinary Lives from History* (O'Brien Press, 2002)
Byrne, Francis J., *Irish Kings and High Kings* (Four Courts Press, 2001)
Fraser, Antonia, *The Warrior Queens: The Legends and the Lives of the Women Who Have Led Their Nations in War* (Anchor, 1990)
McCullough, David W., *Wars of the Irish Kings: A Thousand Years of Struggle, from the Age of Myth through the Reign of Queen Elizabeth I* (Three Rivers Press, 2002)

http://en.wikipedia.org/wiki/Medb

JOAN DENISE MORIARTY
Fleischmann, Ruth, *Joan Denise Moriarty, founder of Irish National Ballet* (Mercier Press & Irish American Book Company, 1998)
'Interview' *Nice Moves*, RTÉ Radio 1, 22 May, 2004
MacLiammoir, Sandra, *The Secret Life of Joan Denise Moriarty: A Biography* (Blackwater Press, 1995)
Wulff, Helena, *Dancing at the Crossroads: Memory and Mobility in Ireland* (Berghahn Books, 2007)

http://en.wikipedia.org/wiki/Joan_Denise_Moriarty

AGNES MORROGH BERNARD

Gallagher, John, *Courageous Irishwomen* (Fiona Books, 1995)

Joyce, Bernie, *Agnes Morrogh Bernard: Foundress of Foxford Woollen Mills* (Foxford I.R.D., 1992)

Murphy, Catherine, 'The Nun, the Mason & The Rug', *Sunday Business Post*, 15 June, 2008

O Céirín, Cyril and Kit, *Women of Ireland: A Biographic Dictionary* (Tir Eolas, 1996)

Ryan, John, 'A Centenary and a Golden Jubilee: Mother Morrogh Bernard and the Providence Woolen Mills', *Studies: An Irish Quarterly Review*, Vol. 31, No. 122, June 1942

NANO NAGLE

Considine, M. Raphael, *One Pace Beyond: the life of Nano Nagle, foundress of the Society of the Congregations of the Presentation of the Blessed Virgin Mary* (Presentation Congregation, 1977)

O'Farrell, Sister Mary Pius, *Woman of the Gospel* (Cork Publishing Limited, 1996)

Walsh, T.J. , *Nano Nagle and the Presentation Sisters* (M.H. Gill and Son, 1959)

Letters of Nano Nagle: *http://www.presentationsistersunion.org/_uploads/rsfil/00060.pdf*

ROSEMARY NELSON

'Interview with the relatives of Rosemary Nelson', *Irish News*, 14 March, 2003

www.anphoblacht.com

www.politics.ie

http://www.rosemarynelsoninquiry.org/

http://cain.ulst.ac.uk/issues/collusion/cory/cory03nelson.pdf

CHRISTINA NOBLE

Noble, Christina, *Bridge Across My Sorrows* (Corgi Books, 1995)

Noble, Christina, *Mama Tina* (Corgi Books, 1999)

http://www.cncf.org

EDNA O' BRIEN

Eckley, Grace, *Edna O' Brien* (Bucknell University Press, 1974)

Greenwood, Amanda, *Edna O' Brien* (Northcote House, 2002)

Jones, Alice, 'Edna O'Brien's latest offering has made it to the stage in full, flaming glory', *The Independent*, 10 April, 2008

O'Brien, Edna, *The Country Girls Trilogy* (Penguin, 1988)

O'Brien, Edna, *Down by the River* (Plume, 1998)

Wolcott, James, 'The Playgirl of the Western World', *Vanity Fair*, June 1992

http://www.salon.com/02dec1995/departments/litchat.html

SINEAD O' CONNOR

Guterman, Jimmy, *Sinead: her life and music* (Warner Books, 1991)

Hayes, Dermott, *Sinéad O'Connor: So Different* (Omnibus, 1991)

Whiteley, Sheila, *Women and Popular Music: Sexuality, Identity and Subjectivity* (Routledge, 2000)

www.sinead-oconnor.com

http://www.rollingstone.com/artists/sineadoconnor/biography

http://www.allmusic.com/cg/amg.dll

http://news.bbc.co.uk/2/hi/entertainment/1406579.stm
http://en.wikipedia.org/wiki/Sin%C3%A9ad_O'Connor
http://www.ilikemusic.com/interviews/Sinead_OConnor_interview_2007_Theology-3797

NUALA O'FAOLAIN

Dodd, Luke, 'Obituary: Nuala O' Faolain', *The Guardian*, 12 May, 2008
O'Faolain, Nuala, *Are You Somebody? The Life and Times of Nuala O'Faolain* (New Island Books, 1996)
O'Faolain, Nuala, *Almost There: the onward journey of a Dublin woman* (Michael Joseph, 2003)

http://us.penguingroup.com/nf/Author/AuthorPage/0,,1000027695,00.html

MAUREEN O'HARA

Barton, Ruth, *Acting Irish in Hollywood: from Fitzgerald to Farrell* (Irish Academic Press, 2006)
O'Hara, Maureen and Nicoletti, John, *Tis Herself – the Autobiography of Maureen O'Hara* (Simon & Schuster, 2004)

www.moharamagazine.com

GRACE O'MALLEY

Broderick, Marian, *Wild Irish Women: Extraordinary Lives from History* (O'Brien Press, 2002)
Chambers, Anne, *Granuaile* (Gill & Macmillan, 2009)
Cook, Judith, *The Pirate Queen: The Life of Grace O' Malley 1530–1603* (Mercier Press, 2004)
Gallagher, John, *Courageous Irishwomen* (Fiona Books, 1995)
Llywelyn, Morgan, *Granuaile* (O'Brien Press, 2001)
Sawyer, Roger, *We Are But Women – Women in Ireland's History* (Routledge, 1993)
Stanley, Jo, *Bold in her breeches: Women Pirates across the Ages* (Pandora/HaperCollins, 1995)

SONIA O'SULLIVAN

Davies, Gareth A., 'My Sport: Sonia O' Sullivan', *Daily Telegraph*, 9 October, 2002
Judge, Yvonne, *Chasing Gold: Sportswomen of Ireland* (Wolfhound Press, 1995)
O'Sullivan, Sonia, with Tom Humphries, *Sonia: My Story* (Penguin Ireland, 2008)

http://en.wikipedia.org/wiki/Sonia_O'Sullivan

ANNA PARNELL

'Anna Parnell Drowned', *The New York Times*, 24 September, 1911
Broderick, Marian, *Wild Irish Women: Extraordinary Lives from History* (O'Brien Press, 2002)
Cote, Jane McL., *Fanny and Anna Parnell: Ireland's Patriot Sisters* (Gill and MacMillan, 1991)
Cullen, Mary and Luddy, Maria, *Women, Power and Consciousness in 19th Century Ireland: Eight Biographical Studies* (Attic, 1995)
O'Shea, Katharine, *Charles Stewart Parnell: His Love Story & Political Life* (Cassell & Co., 1914)
Parnell, Anna, *Tale of a Great Sham* (Arlen House, 1986)
Ward, Margaret, *Unmanageable Revolutionaries; Women and Irish nationalism* (Brandon, 1983)

EDEL QUINN

Forristal, Desmond, *Edel Quinn 1907–1944* (Dominican Publications, 1994)
Suenens, Cardinal Leon Joseph, *Edel Quinn: Envoy of the Legion of Mary to Africa: A Heroine of the Apostolate 1907-1944* (C.J. Fallon, 1955)

http://www.legion-of-mary.ie/
www.edelquinn.org

MARY ROBINSON
Finlay, Fergus, *Mary Robinson: A President with a Purpose* (O'Brien Press, 1990)
Horgan, John, *Mary Robinson: An Independent Voice* (O'Brien Press, 1997)
O'Leary, Olivia and Burke, Helen, *Mary Robinson: The Authorised Biography* (Hodder and Stoughton, 1998)
Siggins, Lorna, *Mary Robinson: The Woman who took Power in the Park* (Mainstream, 1997)

http://en.wikipedia.org/wiki/Mary_Robinson

ADI ROCHE
Roche, Adi, *Children of Chernobyl: The Human Cost of the World's Worst Nuclear Disaster* (Fount, 1996)
Roche, Adi, *Chernobyl Heart: 20 Years On* (New Island, 2006)

Interview with John LeKay: *www.heyokamagazine.com/HEYOKA.9.AdiRoche.1.htm*
www.chernobyl-international.com
www.ccp-intl.org

PEIG SAYERS
O Céirín, Cyril and Kit, *Women of Ireland: A Biographic Dictionary* (Tir Eolas, 1996)
Ó Súilleabháin, Seán, 'Peig Sayers', *Éire – Ireland*, Vol. 5, No 1, 1970
Sayers, Peig, *An Old Woman's Reflections, translated by Seamus Ennis* (Oxford University Press, 1962)
Sayers, Peig, *Peig: the autobiography of Peig Sayers of the Great Blasket Island*; translated by Bryan MacMahon (Talbot Press, 1973)

HANNAH SHEEHY SKEFFINGTON
Broderick, Marian, *Wild Irish Women: Extraordinary Lives from History* (O'Brien Press, 2002)
Sheehy Skeffington, Hanna, *British Militarism As I Have Known It* (Kerryman, 1946)
Ward, Margaret, *Hannah Sheehy Skeffington: A Life* (Attic Press, 1997)

EDITH WILKINS
Doherty, Amanda, 'Street Children's Mother-of-Pearl', *Sunday Mirror*, 25 July, 1999
Hesnan, Anne, 'Research Project into the life of Edith Wilkins, an Irish woman who has made a difference to so many'
McMahon, Leo, 'South County', *The Southern Star*, January 17, 2009

http://www.edithwilkins.org/